THE
PURGATORIO

DANTE ALIGHIERI
Translated by John Ciardi

With an Introduction by
ARCHIBALD T. MACALLISTER
and a New Afterword by
EDWARD M. CIFELLI, PhD

SIGNET CLASSICS

SIGNET CLASSICS
Published by New American Library, a division of Penguin Group (USA) Inc.,
375 Hudson Street, New York, New York 10014, USA
Penguin Group (Canada), 90 Eglinton Avenue East, Suite 700, Toronto,
Ontario M4P 2Y3, Canada (a division of Pearson Penguin Canada Inc.)
Penguin Books Ltd., 80 Strand, London WC2R 0RL, England Penguin Ireland,
25 St. Stephen's Green, Dublin 2, Ireland (a division of Penguin Books Ltd.)
Penguin Group (Australia), 250 Camberwell Road, Camberwell, Victoria 3124,
Australia (a division of Pearson Australia Group Pty. Ltd.)
Penguin Books India Pvt. Ltd., 11 Community Centre, Panchsheel Park,
New Delhi – 110 017, India
Penguin Group (NZ), 67 Apollo Drive, Rosedale, North Shore 0632, New Zealand
(a division of Pearson New Zealand Ltd.)
Penguin Books (South Africa) (Pty.) Ltd., 24 Sturdee Avenue,
Rosebank, Johannesburg 2196, South Africa

Penguin Books Ltd., Registered Offices:
80 Strand, London WC2R 0RL, England

Published by Signet Classics, an imprint of New American Library, a division of
Penguin Group (USA) Inc. Previously published in a Mentor edition.

Acknowledgment is made to *Venture, Italian Quarterly, The Saturday Review, Between
Worlds, The Massachusetts Review, New World Writing,* and *Arbor,* in which excerpts
from the present work first appeared.

First Signet Classics Printing, July 2001
First Signet Classics Printing (Cifelli Afterword), October 2009
10 9 8 7 6 5 4 3 2 1

To Dudley Fitts, *Magister*

Contents

Illustrations

TRANSLATOR'S NOTE

Any theoretical remarks offered by a translator are bound to be an apology for his failures. Obviously no sane translator can allow himself to dream of success. He asks only for the best possible failure.

Translation is, in fact, the wrong word for the process of rendering from one language to another. The idea of "translation" seems to suggest that there exists in Language A some word that will equal any given word in Language B, and that the translator need only find that equivalent word and put it in place, allowing of course for something called "idiom."

But such an assumption ignores the nature of words. The American word "daisy," for example, labels the same flower the French intend by *la marguerite* and the Italians by *la margherita*—or at least approximately so: a botanist might be quick to say that the varieties of the European daisy are distinct from those of the American daisy. Nevertheless, those are the words one would naturally use in these three tongues for labeling any particular daisy. Semantically, that is to say, the denotations are reasonably firm.

But words consist of much more than denotation. Every word has a certain muscularity. That is to say, it involves certain speech muscles. Certainly any man who is word-sensitive is likely to linger over the difference between the long-drawn Italian *carina* and the common, though imprecise, American usage "cute" when applied to an attractive child. The physical gestures the two words invite are at least as different as the Italian child's good-bye wave (*"Fa ciao, carina"*) with the palm of the hand up, and the American child's ("Wave bye-bye") with the back of the hand up. The very difference in ethnic concept between two peoples moves the words about in their mouths. As I once wrote in a poem I am not moved to cherish particularly but whose point remains:

My mother facing a day in Avellino
Tasted it: *una dolce giornata.*

My wife's mother in Protestant Missouri
Judges it: *it is a good day.*

These are two distinct kinds of muscularity. Other kinds could certainly be adduced. And all must function in the effort one must make to find truly equivalent language.

Every word, moreover, has a history. Sometimes the history changes out from under the word very rapidly. English "broadcast" once meant specifically "a way of sowing" and was borrowed by radio as an analogy. Meanwhile new machines all but eliminated the old methods of broadcast-sowing, and the word has just about lost all farm-connotation. What to do then when, to shift examples, one language uses a word denoting anxiety whose essential meaning is based on the history of medieval torture, when the only word in another language that will render that denotation is based on the history of, say, the internal-combustion engine? Pure hypotheticals, to be sure, but how does one find equivalents in any language for such English words as "billingsgate," or "to burke," or "boycott"?—words whose meanings are inseparable from the local scene and local history in which the English language evolved?

Every word has an image locked into its roots. The English word "daisy" is a contraction of the earlier "day's eye," which is to say, "the eye of day"—a lovely root image. *Marguerite* and *margherita* also have a root connotation of all girls named Margaret/Marguerite/Margherita—and bless them all as lovely images. Behind that first suggestion, too, lies the true root of the Greek *margaron,* meaning "pearl"—another fine image. But what happened to "day's eye"? Not that there is any point here in arguing which is the more attractive root image. The point is simply that they are different. And what then does one do for equivalent words?

And to point out only one more of many possibilities within the nature of words, every word connotes a certain level of usage. Italian *antipatico,* for example, is so common a usage that it falls readily from the lips of even very small children, whereas English "antipathetic" is a relatively learned word, and certainly not one for the normal nursery. What weight does one give this element of word usage in seeking equivalents?

We tend to use only the top slice of a word in speech usage. But once the other levels of a word are allowed into consideration, no word is a simple thing. It becomes a complex. But if a single word is a complex, then a phrase is a complex of complexes, and a line is a complex of complexes of complexes, and a stanza, and a poem are . . . and so forth and so on.

I don't honestly know how one makes a theory of translation out of these musings and bewilderments. All I can truthfully say is that such equivalence as I have managed has happened by feel, and that I am more comfortable within specifications than I am in trying to defend theories that distort under every effort to state them.

I began to peck away at Dante because I could find no translation that satisfied my sense of the original. Let nothing in that statement imply that I have now satisfied my sense. When I read the original with my rendering in mind I have no choice but to feel sad. When I read any other translation with my rendering in mind, I feel relatively happy. No one, of course, should trust my sense of it, but I must. Whose sense can I trust else?

In looking at other translations I was distressed by the fact that none of them seemed to be using what I understood to be Dante's vulgate. They seemed rather to fall into literary language, the very sort of thing Dante took such pains to avoid. And none of them, above all else, gave me a satisfying sense of Dante's pace, which is to say, "the rate at which the writing reveals itself to the reader."

I began to experiment out of curiosity. I rendered a number of Cantos in *terza rima* and satisfied myself that it could not do. English is a rhyme-poor language. It was obvious to me that the price of forcing that third rhyme into place in English was ruinous to the language. There are approximately 4,500 lines in each third of the *Divine Comedy*. One must find 1,500 triple-rhymes to render each third into *terza rima,* and English has no such rhyme-resources. Mechanically, it can be done, but not in anything approximating spoken American-English. I could see through what wrestling agonies I had put my own efforts in order to force the language around to that third rhyme, and the same agonies are immediately visible in every extant version in *terza rima.*

Abandoning all thought of *terza rima,* I tried blank verse. But there the language and its movement went askew on another characteristic of English verse. The blank-verse paragraph in English, as nearly as I can determine, runs to an average of about fourteen lines. (Interestingly, the paragraph of Pope's couplets runs to about the same average.) If one thinks of the structure of pauses in a poem as subtotaling points, I take that fact of English poetry to mean that blank verse pauses to complete its sub-thoughts about once every fourteen lines. But Dante sets his pauses (which is to say, his periods, or more usually his semicolons, or sometimes his commas) every three lines, and I take that fact to be, above all else, what determines the pace and sparseness of Dante's writing. If the fundamental unit runs from ten to twenty lines, there is room for all sorts of digression or even self-indulgence. An extra line or two, an extra image or two, an extra flourish or two, are easily possible. But if one is forcing his lines to some sort of summary every three lines, that fact must work to squeeze out all flab. Dante does, to be sure, write any number of run-on tercets, but the three-line unit remains firm as the rigorous basic measure of his way of writing. This writing is of bone and sinew.

I went on to experiment with all sorts of other possibilities. In another effort at *terza rima* I tried assonantal rhyming. Assonance may yet be a possibility for someone else. I can only report that I do not favor it as an English rhyme-method. For a time I tried English couplets, thinking they might be made to render an Italian tercet: they cannot, at least as a sustained measure. I tried various sorts of ballad stanzas: they had no hope of being for anything but the wastebasket. Then I hit on what I may as well call dummy *terza rima,* which is to say, I kept the three-line unit but rhymed only the first and third lines. And with that it began to happen, at least for me. I could persuade myself that what came was reasonably English, reasonably poetry, and reasonably faithful to Dante's pace and to his special way of using language. What is reasonable can, of course, include an awareness of failure, but I could begin to believe this was a good enough failure to be worth investing in.

I had no theory at that point—only a feeling. And I still have no theory I can securely defend. The rest was trial and error: something like learning to walk a tightrope: if one can only manage to grab the rope when he falls, and if he can then manage to get back up, and if he falls only forward, there is always the possibility that he will make it to the other side. To let a single example do for all, the process can be illustrated in the following passage from Canto VIII of the *Purgatorio* which reads, in the original:

> *Ben discerneva in lor la testa bionda;*
> *Ma nella faccia l'occhio si smarria*
> *Come virtù ch'a troppo si confonda.*

The passage is part of the description of two angels that descend to Dante and his companions in the Valley of the Negligent Rulers. It is a simple enough passage as Dante goes, and almost any man with a sense of Latin roots can puzzle out most of the meaning. *Virtù* (virtue) in the Latin sense of "faculty/power/ability/generative force" (*cf.* "by virtue of the power invested in me") is perhaps the one word that might trip the unwary. How is one to render such a passage?

In Pidgin-Literal it might read:

> Well was I discerning in them the head blond
> But in the face the eye dazed itself
> Like a virtue that at too much confounds itself.

Obviously no rendering into any known language has taken place. A more idiomatic literal rendering might read:

    Well did I discern the blondness of their heads
        but in their faces my eye was dazed
        like a faculty which is overcome by excess.

But though such a rendering is idiomatic enough, phrase by phrase, the sequence of phrases is not really intelligible as a communication in English. The passage is still in no spoken tongue but, rather, in an unspeakable hodgepodge neither Italian nor English. So one might work toward a more speakable, which is to say, communicable equivalent:

    I saw clearly that their heads were blond,
        but looking into their faces my eyes grew dazed
        like an overstimulated faculty of the senses.

    That begins to be closer, but now one runs into a peculiarity of the way Dante describes the workings of his senses. If one has been reading from the beginning of the *Divine Comedy* he is used to this way Dante has of describing such matters. By this point in my rendering I have had occasion to supply a number of footnotes on this usage. It is, in fact, a small stylistical formality: Dante often describes the workings of his eyes as if he could focus on, say, the forehead of a distant figure, seeing nothing else, and as if he then had deliberately to move his eyes downward in order to focus on the figure's nose. It is some such thing he is saying here: staring at the angels he can see that their hair is blond, but when he looks down from their hair to their faces, his eyes grow dazzled, overstimulated by the light that shines from them. Obviously, it would be impossible, at any distance, not to be entirely blinded by such light, and the literalist has firm grounds for arguing that Dante could not have seen the hair of the angels. Such a device must be accepted as a well-established mannerism.
    With that much understood, then, the passage may be simplified. Were one simply communicating Dante's thought in an English prose paraphrase it might be stated: "I could make out clearly that their hair was blond, but when I focused on their faces, my eyes were dazzled by the excess of light they gave forth."

Let the rendering remain ragged: it contains the essential intent. But the passage is written as poetry and it must be rendered within meter, rhyme, and in a language sufficient to its emotional intent. And after much scratching and scrambling for a rhyme (and it sometimes happens that the very rhyme you want has been used in the preceding tercet and may not, therefore, be repeated so soon) I came up with the following:

> I could distinctly see their golden hair,
>   but my eyes drew back defeated from their faces
>   like a sense perceiving more than it can bear.

Such a rendering covers the law perhaps, and at times I have been forced to leave some of Dante in no better state than that, but certainly it is nothing to be satisfied with. I especially do not like the feel of that last line in English. As nearly as I can say it, the English word choice is being forced from Dante's Italian rather than being developed in sequence by the normal flow of English.

Whereupon, after more floundering I came to rest on:

> I could see clearly that their hair was gold,
>   but my eyes drew back bedazzled from their faces,
>   defeated by more light than they could hold.

It is simple enough to see that there are all sorts of things literally wrong with such a passage. The original says "the head" and the passage says "hair." There is nothing, at least explicitly, in the original that says the eye "drew back." *Virtù* has disappeared, and "defeated" is certainly not the same thing as "confounded."

And when the charge is put in those terms I have no defense and very little, if any, theory on which to base a defense. Nor any hope of arguing that I have achieved a perfect rendering. All I can really argue, as lamely as need be, is that within the essential failure, this final version *feels* enough like the original, and *feels* enough like English poetry (or at least verse) to allow me to conclude that I have probably caught it as well as I shall be able to. There must be some theory of translation implicit in these feelings, but in practice I suspect any translation turns out to be a long series of such individual cases, each met on its own grounds, and that each is finally settled by *feel*. What has any poet to trust more than that *feel* of the thing? Theory concerns him only until he picks up his pen, and it begins to concern him again as soon as he lays it down, but when the pen is in his hand he has to write by itch and twitch, though certainly his itch and twitch are intimately conditioned by all his past itching and twitching, and by all his past theorizing about them.

I should be an ingrate were I to omit my thanks to Professor Giorgio de Santillana and to Professor Archibald MacAllister, both of whom read the manuscript of this text and made detailed comments. Their learning has guarded me time and again from the pitfalls of my own ignorance.

—John Ciardi

How to Read Dante

In the opening allegory of the *Divine Comedy,* Dante finds himself lost and in darkness:

> Midway in our life's journey, I went astray
>   from the straight road and woke to find myself
>   alone in a dark wood.

These are familiar allegorical devices and no sensitive reader will fail to understand that "the straight road" has something to do with rectitude ("the straight and narrow"), that "the dark wood" has something to do with error/sinfulness/ loss of purpose, and—by extension—that the proper course must lie in finding the light.

Having "something to do with" is not close enough, however. Dante demands more careful reading. Because of that demand, because of the immense and minute scholarship that has been expended upon Dante, and because too few English readers have been pointed in the right direction to him, Dante has acquired a reputation as an immensely difficult poet.

It is true that Dante writes in depth. Though his language is normally simple, his thought is normally complex. But if the gold of Dante runs deep, it also runs right up to the surface. A lifetime of devoted scholarship will not mine all that gold; yet enough lies on the surface—or just an inch below— to make a first reading a bonanza in itself. All one really needs is some first instruction in what to look for. Thereafter he need only follow the vein as it goes deeper and deeper into the core of things.

The instruction may properly begin with those opening lines. "Midway in our life's journey," writes Dante. The reader must understand that Dante is not tossing off a poetic generalization. "Our life's journey" means specifically the "three-score years and ten" of the Biblically allotted life span. "Midway," therefore, means that Dante was thirty-five years old at the time of which he writes. Since he was born in 1265, it follows that the poem opens in the year 1300. And from a number of statements that can be culled from the poem, the careful reader can learn that the exact time is just before dawn of Good Friday.

By culling certain other statements, most of which are made at once, the reader may further learn that the sun is at the vernal equinox, that it is in the sign of Aries (the zodiacal sign in which God placed it at the Creation), and that the moon is full. These elements, added to the fact that it is the hour of the dawn and the season of Easter, clearly compound a massive symbol of rebirth. All things are at their regenerative peak when the lost soul realizes it has gone astray, for that realization is itself the beginning of the soul's rebirth.

Scholars have since shown that there was no Friday in the year 1300 on which all these conditions obtained. Dante, moreover, was a close student of astronomy and astrology. He knew that no such conjunction of sun, moon, zodiacal sign, and Easter season had taken place. He invented that conjunction as a full-swelling introductory theme in what amounts to a symphonic structure. The poem sounds its first chords with first light striking through darkness. In what follows, the darkness must grow more and more absolute to the very depth of dark (Hell); the light must then begin to overcome the darkness (Purgatory); and finally the "music" must mount from light to light to the ultimate indescribable glory of the all-blazing presence of God at the peak of Heaven.

As soon as Dante recognizes that he is lost and in darkness, he looks up and sees the first light of the new day glowing on the shoulders of a little hill. Throughout the *Divine Comedy,* the sun ("that planet/whose virtue leads men straight on every road") is a symbol for God, for Divine Illumination. In the *Purgatorio,* for example, souls may climb only in the light of the sun: once it has set, it is possible for them to descend, but they lack the power to move upward even so much as an inch. Only in the light of God may one ascend that road, for that is the light to which the soul must win.

Another allegorical theme begins immediately. Dante, in his passion to reach the light (God), races straight up the hill to it. He uses a grand and typical synechdoche to describe his speed, saying that he raced up that slope at such a pace "that the fixed foot was ever the lower."

Synechdoche is that figure of speech in which a part is taken to represent the whole. A less certain writer might have reached for all sorts of great metaphors to describe the speed of his climb. Dante focuses on a single detail that does for all. If the feet of a man climbing a steep slope move in such a way that the moving foot is forever above the one that is pausing, it follows that the climb must be taking place at a blurring speed—in fact, at an impossible rate, whereby hyperbole must be added to synechdoche as a reinforcement of the poetic effect. The point for the reader to remember is that it will not do to slide over Dante's details. They will take thinking about because they took thought to find.

There is perhaps nothing so entirely impressive about the *Divine Comedy* as its power of mind. The true mark of any writer is in the choices he makes. Having written three words, he must choose a fourth. Having written four, he must choose a fifth. Nothing happens into a good poem; everything must be chosen into it. A poem may be thought of as a construction for making choices, and it is in the quality of his choices that Dante makes his greatness known. His language and his prosody can be rough and awkward. Anyone who reads the original will wonder at times if this is really "poetry." Very well, then, let it be prose, if one insists on folly. But if it is prose, it is prose of a previously unknown order, for the depth and multiplicity of mind that seem to function at every choice have not been matched in any piece of Western writing.

Meanwhile, back at the narrative, Dante is racing up the slope to what would be immediate salvation, could he manage to reach that light. The sinner has realized he is in darkness, he has seen the light, he ardently desires it, and he races to be received by it. But salvation is not to be had that easily:

Dante finds his way blocked by three beasts. There is a She-Wolf that represents the sins of Incontinence, a Lion that represents the sins of Violence and Bestiality, and a Leopard that represents Fraud. The beasts themselves are derived from Jeremiah; the three categories of sin are derived from Aristotle. Into these three categories fall all the sins of the world. The Three Beasts, therefore, represent the total blindness of which the world is capable. Symphonically, they also foreshadow the three divisions of Hell through which Dante must journey. In the Hell of the She-Wolf are punished the sins of excessive animal appetite. In the lower Hell, the Hell of the Lion, are punished the sins of bestial violence. In the lowest Hell, the Hell of the Leopard, are punished the sins of fraud, worse than the sins of bestiality because they involve the perversion of the higher gift of intellect—a beast, that is to say, can murder; but only a rational being, by perverting the gift of rationality, can commit a fraudulent act.

These three beasts drive Dante back into the darkness, blocking the direct and easy way to that light. In that darkness, when all seems to have been lost, and when Dante can find no way around those beasts of worldliness, there appears to him the figure of Virgil.

Virgil is a complex figure, combining within himself, among other things, the classical heritage, genius, magic powers, and Dante's personal devotion. On the first level, however, it will do to take him as representing Human Reason in its best development. More subtly, he may be taken as Esthetic Wisdom, the knowledge of the true poet. For present purposes let him be taken simply as representing Human Reason. In that role, he points out that there is no such express road to God as Dante had imagined in racing up the hill: "He must go by another way who would escape/this wilderness."

The other way—the long way round—is the total journey into ultimate darkness and out again to ultimate light. Such is the arduous road of the *Divine Comedy*. It is the painful descent into Hell—to the recognition of sin. It is the difficult ascent of Purgatory—to the renunciation of sin. Then only may Dante begin the soaring flight into Paradise, to the rapturous presence of God. God, that is to say, may be found only on the other side of the total self-searching experience of a zealous life. There are no shortcuts to that totally encompassing experience. Salvation must grow out of understanding, total understanding can follow only from total experience, and experience must be won by the laborious discipline of shaping one's absolute attention. The object is to achieve God, and Dante's God exists in no state of childlike innocence: He is total knowledge and only those who have truly experienced knowledge can begin to approach Him.

Virgil, as Human Reason, is the first guide to that ultimate knowledge, but Virgil cannot guide Dante all the way. Reason is finite and God is infinite. The greater guide, in the medieval concept, was Faith. Reason was merely the handmaiden of Faith. Virgil can guide Dante to the recognition of sin and to its renunciation, which is to say, through Hell and to the top of Purgatory. But once at that summit, the soul has achieved purity. It has risen beyond Reason. It is ready to enter the Divine Mysteries. And there Beatrice (call her Divine Love) must take over.

It was in her infinite compassion as Divine Love that Beatrice sent Reason to the man's soul in his hour of darkness, that Reason might serve as his guide to bring him into her higher presence. One may not simply wish himself into that higher presence. That presence must be won by devout labor.

That devout labor is what might be called the basic plot and the basic journey of the *Divine Comedy*. All that follows, once the journey has begun, is an amplification of themes that have already been established. That much understood, the writing itself will best explain itself as it unfolds—always, of course, with the help of those indispensable footnotes.

When, however, one has read all the way through the poem and has returned to reread these first Cantos, he will find many other themes rooted in them. There are four such themes that any beginning reader will do well to grasp as particularly able to enrich his first experience.

The first has to do with Dante's sinfulness. What sin was it that had brought him into the dark wood of Error? Dante was expelled from Florence on charges of having been a grafter, and some commentators have tried to identify his guilt in that charge. In the *Purgatorio* Dante himself recognizes that he is guilty of Pride, and to some extent of Wrath. He has both those offenses to pay for when he returns to Purgatory after his death. But the charges against Dante were certainly trumped up by his political enemies, and no specific act of Pride or Wrath can be cited to account for Dante's opening mood. His offense was, rather, Acedia. Let it serve to label this first theme.

The Seven Deadly Sins for which souls suffer in Purgatory are—in ascending order—Pride, Envy, Wrath, Acedia, Avarice, Gluttony, and Lust. Acedia is the central one, and it may well be the sin the twentieth century lost track of. Acedia is generally translated as Sloth. But that term in English tends to connote not much more than laziness and physical slovenliness. For Dante, Acedia was a central spiritual failure. It was the failure to be sufficiently active in the pursuit of the recognized Good. It was to acknowledge Good, but without fervor.

The spiritual awakening to which Dante comes in the Dark Wood—the enormous rebirth—is the awareness of the fact that he has not been sufficiently zealous in his pursuit of the Good. The *Divine Comedy* is the zealous journey from the man's recognized spiritual torpor (neglect of God) to the active pursuit of his soul's good (love of God). Every step of that journey may simultaneously be understood as the man's active embrace of his Godly experience, as the soul's active pursuit of the love of Good, and as the artist's pursuit of form.

The second theme—perhaps it is not so much a theme as a method—is inseparable from the others. Call it the Five Levels. In a letter to his patron, Can Grande della Scala, Dante explicitly names four levels of meaning that he intends all the way through the *Divine Comedy—narrative, allegorical, moral,* and *anagogical.* That letter may, as many scholars contend, be a forgery. Whether genuine or not, what it states explicitly is clearly implicit in the writing. And to those four stated levels may be added a fifth: the journey seen as a *progress of the soul.*

Dante was a parochial man. He was persuaded that the One Truth had been revealed to him, and he was intolerant of all non-Catholic views. He refused, for example, to think of

Mohammed as a religious leader but dismissed him as schismatic and heretic and assigned to him a particularly grotesque punishment in Hell.

But if the man was parochial, the artist was universal as only art can be. The *Divine Comedy* is a triumph of art over creed. And that triumph—to paraphrase terms that Dante himself might have used—arises from the force of the Esthetic Mysteries, which is to say, the power of form in the interplay of its structures and its levels of meaning.

The first obvious level, for example, is narrative: a travelogue. But that journey is through a country populated by second meanings. On one level Dante writes of Hell as a literal place of sin and punishment. The damned are there because they offended a theological system that enforces certain consequences of suffering. But part of that theological system has also decreed that salvation was available to all men. Christ in his ransom had procured endless mercy. One need only wish to be saved, need only surrender his soul to God in a last gasp of contrition, and he will be saved. He may have to suffer at length in Purgatory, but, once there, his place is reserved in Heaven and he will in time arrive there. Purgatory is like our modern colleges: no one can flunk out of them.

It follows, then, that the only way to get into Hell is to insist upon it. One must deliberately exclude himself from grace by hardening his heart against it. Hell is what the damned have actively and insistently wished for.

Thus, allegorically, Hell is the true goal of the damned. On the surface the state of the sinners is described in terms of sin. The wonder and the universality of it are that a reader who does not care for those terms may restate them in terms of behavior, and the *Inferno* remains entirely coherent as a dramatic treatise on self-destructive behavior. Like addicts, the damned both hate and love their self-destruction. "They yearn for what they fear," says Dante.

Thus Hell is not only a specific place but a moral and anagogical allegory of the guilty conscience of the damned. It is the projection into a physical reality of the inner state of the damned. As Purgatory is such a projection of the inner state of those who suffer toward grace. As Heaven is such another projection of the inner state of those who have achieved

grace. Each environment is an allegory and a moral and ana-
gogical commentary on the essential nature of the souls one
finds in each. Hell exists from within.

In a detailed discussion in the *Purgatorio,* Dante rein-
forces these levels of meaning by pointing out that though
mortal man may deceive by hiding his true nature under false
semblances, the dead, by the very nature of their aerial bod-
ies, can only appear to be exactly what they are. The dead
cannot dissemble. *What* they appear to be and *where* they ap-
pear, they are.

The third theme—let it be called the Moral Universe or
the Sentient Universe—is the vast, overriding concept of the
total universe that makes the *Divine Comedy* the massive ve-
hicle it is. Every artist seeks the vehicle that will best engage
all his possibilities, just as every actor seeks the perfect role
for himself. So, any actor would rather play Hamlet than Un-
cle Tom. Hamlet gives him more chances to act.

Dante's vehicle is nothing less than the total universe.
Where in all poetry is there an equivalent subject-structure?
Dante not only draws a map of his universe; he walks it from
end to end. But his map is both of a physical geography and
of a structure of values. That universe exists on all five levels
of meaning.

For Dante, as for classical man, there was no real distinc-
tion between moral and physical law; between, say, the moral
law against incest and the physical law of gravity. All of
matter was a projection of God's will, and what we call physi-
cal law and what we call moral law derived equally from
that will. When Oedipus, though unknowingly, transgressed
moral law by killing his father and marrying his mother, a
plague descended upon Thebes. It would not have occurred to
the Greeks that to think of a flight of locusts as a consequence
of what happened in the king's bedroom was to cross cate-
gories.

Dante's physical universe is Ptolemaic. It consists of nine
concentric circles (spheres) with the Earth as the center. In
ascending order those spheres are: the Moon, Mercury, Venus,
the Sun, Mars, Jupiter, Saturn, the Fixed Stars, and the Primum
Mobile. Beyond the Primum Mobile lies the Empyrean, which

is the dwelling and presence of God. God is an essence that
entirely surrounds and contains creation.

If God is the circumference of this nine-layered sphere,
the center is the greatest distance one can travel from God.
That center is the Earth, and the center of that center is the
bottom of Hell. Inevitably, it is there, at the Ultimate bottom
of the universe, that Dante places Satan.

Satan is a powerful symbol. He is described as an unholy
reverse-Trinity with three foul heads and three pairs of
wings. He has been flung from Heaven to the farthest dis-
tance one can go from God. To his dark center drain all the
waters of the earth, bearing the filthy sediment of all sin and
uncleanliness. Satan's six wings beat madly in his efforts to
escape from that foul lake but they succeed only in whipping
up a freezing gale that turns all to ice, fixing him ever more
securely in the bottom ice-tray. From the top of Purgatory,
moreover, there flow down to him the waters of Lethe, in
which the finally purified souls bathe and are washed clean of
every memory of sin. That memory, too, is frozen into the
filthy ice about Satan.

Thus that center is the center of all weight, of all sin, of all
darkness, and of all cold. And to it flows all the filth of time.
Weight, sin, dark, cold, and filth are, of course, the five things
farthest from God. And thus the universe becomes a scale of
precise values: the closer a thing is to the center, the lower it
is on that scale; the closer a thing is to the circumference, the
higher it is.

The existence of that scale makes possible an enormous
economy in Dante's writing. Dante need only place his finger
on that map and say what he saw there. The very act of place-
ment becomes the value judgment.

That economy is further assisted by the firm laws of the
other world. As one sins, so is he punished; as he strove for
grace, so is he rewarded. In Hell, then, each punishment is a
symbolic analysis of the nature of the sin and of the state of
the sinner's soul. The reader need only be told, for example,
that the punishment of the Lustful is highest in the Infernal
scale, and that it consists of being buffeted eternally round
and round by a dark whirlwind. The reader knows at once
that this sin, though sufficient for damnation, is the least

weighty of all the sins of Hell proper, and that the nature of the sin is to allow one's soul to be buffeted round and round by the dark winds of immoderate passion. Love is a sweet human state, but by excessive physical love these sinners shut their souls from God, surrendering "reason to their appetites."

Dante's Cantos average about 140 lines. As a general thing he requires no more than twenty or thirty lines to identify the sinner and to describe the punishment. Since the value judgment is already established by the map, and since the punishment is a symbolic analysis of the sin, these essential matters are settled in short order, and Dante has the rest of his Canto available for all sorts of matters that attract his ranging mind.

Dante had once set out to be an encyclopedist. His *Il Convivio*—never finished—was an effort to set down in Italian all human "science." There is nothing that does not interest him. As a poet, moreover, he would naturally look for chances to use his dramatic, lyric, and didactic powers. So, with his structure firmly determined by its basic economy, Dante is free to range at will, packing every rift with those fascinating details that add so much to his poem. He has time for gossip, for prophecies, for marvelous dramatic interplays, for treatises on history, for analyzing the French monarchy, the corruption of the Church, the decay of Italian politics. He has time for all sorts of metaphysical treatises on such matters as the nature of the generative principle, literary criticism, meteorology— in short, for his whole unfinished encyclopedia. And he still has time to invent a death for Ulysses, to engage in a metamorphic contest with Ovid, to make side remarks to his friends. He can give full rein to his powers because he has found the inexhaustible vehicle.

The fourth principal theme will inevitably reveal itself to the careful reader, but he will lose nothing by having it in mind from the start. Call it the Architectonics. The *Divine Comedy* has often been compared to a cathedral, and, whether or not the comparison is finally apt, it is certainly true that Dante's details keep acquiring significance as one goes on and learns to look back at them from some corresponding point in the later structure. The structure, that is to say, produces a *back-illumination*.

Charon, for example, is the boatman of the damned, ferrying them across Acheron into Hell proper. He is a memorable figure. Later, one meets the Angel-Pilot who ferries souls to Purgatory. He, too, is a memorable figure. But no reasonably careful reader can fail to see that one ferryman stands in meaningful relation to the other. Thus, the Angel is not only himself, but an opposite figure to Charon, and Charon seen backwards from the figure of the Angel acquires a dimension he did not have as an isolated figure. The development of these structural correspondences—of an endless number of them—is an everlasting and ever-enlarging source of the power of the *Divine Comedy.*

The supreme art of poetry is not to *assert* meaning but to *release* it by the juxtaposition of poetic elements. Form, in its interrelations, is the most speaking element. Because in any extended poetic structure these juxtapositions will fall into different perspectives when looked at from different points of vantage, that release of meaning is subject to endless meaningful reinterpretation. The inexhaustibility of the *Divine Comedy* is a consequence of this structural quality. It is for that reason that no one can ever finish reading it. There will always be a new way of viewing the elements. But if no man can finish the poem, any man may begin it and be the richer for having begun. The present imperfect gloss—skimming though it be—is really about all one needs to start with. And, having started, all he needs is to pay attention. The poem itself is the rest of the way, and the way is marked.

—John Ciardi

INTRODUCTION

One of the qualities which distinguish Dante's *Divine Comedy* from most other long narrative poems is the individual character and, as it were, physiognomy peculiar to each of its three great divisions. Readers of the *Inferno* will recall its frequently harsh materialism, the great variety of intonation, the vivid realism, in which its ghostly figures rapidly seem to become people and the whole scene appears the "hell on earth" Dante probably wished it to represent.

To understand the *Inferno,* some historical background was obviously essential. It was important to know that Dante, by being born an upper-middle-class Alighieri in the independent commune of Florence in 1265, had inherited the political loyalties of a Guelph and that he had also acquired hereditary enemies called Ghibellines. The history of the civil strife between these parties was of equal importance, for, even if it culminated in a Guelph victory just after Dante's birth, talk of it and of fears lest it flare up again filled his mind during his formative years. Outstanding members of the preceding generation of both parties such as the great Ghibelline Farinata degli Uberti, and the Guelph statesman and scholar Brunetto Latini, were to supply a number of his infernal figures, and allusions to victories, exiles, and defeats fill its pages.

Since participation in public life would determine Dante's fate, we had to be aware of new dissension among the Guelphs, now divided among themselves into the "Blacks" and the "Whites" to which he belonged, and to follow the strange fatal parallel between his political progress and the growth of this new partisan strife. We saw the irony of his rise to the highest magistracy just as violence broke out in 1300, so his prominence made him a prime target for his foes.

What happened next, however, was of fundamental importance for all parts of the *Comedy* and, indeed, for all Dante's thinking thereafter. The Blacks schemed to interest the Pope in intervening in the dispute. Boniface VIII, ever alert for an opportunity to strengthen his political influence, ignored the protests of the Whites, and invited a supposedly neutral third party, Charles of Valois, to enter Florence in the role of impartial arbitrator and peacemaker. What the Pope's secret orders had been became instantly apparent when Charles was admitted in November 1301. After seizing and disarming the Whites, he opened the gates to the banished Blacks, and stood by as they gave themselves over to murder and pillage. Dante was absent on a political mission and, fortunately for him and for posterity, he preferred exile to the sort of justice he would have faced had he returned.

This experience, crushing and embittering to most of its victims—and Dante's share of bitterness can be tasted in the *Comedy*'s invectives and many ironic allusions—launched Dante's mind on one of its greatest drives: to understand the problem of evil, and to try to solve it. What could lead the head of the Church, of all Christendom, vicar of the Christ who scorned the hypocrites and drove the money-changers and shopkeepers from the Temple, to engage in the fraud and perfidy of the Florentine conspiracy? How could such a man rise to such a position? What hope was there that men in general might be persuaded to a just life in this world and salvation in the next when they saw their spiritual leaders behave in such a way? Surely such a marvelously ordered physical universe, created for man's enjoyment, must contain somewhere a clue to a better political organization or government than that of Dante's day.

Exploration of these questions led Dante through the Scriptures with their commentators, the Church Fathers, notably Anselm, Bonaventure, and Augustine, to Boethius and beyond to Lucan, Statius, Ovid, Horace, and his beloved and revered Virgil. Cicero's treatises were a wonderful discovery ("like happening upon gold while looking for silver") but bristling with difficulties both stylistic and conceptual. This was the new and alien material—philosophy—that the Church had repeatedly proscribed until the recent appearance of Aquinas' Christian explanation of Aristotle.

The fruits of his long and painstaking exploration of the problem of evil formed the substance of Dante's *Inferno*. In this remarkable amalgam of the *Nicomachaean Ethics* and Cicero there is little that is peculiarly Christian except for a few borrowings from St. Thomas and the implicit application of St. Paul's *"Radix enim omnium malorum est cupiditas"* as the principle underlying the worst categories. It is not a theological arrangement but a philosophical one; not a theoretical exposition—save for the marvelously concise discourse of Virgil in Canto XI—but what might be called a case-system presentation of classic examples of evil in its outward social manifestations. The theoretical approach had already been tried in Dante's first work after his exile, the unfinished *Banquet* (*Il Convivio*). Here he had set out along the scholiast's favorite way—a commentary on an established text—with the purpose of making available to the un-Latined the corpus of philosophy as he had found it. Yet when only about one-third complete, this ambitious task had been abandoned, with no word of explanation such as that which terminated his only preceding work, the *Vita Nuova*.

These two works together, the tender autobiographical effusion and the unfinished encyclopedia, or more precisely the experiences they represent, are of central importance to the *Comedy*. The *Vita Nuova* in particular is as essential to a deeper understanding of the *Purgatorio* as the Florentine events and Dante's part in them are to an understanding of the *Inferno*. Without a knowledge of at least the outline of his rapturous, remote love for Beatrice, the many allusions to her lose their meaning and the growing tension as the poet mounts to the top of Purgatory cannot be fully felt. Of even greater significance is the knowledge that Beatrice died in 1290, and that, in the ten years between then and the supposed date of the *Comedy,* Dante had been unfaithful to her memory; without it, we are puzzled by her severe reproof when she confronts him in the Earthly Paradise. An understanding of the allegorical meaning with which Dante invested

both earlier works and their relationship explains another of
her reproofs and illuminates the poet's spiritual biography.
No one reading the *Vita Nuova* can doubt that its characters
are real persons, especially the object of its idealized love.
Likewise when Dante describes how deeply he was affected,
in his grief after Beatrice's death, by the obvious compassion
shown by the "Lady of the Window," he was clearly describ-
ing how his grief was being lessened by his interest in an-
other woman; and the remorse with which this little book
closes is obviously sincere. Twelve or more years later, when
he begins the *Banquet,* Beatrice has gradually become a sa-
cred abstraction relegated to Heaven, having no further role
in this life, while the "Lady of the Window" has become
"daughter of God, queen of everything, most fair and noble
Philosophy."

Dante threw himself into his new love with such character-
istic single-mindedness that, soon, as he himself tells us, "it
drove out and destroyed every other thought" (*Banquet,* II,
xii). At some point thereafter—and, since so little of this
book dedicated to philosophy was written, it was probably
not many years—there must have occurred another crisis like
that at the end of the *Vita Nuova,* but much greater. Dante
must have realized the peril in his overdependence on secular
wisdom and on his own faculties, and he readjusted his scale
of values in such a way as to reestablish the superiority of re-
vealed truth. This crisis is probably represented in Canto I of
the *Comedy,* for it is doubtless from this futile and dangerous
self-reliance that Dante is there rescued by Virgil. In the
Comedy it is evident that the lover, now definitely returned—
both to Beatrice and to her sacred significance—wished to
make public confession and amends for his error by weaving
it very fittingly into the fabric of his Mount of Purification.
Indeed, to the reader thus prepared to understand it, this sec-
ond *cántica* can be seen to contain a monumental act of
atonement. To clarify his intent and achieve greater effect,
Dante planned this episode to occur in a sequence similar to
the original. Since all the deviations sprang from the *Vita
Nuova,* some way had to be found to recall that work and its
experiences to the reader without disrupting the poem's artis-
tic unity. This he achieved by a device so effective, so subtle,

and at the same time so obvious that its secret has rarely been perceived. To see this we must examine the *Purgatorio* itself.

Among the distinguishing features of this division of the *Comedy* is what might be called its "middle" character. Whereas the *Inferno* is all darkness and the *Paradiso* is all light, the *Purgatorio* is a mixture of the two in its alternation of day and night. This comes about naturally, since it is imagined as a mountain rising in the middle of Earth's southern hemisphere opposite Jerusalem. Arriving there at dawn on Easter Sunday, Dante and Virgil spend four days and three nights in its ascent. As Hell had its vestibule, so Purgatory begins with an "ante-Purgatorio," the whole base of the mountain up to a certain height. Then comes a gate, and Purgatory itself begins. The poets reach this point in the first night, during Dante's sleep; it is Canto IX. During the second night they are in the fourth or middle one of the seven vices, Sloth, and again Dante falls asleep; this is Canto XVIII. The end of Purgatory itself is reached, and Dante falls asleep for the final time, in Canto XXVII. The scheme thus revealed is a series of 9's. At this point, no one familiar with the *Vita Nuova* can fail to be alerted, remembering the pains its young author had taken to associate the number 9 with Beatrice, because she was herself "a nine, that is, a miracle." When one sees further that there are precisely three of these 9's, and that each has a vision associated with it, he cannot help recalling how Dante first saw Beatrice at age 9, saw her again at 18, and concluded the *Vita Nuova* at 27; and that there was a vision associated with each of those three 9's. Dante has accomplished his purpose; the alert and knowledgeable reader is prepared for the confrontation with Beatrice. To make this doubly sure, he has the latter say, in her rebuke,

"This man was such, in his *vita nova*,"

where the last two words have the unaccustomed, though legitimate, meaning of "childhood" or "youth." The only specific term Beatrice employs here to identify Dante's transgressions is *pargoletta,* an endearment used by the poet in a love lyric not addressed to Beatrice. That they are meant to include Dante's overemphasis on secular studies is made clear two cantos later, where she explains her use of lofty words and concepts:

> "They fly so high," she said, "that you may know
>   what school you followed, and how far behind
>   the truth I speak its feeble doctrines go;
>
> and see that man's ways, even at his best,
>   are far from God's as earth is from the heaven
>   whose swiftest wheel turns above all the rest."
>   [XXXIII, 85–90]

It should be emphasized that Dante is not here denying the great value of secular wisdom, especially philosophy, for without it he could not have written the *Comedy.* His purpose is to put such wisdom in its proper place by making it subservient to God, by whom it was ordained to minister to man's practical intellectual needs, and by excluding it from all questions touching matters of faith. This message, aside from informing the *Comedy* as a whole, finds its most eloquent expression in the tragic story of Ulysses. It is in the *Purgatorio,* however, that Dante demonstrates systematically the interrelation of the two wisdoms he believes necessary for the education of mankind for the enjoyment of this life and the life to come.

In contrast with the turbulent complexity of Hell, Dante's Purgatory is simple, regular, and serene. On the lower reaches below the gate are kept in exile for varying lengths of time those souls who, for various reasons and in various conditions, sought salvation at the last moment. Above, within Purgatory, we find not the multifarious crimes by which vice or sin manifests itself in Hell (or on Earth), but simply the seven Capital Vices that lead to sinful acts. Since the souls here are all saved, and eager to act in accordance with divine will, there is no place among them for violence, malice, fraud, rebelliousness, etc. Each vice is treated on a specific ledge (*cornice*) that circles the mountain. Souls remain on a given ledge until they feel purged of all slightest subconscious taint of that particular vice, at which point they move up spontaneously.

The educative system employs, first, examples of the virtue

opposed to the vice, then examples of the vice punished; the method of presentation is different for each vice, and particularly suited to the posture and condition of the souls undergoing purgation. The Proud, bowed under loads that are proportionate to the gravity of their vice, have ample time, as they creak slowly around, to contemplate marvelously realistic carvings; the Envious, sitting together with their eyes, misused to their sorrow on earth, sewn shut, hear their lessons called out; the Slothful, rushing with the zeal they lacked in life, shout theirs aloud, and so on.

The ingenuity thus called for was admirable enough, but the truly significant feature is the steady pattern of duality, of the interaction of two sets of values. This is most clearly observable in the ordering of the lessons, or examples. First, in every instance, is an example from the life of the Virgin who, Bonaventure said, ". . . shone with every virtue . . . and was most free from the seven Capital Vices." Priority is thus given to sacred learning. Thereafter on every ledge the lessons are drawn alternately from the Bible and classical history, mythology, or literature. Progress up the mountain is possible only while the sun shines, *i.e.,* under the inspiration of divine wisdom. At the same time we know that the stars representing the four Cardinal Virtues are overhead, though made invisible by the sun's brightness. In other words, divine wisdom is the *sine qua non* of education, but the virtues Dante identifies with ancient Rome form its subject matter. At night, when no progress is possible in the active way, the stars representing the Theological Virtues are overhead, and men receive divine wisdom through mystical means, such as dreams and visions. At the end of Purgatory proper, Canto XXVII, Dante is awarded his diploma by Virgil, who, telling him that because his will is now free, healthy, and straight he may follow it freely, adds,

"Lord of yourself I crown and mitre you."

In other words, Dante is henceforth his own philosopher-king and his own bishop-pope; completely educated in the cardinal and theological virtues, he needs no further formal guidance in this life.

The principle of interaction between the classical and the Christian worlds is repeated once again in the pageant at the end of the *cántica*. Here Dante recapitulates his theory of the history of man's fall and redemption and the vicissitudes of the Church, ending in its contemporary degradation, the "Babylonian Captivity" of the Papacy in Avignon. To represent the Church, Dante uses a triumphal two-wheeled chariot. Around the right wheel—indication of their superiority—dance the three Theological Virtues, as maidens each dressed in her appropriate color; around the left wheel dance four others identified as the Cardinal Virtues by their imperial purple. A few *terzine* later the union of Biblical and classical authority is underlined again by the verses which herald the approach of Beatrice. The first is a paraphrase of *Matthew,* xxi, "Blessed art thou that comest"; the second are the words of Anchises in the *Aeneid,* VI, 833: "Oh scatter handfuls of lilies."

To most modern readers, all this may seem of little importance, and certainly not dangerously controversial; things were quite different in the early 1300's. To form an idea of how different, we do not need to strain our imaginations; we have only to think of certain fundamentalist groups of our own day and in our own country, among whom to suggest that the Bible is not sufficient by itself for every need is to invite serious trouble. Yet Dante was not content with challenging the Church's adequacy, though in a figurative and more or less covert form. His insistence that secular wisdom stand beside sacred wisdom in the education of the individual implied a much more dangerous challenge: that secular government stand beside sacred government. In simple terms, the world needed a strong civil state independent of the Church. Such a theory ran counter to the policy and pronouncements of the Holy See, supreme since its defeat of the last of the Hohenstaufen emperors. Now if an author should propound such an unpalatable theory openly, and add to it a proposal to remove and exclude from the Church all of its temporal power now and in the future, we have a book that's fit for burning, with an author not far removed. Such indeed was to be the fate, so far as possible, of Dante's last treatise, *De Monarchia.* Written in Latin, and hence worthy of official notice, in the last years before its author's death in 1321, it contained the conclusions of Dante's many years of study and meditation concerning God's plan for the proper governing of the world. It not only argued the divine authorization of the Empire, the advantages of such a system, its duties in providing civil peace and education; it denied and denounced in strongest terms the official dogma published by Innocent III, which likened the emperor to the Moon, deriving all authority from the Pope as the Sun. Instead, it maintained that emperor and Pope represented two Suns, each receiving light—and authority—directly from God. The world would thus have "the Supreme Pontiff to lead the human race by means of revelation, and the Emperor to guide it to temporal felicity by means of philosophic education." Since the emperor would be the supreme civil authority and power, there would exist in the world no one for him to envy, no one with greater possessions for him to covet. With nothing to arouse *cupiditas,* "root of all evils," he would himself be just, and would stamp out injustice in his subjects. Mankind would thus be able freely to develop its full potential for the enjoyment of this life in which Dante firmly believed. More important *sub specie aeternitatis* would be the inability of the clergy and the Church to acquire wealth, property, and any but spiritual power. In these circumstances its example would encourage men to follow its preachings of the unimportance of worldly goods, and would not have the opposite effect, as under actual conditions.

As Dante no doubt foresaw, the *De Monarchia* was not popular with ecclesiastical authorities. As a matter of fact, they destroyed every manuscript they could get their hands on, and later included it in the first *Index librorum prohibitorum.* As for the author, many persons believe there to be a connection between this attitude and the mystery which long surrounded the whereabouts of his remains.

It is a curious fact that in the *Purgatorio* the reasons for unhappy world conditions are much more outspoken in form than is the principle of interaction between the two sets of virtues. Here are some examples:

> What does it matter that Justinian came
> to trim the bit, if no one sits the saddle?
> Without him you [Italy] would have less cause for shame!

> You priests who, if you heed what God decreed,
> > should most seek after holiness and leave
> > to Caesar Caesar's saddle and his steed—
>
> see how the beast grows wild now none restrains
> > its temper, nor corrects it with the spur
> > since you set meddling hands upon its reins! [VI, 91–99]

And again, speaking of the causes of injustice and discord:

> Men, therefore, need restraint by law, and need
> > a monarch over them who sees at least
> > the towers of The True City. Laws, indeed,
>
> there are, but who puts nations to their proof?
> > No one. The shepherd who now leads mankind
> > can chew the cud, but lacks the cloven hoof.
>
> The people, then, seeing their guide devour
> > those worldly things to which their hunger turns
> > graze where he grazes, and ask nothing more.
>
> The bad state of the modern world is due—
> > as you may see, then—to bad leadership;
> > and not to natural corruption in you.
>
> Rome used to shine in two suns when her rod
> > made the world good, and each showed her its way:
> > one to the ordered world, and one to God.
>
> Now one declining sun puts out the other.
> > The sword and crook are one, and only evil
> > can follow from them when they are together;
>
> for neither fears the other, being one. [XVI, 94–112]

    The reason why such passages have not incurred official wrath lies probably in their being sporadic outbursts; they need not be interpreted as part of a systematic presentation, as in the case of the scheme for education.

In addition to such matters—and let it be said without wishing to lessen their very real importance—there was other material of much more crucial significance to be presented. In the *Comedy*'s imitation of the Holy Trinity, this second *cántica* represents the Second Person, and one of His chief attributes is Wisdom; this is the logical division in which to offer intellectual wisdom. Furthermore, in a poem dedicated to the demonstration of how, by their merits or demerits, men make themselves subject to reward or punishment, there is one central, all-important question to be treated—that of Free Will and the individual's responsibility for his actions. In introducing the *Inferno,* I had occasion to point out the care with which it had been constructed so as to give maximum expression to the Trinity, the Perfect Number, and so on. Now I must ask the forbearance of those readers intolerant of all such antic devices while I call attention to the way in which Dante arranged the present discussions. He begins the explanation of responsibility in Canto XVI, continues it in Canto XVII, and concludes it in Canto XVIII. Since there are 33 cantos in the *Purgatorio,* these are, respectively, the last of the first 16, the 17th or middle, and the first of the second 16. But added significance can be had by looking at the three *cántiche,* or the main body of the poem, less the introductory first canto. What has been said of the *Purgatorio* then becomes true for the whole; the discussion begins in Canto 49, continues in Canto 50, and concludes in Canto 51, the first of the remaining 49. The subject of the middle canto, either way, is Love as the moving force behind every action of mankind, whether good or evil.

For such instruction as was offered in the *Inferno,* Aristotle was much the preferred authority. In the presentations of metaphysics, psychology, and physiology which comprise most of the instruction that Dante was making available in the *Purgatorio* to readers of the vernacular, Aquinas is absolute and unchallenged. This does not mean, naturally, that much of the material was not originally Aristotelian, but rather that in form it is the version, reading, or interpretation chosen or elaborated by St. Thomas.

The first lesson, having established man's freedom from predestination, shows the need of the free will for discipline administered by an independent civil authority which will curb and direct his inclinations from childhood on. Since a child turns instinctively to anything pleasant, knowing no better, it will pursue valueless pleasures excessively and exclusively unless properly schooled. It is characteristic of Dante's method that the reader, now halfway through the book, suddenly realizes that he has already had an object lesson back in Canto II. There, among a boatload of souls arrived just after the two poets, Dante meets a dear friend, the musician Casella. All the souls are essentially childlike in their lack of sophistication and experience of the new environment; instead of pursuing their arduous upward path, they sit and indulge in the most innocent of pleasures by listening to the singing of one of Dante's best lyrics. The necessary discipline is suddenly administered by the stern Cato, and the group hastens off in pursuit of more substantial goods, with Virgil very red of face.

The lesson on Love distinguishes natural, instinctive love from the intellectual love peculiar to man, and explains how the latter can err. The most ingenious feat, however, is the explanation of how the infliction of wrong on one's neighbor, as it was spoken of in the *Inferno,* is really the pursuit of what appears to the distorted vision as a good. The discussion thus ends in a definition of the Capital Sins or Vices.

The third great lesson (XVIII) was directed against Christianity's most dangerous domestic foes at the time, the Epicureans. Readers of the *Inferno* will remember how Epicurus is dealt a much harsher fate than the other Greek philosophers, and placed in the burning tombs of Canto X instead of in the pleasant, though hopeless, serenity of Limbo. An incredibly large proportion of Dante's townsmen shared this materialist heresy which denied the immortality of the soul and man's responsibility for his acts. The lesson is probably the most difficult in the whole *Comedy.* Having made the point that attraction toward a pleasurable stimulus is not necessarily a good, according to Epicurus, but merely a natural reaction, Dante must justify the concept of man's being held responsible for simply following a natural impulse. To accomplish this, the principle of the Substantial Form must be explained, together with the concept of Pure Act versus Potentiality. To have done all this concisely, clearly, and with poetry intact is one of Dante's greater achievements.

The last lesson of this general type is on human reproduction and the creation of the individual soul. It is introduced ingeniously by Dante's supposed curiosity as to how incorporeal souls could still reflect so vividly and painfully the effects of tantalized hunger and thirst as are seen among the Gluttonous. From this starting point, and with the ostensible purpose of describing how, after death, memory, intellect, and will, stronger than before, impress on the surrounding air a fictive body with senses operative, Dante launches what is really a refutation of the other important heretical group of the day, the Averroists. Comparable to the Epicureans in numbers and influence, they shared with them a nonbelief in the immortality of the soul *as an individual entity.* They differed from them, however, in that the basis of their belief was what we might call today "scientific" rather than philosophical. The founder of the sect was a famed Arabian scholar who died about 1200, traditionally called Averroës, but known increasingly today as Ibn-Roschd. Physician as well as philosopher, he denied the existence of a conscious soul because he could find no organ or place for it in the body. His solution (simplified) to the obvious fact of man's intellectual ability posited a universal intellect, with part of which the soul was endowed, and to which each share returned at death. For decades, Christendom floundered in refuting him, till Aquinas accomplished it with the argument of self-consciousness or awareness used by Dante (XXV, 67–75), who himself has often been accused of Averroism. In this canto, then, Dante has given the best current explanation of human generation, and has established the unity of the soul, the survival of its individuality, and its capacity to suffer the sort of punishment calculated to impress at least his contemporary readers.

It should be noted, in this connection, that Virgil no longer enjoys the position he had in the *Inferno,* where he appeared as the quasi-omniscient, unique purveyor of wisdom. This was fitting in such a predominantly pre-Christian realm, peopled almost exclusively by souls who had lost *il bene dell' intelletto,* and where Virgil is the rescuer of one who had almost suffered that fate. As the poets emerge into the dawn light of the *Purgatorio,* the change is immediate and striking. The confident guide becomes another pilgrim; wise and experienced, however, he serves Dante and his readers as an example of the disciplined mind at work deducing the rules of this Christian territory. So, although Dante has him deliver the great central lectures on Love, the earlier one on Free Will versus Predestination is given (with characteristic irascibility) by one Marco Lombardo, whom we never see because of the dense smoke on the ledge of Anger. The last, in Canto XXV, Virgil graciously entrusts to Statius, a Latin poet a generation and more later than Virgil. Presented by Dante as the older poet's ardent admirer, and a "crypto-Christian" through him, Statius represents a poet of the ancient, pagan world redeemed by the coming of Christ; the union of Empire with Christianity, of Cardinal Virtues with Theological Virtues. He is, thus, the obverse of Dante and his goal: the union of Christianity with the revived Empire, and of the Theological Virtues with the Cardinal Virtues to be restored under it. Artistically, he contributes a great new dramatic interest at a point where it is most welcome.

Quite apart from inevitable limitations of space, I have deliberately refrained from commenting on the poetry, the style, and (so far as possible) the unfolding story. I feel that everyone is entitled to make his own private initial approach to the intimate author-reader relationship. Happily, in the *Purgatorio* as in the preceding *cántica,* Mr. Ciardi's perceptive and sensitive translation makes that relationship more accessible than has hitherto been possible without a good command of the original Italian.

—Archibald T. MacAllister

THE
PURGATORIO

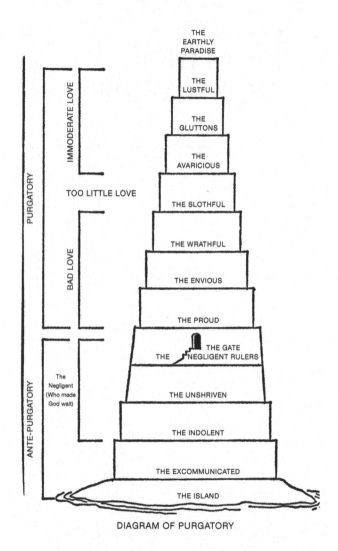

DIAGRAM OF PURGATORY

Canto I

ANTE-PURGATORY:
THE SHORE OF THE ISLAND   *Cato of Utica*

*The Poets emerge from Hell just before dawn of Easter Sunday
(April 10, 1300), and Dante revels in the sight of the rediscov-
ered heavens. As he looks eagerly about at the stars, he sees
nearby an old man of impressive bearing. The ancient is
CATO OF UTICA, guardian of the shores of Purgatory. Cato
challenges the Poets as fugitives from Hell, but Virgil, after
first instructing Dante to kneel in reverence, explains Dante's
mission and Beatrice's command. Cato then gives them in-
structions for proceeding.*

*The Poets have emerged at a point a short way up the
slope of Purgatory. It is essential, therefore, that they de-
scend to the lowest point and begin from there, an alle-
gory of Humility. Cato, accordingly, orders Virgil to lead
Dante to the shore, to wet his hands in the dew of the new
morning, and to wash the stains of Hell from Dante's face
and the film of Hell's vapors from Dante's eyes. Virgil is
then to bind about Dante's waist one of the pliant reeds
(symbolizing Humility) that grow in the soft mud of the
shore.*

*Having so commanded, Cato disappears. Dante arises in
silence and stands waiting, eager to begin. His look is all the
communication that is necessary. Virgil leads him to the
shore and performs all that Cato has commanded. Dante's
first purification is marked by a miracle: when Virgil breaks
off a reed, the stalk immediately regenerates a new reed,
restoring itself exactly as it had been.*

3

For better waters now the little bark
   of my indwelling powers raises her sails,
   and leaves behind that sea so cruel and dark.

Now shall I sing that second kingdom given
   the soul of man wherein to purge its guilt   5
   and so grow worthy to ascend to Heaven.

Yours am I, sacred Muses! To you I pray.
   Here let dead poetry rise once more to life,
   and here let sweet Calliope rise and play

some fair accompaniment in that high strain   10
   whose power the wretched Pierides once felt
   so terribly they dared not hope again.

Sweet azure of the sapphire of the east
   was gathering on the serene horizon
   its pure and perfect radiance—a feast   15

to my glad eyes, reborn to their delight,
   as soon as I had passed from the dead air
   which had oppressed my soul and dimmed my sight.

The planet whose sweet influence strengthens love
   was making all the east laugh with her rays,   20
   veiling the Fishes, which she swam above.

I turned then to my right and set my mind
   on the other pole, and there I saw four stars
   unseen by mortals since the first mankind.

The heavens seemed to revel in their light.   25
   O widowed Northern Hemisphere, bereft
   forever of the glory of that sight!

As I broke off my gazing, my eyes veered
   a little to the left, to the other pole
   from which, by then, the Wain had disappeared.   30

I saw, nearby, an ancient man, alone.
  His bearing filled me with such reverence,
  no father could ask more from his best son.

His beard was long and touched with strands of white,
  as was his hair, of which two tresses fell   35
  over his breast. Rays of the holy light

that fell from the four stars made his face glow
  with such a radiance that he looked to me
  as if he faced the sun. And standing so,

he moved his venerable plumes and said: 40
  "Who are you two who climb by the dark stream
  to escape the eternal prison of the dead?

Who led you? or what served you as a light
  in your dark flight from the eternal valley,
  which lies forever blind in darkest night?   45

Are the laws of the pit so broken? Or is new counsel
  published in Heaven that the damned may wander
  onto my rocks from the abyss of Hell?"

At that my Master laid his hands upon me,
  instructing me by word and touch and gesture   50
  to show my reverence in brow and knee,

then answered him: "I do not come this way
  of my own will or powers. A Heavenly Lady
  sent me to this man's aid in his dark day.

But since your will is to know more, my will   55
  cannot deny you; I will tell you truly
  why we have come and how. This man has still

to see his final hour, though in the burning
  of his own madness he had drawn so near it
  his time was perilously short for turning.   60

As I have told you, I was sent to show
   the way his soul must take for its salvation;
   and there is none but this by which I go.

I have shown him the guilty people. Now I mean
   to lead him through the spirits in your keeping,   65
   to show him those whose suffering makes them clean.

By what means I have led him to this strand
   to see and hear you, takes too long to tell:
   from Heaven is the power and the command.

Now may his coming please you, for he goes   70
   to win his freedom; and how dear that is
   the man who gives his life for it best knows.

You know it, who in that cause found death sweet
   in Utica where you put off that flesh
   which shall rise radiant at the Judgment Seat.   75

We do not break the Laws: this man lives yet,
   and I am of that Round not ruled by Minos,
   with your own Marcia, whose chaste eyes seem set

in endless prayers to you. O blessed breast
   to hold her yet your own! for love of her   80
   grant us permission to pursue our quest

across your seven kingdoms. When I go
   back to her side I shall bear thanks of you,
   if you will let me speak your name below."

"Marcia was so pleasing in my eyes   85
   there on the other side," he answered then,
   "that all she asked, I did. Now that she lies

beyond the evil river, no word or prayer
   of hers may move me. Such was the Decree
   pronounced upon us when I rose from there.   90

But if, as you have said, a Heavenly Dame
    orders your way, there is no need to flatter:
    you need but ask it of me in her name.

Go then, and lead this man, but first see to it
    you bind a smooth green reed about his waist   95
    and clean his face of all trace of the pit.

For it would not be right that one with eyes
    still filmed by mist should go before the angel
    who guards the gate: he is from Paradise.

All round the wave-wracked shore-line, there below,   100
    reeds grow in the soft mud. Along that edge
    no foliate nor woody plant could grow,

for what lives in that buffeting must bend.
    Do not come back this way: the rising sun
    will light an easier way you may ascend."   105

With that he disappeared; and silently
    I rose and moved back till I faced my Guide,
    my eyes upon him, waiting. He said to me:

"Follow my steps and let us turn again:
    along this side there is a gentle slope   110
    that leads to the low boundaries of the plain."

The dawn, in triumph, made the day-breeze flee
    before its coming, so that from afar
    I recognized the trembling of the sea.

We strode across that lonely plain like men   115
    who seek the road they strayed from and who count
    the time lost till they find it once again.

When we had reached a place along the way
    where the cool morning breeze shielded the dew
    against the first heat of the gathering day,   120

with gentle graces my Sweet Master bent
   and laid both outspread palms upon the grass.
   Then I, being well aware of his intent,

lifted my tear-stained cheeks to him, and there
   he made me clean, revealing my true color   125
   under the residues of Hell's black air.

We moved on then to the deserted strand
   which never yet has seen upon its waters
   a man who found his way back to dry land.

There, as it pleased another, he girded me.   130
   Wonder of wonders! when he plucked a reed
   another took its place there instantly,

arising from the humble stalk he tore
so that it grew exactly as before.

NOTES

4. *that second kingdom:* Purgatory.

5. *to purge its guilt:* (See also line 66: *those whose suffering makes them clean.*) There is suffering in Purgatory but no torment. The torment of the damned is endless, produces no change in the soul that endures it, and is imposed from without. The suffering of the souls in Purgatory, on the other hand, is temporary, is a means of purification, and is eagerly embraced as an act of the soul's own will. Demons guard the damned to inflict punishment and to prevent escape. In Purgatory, the sinners are free to leave off their sufferings: nothing but their own desire to be made clean moves them to accept their pains, and nothing more is needed. In fact, it is left to the suffering soul itself (no doubt informed by Divine Illumination) to decide at what point it has achieved purification and is ready to move on.

8. *dead poetry:* The verses that sang of Hell. Dante may equally have meant that poetry as an art has long been surpassed by history

as the medium for great subjects. Here poetry will return to its classic state.

7–12. THE INVOCATION. Dante invokes all the Muses, as he did in *Inferno,* II, 7, but there the exhortation was to his own powers, to High Genius, and to Memory. Here he addresses his specific exhortation to Calliope, who, as the Muse of Epic Poetry, is foremost of the Nine. In *Paradiso* (I, 13) he exhorts Apollo himself to come to the aid of the poem.

Dante exhorts Calliope to fill him with the strains of the music she played in the defeat of the Pierides, the nine daughters of Pierius, King of Thessaly. They presumed to challenge the Muses to a contest of song. After their defeat they were changed into magpies for their presumption. Ovid (*Metamorphoses,* V, 294–340 and 662–678) retells the myth in detail.

Note that Dante not only calls upon Calliope to fill him with the strains of highest song, but that he calls for that very song that overthrew the arrogant pretensions of the Pierides, the strains that humbled false pride. The invocation is especially apt, therefore, as a first sounding of the theme of Humility.

17. *the dead air:* Of Hell.

19–21. *The planet whose sweet influence strengthens love:* Venus. Here, as morning star, Venus is described as rising in Pisces, the Fishes, the zodiacal sign immediately preceding Aries. In Canto I of the *Inferno* Dante has made it clear that the Sun is in Aries. Hence it is about to rise.

Allegorically, the fact that Venus represents love is, of course, indispensable to the mood of the *Purgatorio.* At no time in April of 1300 was Venus the morning star. Rather, it rose after the Sun. Dante's description of the first dawn in Canto I of the *Inferno* similarly violates the exact detail of things. But Dante is no bookkeeper of the literal. In the *Inferno* he violated fact in order to compile a perfect symbol of rebirth. Here, he similarly violates the literal in order to describe an ideal sunrise, and simultaneously to make the allegorical point that Love (Venus) leads the way and that Divine Illumination (the Sun) follows upon it.

23. *four stars:* Modern readers are always tempted to identify these four stars as the Southern Cross, but it is almost certain that Dante did not know about that formation. In VIII, 89, Dante mentions

three other stars as emphatically as he does these four and no one has been tempted to identify them on the star-chart. Both constellations are best taken as allegorical. The four stars represent the Four Cardinal Virtues: Prudence, Justice, Fortitude, and Temperance. Dante will encounter them again in the form of nymphs when he achieves the Earthly Paradise.

24. *the first mankind:* Adam and Eve. In Dante's geography, the Garden of Eden (the Earthly Paradise) was at the top of the Mount of Purgatory, which was the only land in the Southern Hemisphere. All of what were called "the southern continents" were believed to lie north of the equator. When Adam and Eve were driven from the Garden, therefore, they were driven into the Northern Hemisphere, and no living soul since had been far enough south to see those stars.

Ulysses and his men (*Inferno,* XXVI) had come within sight of the Mount of Purgatory, but Ulysses mentioned nothing of having seen these stars.

29. *the other pole:* The North Pole. The Wain (Ursa Major, *i.e.,* the Big Dipper) is below the horizon.

31 ff. CATO OF UTICA. Marcus Porcius Cato, the younger, 95–46 B.C. In the name of freedom, Cato opposed the policies of both Caesar and Pompey, but because he saw Caesar as the greater evil joined forces with Pompey. After the defeat of his cause at the Battle of Thapsus, Cato killed himself with his own sword rather than lose his freedom. Virgil lauds him in the *Aeneid* as a symbol of perfect devotion to liberty, and all writers of Roman antiquity have given Cato a similar high place. Dante spends the highest praises on him both in *De Monarchia* and *Il Convivio.*

Why Cato should be so signally chosen by God as the special guardian of Purgatory has been much disputed. Despite his suicide (and certainly one could argue that he had less excuse for it than had Pier delle Vigne—see *Inferno,* XIII—for his) he was sent to Limbo as a Virtuous Pagan. From Limbo he was especially summoned to his present office. It is clear, moreover, that he will find a special triumph on Judgment Day, though he will probably not be received into Heaven.

The key to Dante's intent seems to lie in the four stars, the Four Cardinal Virtues, that shine so brightly on Cato's face when Dante first sees him. Once Cato is forgiven his suicide (and a partisan could argue that it was a positive act, a death for freedom), he may certainly be taken as a figure of Prudence, Justice, Fortitude, and Temperance. He does very well, moreover, as a symbol of the natural love of freedom; and Purgatory, it must be remembered, is the road to Ultimate Freedom. Cato may be taken, therefore, as representative of supreme virtue short of godliness. He has accomplished everything but the purifying total surrender of his will to God. As such he serves as an apt transitional symbol, being the highest rung on the ladder of natural virtue, but the lowest on the ladder of those godly virtues to which Purgatory is the ascent. Above all, the fact that he took Marcia (see line 78, note) back to his love, makes him an especially apt symbol of God's forgiveness in allowing the strayed soul to return to him through Purgatory.

53. *A Heavenly Lady:* Beatrice.

77. *Minos:* The Judge of the Damned. The round in Hell not ruled by Minos is Limbo, the final resting place of the Virtuous Pagans. Minos (see *Inferno,* V) is stationed at the entrance to the second circle of Hell. The souls in Limbo (the first circle) have never had to pass before him to be judged.

78. *Marcia.* The story of Marcia and of Cato is an extraordinary one. She was the daughter of the consul Philippus and became Cato's second wife, bearing his three children. In 56 B.C., in an unusual transaction approved by her father, Cato released her in order that she might marry his friend Hortensius. (Hence line 87: "that all she asked, I did.") After the death of Hortensius, Cato took her back.

In *Il Convivio,* IV, 28, Dante presents the newly widowed Marcia praying to be taken back in order that she may die the wife of Cato, and that it may be said of her that she was not cast forth from his love. Dante treats that return as an allegory of the return of the strayed soul to God (that it may die "married" to God, and that God's love for it be made manifest to all time). Virgil describes Marcia as still praying to Cato.

89. *the Decree:* May be taken as that law that makes an absolute separation between the damned and the saved. Cato cannot be referring here to *Mark,* xii, 25 ("when they shall rise from the dead, they neither marry, nor are given in marriage") for that "decree" was not pronounced upon his ascent from Limbo.

98. *filmed by mist:* Of Hell.

100 ff. THE REED. The pliant reed clearly symbolizes humility, but other allegorical meanings suggest themselves at once. First, the Reed takes the place of the Cord that Dante took from about his waist in order to signal Geryon. The Cord had been intended to snare and defeat the Leopard with the Gaudy Pelt, a direct assault upon sin. It is now superseded by the Reed of submission to God's will. Second, the reeds are eternal and undiminishable. As such they must immediately suggest the redemption purchased by Christ's sufferings (ever-abounding grace), for the quantity of grace available to mankind through Christ's passion is, in Christian creed, also eternal and undiminishable. The importance of the fact that the reeds grow at the lowest point of the Island and that the Poets must descend to them before they can begin, has already been mentioned. Curiously, the reed is never again mentioned, though it must remain around Dante's waist. See also *Matthew,* xxvii, 29.

119. *breeze shielded the dew:* The dew is a natural symbol of God's grace. The morning breeze shields it in the sense that, being cool, it retards evaporation.

Even more naturally, being bathed in the dew may be taken to signify baptism. The structure of Purgatory certainly suggests a parable of the soul's stages of sacred development: the dew, baptism; the gate of Purgatory, above, first communion; Virgil's certification of Dante as lord of himself (XXVII, 143), confirmation; and Dante's swoon and awakening (XXXI, 89), as extreme unction and the reception into the company of the blessed.

Canto II

———◆◇◆———

*It is dawn. Dante, washed, and girded by the reed, is standing
by the shore when he sees a light approaching at enormous
speed across the sea. The light grows and becomes visible as
THE ANGEL BOATMAN who ferries the souls of the elect
from their gathering place at THE MOUTH OF THE TIBER
to the shore of Purgatory.*

    *The newly arrived souls debark and, taking the Poets as
familiars of the place, ask directions. Virgil explains that he
and Dante are new arrivals but that they have come by the
dark road through Hell. The newly arrived souls see by his
breathing that Dante is alive and crowd about him. One of
the new souls is CASELLA, a musician who seems to have
been a dear friend of Dante's. Dante tries three times to clasp
him to his bosom, but each time his arms pass through empty
air. Casella explains the function of the Angel Boatman and
then, at Dante's request, strikes up a song, one of Dante's own
canzoni that Casella had set to music. Instantly, CATO de-
scends upon the group, berating them, and they break like
startled pigeons up the slope toward the mountain.*

The Sun already burned at the horizon,
    while the high point of its meridian circle
    covered Jerusalem, and in opposition

equal Night revolved above the Ganges
    bearing the Scales that fall out of her hand   5
    as she grows longer with the season's changes:

thus, where I was, Aurora in her passage
    was losing the pale blushes from her cheeks
    which turned to orange with increasing age.

We were still standing by the sea's new day   10
    like travelers pondering the road ahead
    who send their souls on while their bones delay;

when low above the ocean's western rim,
    as Mars, at times, observed through the thick vapors
    that form before the dawn, burns red and slim;   15

just so—so may I hope to see it again!—
    a light appeared, moving above the sea
    faster than any flight. A moment then

I turned my eyes to question my sweet Guide,
    and when I looked back to that unknown body   20
    I found its mass and brightness magnified.

Then from each side of it came into view
    an unknown something-white; and from beneath it,
    bit by bit, another whiteness grew.

We watched till the white objects at each side   25
    took shape as wings, and Virgil spoke no word.
    But when he saw what wings they were, he cried:

"Down on your knees! It is God's angel comes!
    Down! Fold your hands! From now on you shall see
    many such ministers in the high kingdoms.   30

See how he scorns man's tools: he needs no oars
    nor any other sail than his own wings
    to carry him between such distant shores.

See how his pinions tower upon the air,
    pointing to Heaven: they are eternal plumes   35
    and do not moult like feathers or human hair."

Then as that bird of heaven closed the distance
    between us, he grew brighter and yet brighter
    until I could no longer bear the radiance,

and bowed my head. He steered straight for the shore,   40
    his ship so light and swift it drew no water;
    it did not seem to sail so much as soar.

Astern stood the great pilot of the Lord,
    so fair his blessedness seemed written on him;
    and more than a hundred souls were seated forward,   45

singing as if they raised a single voice
    in exitu Israel de Aegypto.
    Verse after verse they made the air rejoice.

The angel made the sign of the cross, and they
    cast themselves, at his signal, to the shore.   50
    Then, swiftly as he had come, he went away.

The throng he left seemed not to understand
    what place it was, but stood and stared about
    like men who see the first of a new land.

The Sun, who with an arrow in each ray   55
    had chased the Goat out of the height of Heaven,
    on every hand was shooting forth the day,

when those new souls looked up to where my Guide
    and I stood, saying to us, "If you know it,
    show us the road that climbs the mountainside."   60

Virgil replied: "You think perhaps we two
    have had some long experience of this place,
    but we are also pilgrims, come before you

only by very little, though by a way
   so steep, so broken, and so tortuous   65
   the climb ahead of us will seem like play."

The throng of souls, observing by my breath
   I was still in the body I was born to,
   stared in amazement and grew pale as death.

As a crowd, eager for news, will all but smother   70
   a messenger who bears the olive branch,
   and not care how they trample one another—

so these, each one of them a soul elect,
   pushed close to stare at me, well-nigh forgetting
   the way to go to make their beauty perfect.   75

One came forward to embrace me, and his face
   shone with such joyous love that, seeing it,
   I moved to greet him with a like embrace.

O solid-seeming shadows! Three times there
   I clasped my hands behind him, and three times   80
   I drew them to my breast through empty air.

Amazed, I must have lost all color then,
   for he smiled tenderly and drew away,
   and I lunged forward as if to try again.

In a voice as gentle as a melody   85
   he bade me pause; and by his voice I knew him,
   and begged him stay a while and speak to me.

He answered: "As I loved you in the clay
   of my mortal body, so do I love you freed:
   therefore I pause. But what brings you this way?" 90

"Casella mine, I go the way I do
   in the hope I may return here," I replied.
   "But why has so much time been taken from you?"

And he: "I am not wronged if he whose usage
   accepts the soul at his own time and pleasure   95
   has many times refused to give me passage:

his will moves in the image and perfection
   of a Just Will; indeed, for three months now
   he has taken all who asked, without exception.

And so it was that in my turn I stood   100
   upon that shore where Tiber's stream grows salt,
   and there was gathered to my present good.

It is back to the Tiber's mouth he has just flown,
   for there forever is the gathering place
   of all who do not sink to Acheron."   105

"If no new law has stripped you of your skill
   or of the memory of those songs of love
   that once could calm all passion from my will,"

I said to him, "Oh sound a verse once more
   to soothe my soul which, with its weight of flesh   110
   and the long journey, sinks distressed and sore."

"Love that speaks its reasons in my heart,"
   he sang then, and such grace flowed on the air
   that even now I hear that music start.

My Guide and I and all those souls of bliss   115
   stood tranced in song; when suddenly we heard
   the Noble Elder cry: "What's this! What's this!

Negligence! Loitering! O laggard crew,
   run to the mountain and strip off the scurf
   that lets not God be manifest in you!"   120

Exactly as a flock of pigeons gleaning
   a field of stubble, pecking busily,
   forgetting all their primping and their preening,

will rise as one and scatter through the air,
    leaving their feast without another thought   125
    when they are taken by a sudden scare—

so that new band, all thought of pleasure gone,
    broke from the feast of music with a start
    and scattered for the mountainside like one

who leaps and does not look where he will land.   130
Nor were my Guide and I inclined to stand.

Notes

1–9. The bit of erudite affectation in which Dante indulges here
means simply, "It was dawn." To understand the total figure, one
must recall the following essentials of Dante's geography: (1)
Jerusalem is antipodal to the Mount of Purgatory. Thus it is sunset at
Jerusalem when it is sunrise on the mountain. (2) All the land of the
earth is contained in one half of the Northern Hemisphere. That is to
say, there is no land (except the Mount of Purgatory) anywhere in
the Southern Hemisphere and of the total circle of the Northern
Hemisphere (360°) only half (180°) is land. Jerusalem is at the exact
center of this 180° arc of land. Spain, 90° to one side, is the West, and
India (Ganges), 90° to the other, is the East.

Every fifteen degrees of longitude equals one hour of time. That
is to say, it takes the Sun an hour to travel fifteen degrees. Thus at
sunset over Jerusalem it is midnight (six hours later) over India,
and noon (six hours earlier) over Spain. The journey, moreover,
is conceived as taking place during the vernal equinox, when the
days and nights are of the same length. Thus it is "equal Night"
(line 4).

Finally, when the Sun is in Aries, midnight is in Libra (the
Scales). Thus the night bears the Scales in her hand (*i.e.,* that con-
stellation is visible), but Libra will no longer be the sign of the night
as the season changes, and thus it may be said that the Scales will
fall from her hand (*i.e.,* will no longer be visible).

47. *in exitu Israel de Aegypto:* When Israel out of Egypt came.
Psalm CXIII.

50. *cast themselves, at his signal, to the shore:* Note that this is exactly what Dante says of the sinners leaving Charon's ferry in *Inferno,* III, 113. In Dante there is no accident in such correspondence. Such parallels between the *Purgatorio* and the *Inferno* are essential parts of the poem's total structure.

56. *the Goat:* Capricorn.

71. *who bears the olive branch:* In Dante's time couriers bore the olive branch to indicate not only peace but good news in general.

79–84. *O solid-seeming shadows!:* As always, Dante treats the substance of the souls to suit his own dramatic convenience, at times giving them the attributes of fleshly bodies, at others treating them as mirages.

91. *Casella:* Practically all that is known about Casella has been drawn from the text itself. He seems to have died several months before Dante began his journey, hence early in 1300 or late in 1299. There is no explanation of his delay in reaching Purgatory (the time that has been taken from him). Dante later meets several classes of sinners who must spend a certain period of waiting before they can begin their purification. Clearly it is Dante's conception that the souls bound for Purgatory do not always proceed instantly to their destination, but may be required to expiate by a delay at their gathering point by the mouth of the Tiber (line 101).

Casella was a musician and is known to have set some of Dante's *canzoni* to music. The song he strikes up (line 112) is such a *canzoni.*

99. *he has taken all who asked:* Boniface VIII decreed a Jubilee Year from Christmas 1299 to Christmas 1300. (See *Inferno,* XVIII, 28–33 and note.) His decree extended special indulgences even to the dead. Hence the Angel's permissiveness.

Note, however, that he has taken all who wished to go, all who asked. It follows that some souls did not express such a wish, almost certainly because they did not feel themselves to be ready. As in note to I, 5, the souls of Purgatory decide for themselves when they are ready to progress from one stage to the next.

Canto III

ANTE-PURGATORY:
THE BASE OF THE CLIFF   *The Late-Repentant*
                        Class One: The Contumacious
                                    Manfred

The souls scatter for the mountain, and Dante draws close to Virgil as they both race ahead. The newly risen sun is at Dante's back. He runs, therefore, with his shadow stretched long and directly before him. Suddenly he becomes aware that there is only one shadow on the ground and he turns in panic, thinking Virgil is no longer at his side. Virgil reassures him, explaining that souls are so made as to cast no shadow. His remarks on the nature of souls give him occasion to define THE LIMITS OF REASON IN THE SCHEME OF CREATION.

The Poets reach THE BASE OF THE CLIFF and are dismayed to find that it rises sheer, offering no way by which they may climb. While Virgil is pondering this new difficulty, Dante looks about and sees a band of souls approaching so slowly that they seem scarcely to move. These are the first of THE LATE-REPENTANT souls the Poets will encounter. In life they put off the desire for grace: now, as they were laggard in life, so must they wait before they may begin their purification. The souls in this band are all souls of THE CONTUMACIOUS: they died excommunicated, but surrendered their souls to God when they were at the point of death. Their punishment is that they must wait here at the Base of the Cliff for thirty times the period of their contumacy.

One soul among them identifies himself as MANFRED and begs Dante to bear a message to his daughter Constance in

order that she may offer prayer for Manfred's soul and
thereby shorten his period of waiting. Manfred explains that
prayer can greatly assist the souls in Purgatory. He also ex-
plains how it is that though contumacy is punished, no act of
priest or Pope may keep from salvation a soul that has truly
given itself to God.

Those routed souls scattered across the scene,
    their faces once again turned toward the mountain
    where Reason spurs and Justice picks us clean;

but I drew ever closer to my Guide:
    and how could I have run my course without him?   5
    who would have led me up the mountainside?

He seemed gnawed by remorse for his offense:
    O noble conscience without stain! how sharp
    the sting of a small fault is to your sense!

When he had checked that haste that urges men   10
    to mar the dignity of every act,
    my mind, forced in upon itself till then,

broke free, and eager to see all before me,
    I raised my eyes in wonder to that mountain
    that soars highest to Heaven from the sea.   15

Low at my back, the Sun was a red blaze;
    its light fell on the ground before me broken
    in the form in which my body blocked its rays.

I gave a start of fear and whirled around
    seized by the thought that I had been abandoned,   20
    for I saw one shadow only on the ground.

And my Comfort turned full to me then to say:
    "Why are you still uncertain? Why do you doubt
    that I am here and guide you on your way?

Vespers have rung already on the tomb   25
    of the body in which I used to cast a shadow.
    It was taken to Naples from Brindisium.

If now I cast no shadow, should that fact
    amaze you more than the heavens which pass the light
    undimmed from one to another? We react   30

within these bodies to pain and heat and cold
    according to the workings of That Will
    which does not will that all Its ways be told.

He is insane who dreams that he may learn
    by mortal reasoning the boundless orbit   35
    Three Persons in One Substance fill and turn.

Be satisfied with the *quia* of cause unknown,
    O humankind! for could you have seen All,
    Mary need not have suffered to bear a son.

You saw how some yearn endlessly in vain: 40
    such as would, else, have surely had their wish,
    but have, instead, its hunger as their pain.

I speak of Aristotle and Plato," he said.
    "—Of them and many more." And here he paused,
    and sorrowing and silent, bowed his head.   45

Meanwhile we reached the mountain's foot; and there
    we found so sheer a cliff, the nimblest legs
    would not have served, unless they walked on air.

The most forsaken and most broken goat-trace
    in the mountains between Lerici and Turbia   50
    compared to this would seem a gracious staircase.

My Guide exclaimed: "Now who is there to say
    in which direction we may find some slope
    up which one without wings may pick his way!"

While he was standing, head bowed to his shoulders,   55
   and pondering which direction we might take,
   I stood there looking up among the boulders,

and saw upon my left beside that cliff-face
   a throng that moved its feet in our direction,
   and yet seemed not to, so slow was its pace.   60

"Master," I said, "look up and you will find
   some people coming who may solve the problem,
   if you have not yet solved it in your mind."

He looked up then and, openly relieved,
   said: "Let us go to them, since they lag so.   65
   And you, dear son, believe as you have believed."

We were as far off yet from that slow flock
   (I mean when we had gone a thousand paces)
   as a strong slingsman could have thrown a rock,

when they drew in against the cliff and stood there   70
   like men who fear what they see coming toward them
   and, waiting for it, huddle close and stare.

"O well-concluded lives! O souls thus met
   already among the chosen!" Virgil said,
   "By that sweet crown of peace that shall be set   75

on each of you in time, tell us which way
   leads to some slope by which we two may climb.
   Who best knows time is most grieved by delay."

As sheep come through a gate—by ones, by twos,
   by threes, and all the others trail behind,   80
   timidly, nose to ground, and what the first does

the others do, and if the first one pauses,
   the others huddle up against his back,
   silly and mute, not knowing their own causes—

just so, I stood there watching with my Guide,   85
   the first row of that happy flock come on,
   their look meek and their movements dignified.

And when the souls that came first in that flock
   saw the light broken on the ground to my right
   so that my shadow fell upon the rock,   90

they halted and inched back as if to shy,
   and all the others who came after them
   did as the first did without knowing why.

"Let me confirm the thought you leave unspoken:
   it is a living body you see before you   95
   by which the sunlight on the ground is broken.

Do not be astonished: you may rest assured
   he does not seek the way to climb this wall
   without a power from Heaven."—Thus my Lord

addressed them, and those worthy spirits said,   100
   waving the backs of their hands in our direction:
   "First turn around, and then go straight ahead."

And one soul said to me: "Whoever you are,
   as you move on, look back and ask yourself
   if you have ever seen me over there."   105

I studied him with care, my head turned round:
   gold-blond he was, and handsomely patrician,
   although one brow was split by a sword wound.

When I, in all humility, confessed
   I never before had seen him, he said, "Look"   110
   —and showed me a great slash above his breast.

Then, smiling, added: "I am Manfred, grandson
   of the blessed Empress Constance, and I beg you,
   when you return there over the horizon,

go to my sweet daughter, noble mother   115
   of the honor of Sicily and of Aragon
   and speak the truth, if men speak any other.

My flesh had been twice hacked, and each wound
    mortal,
   when, tearfully, I yielded up my soul
   to Him whose pardon gladly waits for all.   120

Horrible were my sins, but infinite
   is the abiding Goodness which holds out
   Its open arms to all who turn to It.

If the pastor of Cosenza, by the rage
   of Clement sent to hunt me down, had first   125
   studied the book of God at this bright page,

my body's bones would still be in the ground
   there by the bridgehead outside Benevento,
   under the heavy guard of the stone mound.

Now, rattled by the wind, by the rain drenched,   130
   they lie outside the kingdom, by the Verde,
   where he transported them with tapers quenched.

No man may be so cursed by priest or Pope
   but what the Eternal Love may still return
   while any thread of green lives on in hope.   135

Those who die contumacious, it is true,
   though they repent their feud with Holy Church,
   must wait outside here on the bank, as we do,

for thirty times as long as they refused
   to be obedient, though by good prayers   140
   in their behalf, that time may be reduced.

See, then, how great a service you may do me
   when you return, by telling my good Constance
   of my condition and of this decree

that still forbids our entrance to the kingdom.   145
For here, from those beyond, great good may come."

NOTES

1–3. The original lines are in Dante's densest style, and every commentator has felt the need to discuss this passage at length. *once again turned:* Dante's intent here seems clear enough. On their arrival the souls had looked straight ahead at the mountain. The distraction for which Cato chastised them had led them to look away. *where Reason spurs and Justice picks us clean:* The original phrasing is *ove ragion ne fruga.* If *ragion* is taken to mean "reason" and *fruga* in one of its senses to mean "to prick on," then one meaning follows clearly enough. If, however, *ragion* is taken in context to mean Divine Justice—and many commentators have argued that it must so be taken—and if *fruga* (a very complex word) is taken in its first sense of "to probe, to search minutely, to pick clean"—then a second meaning follows. I am inclined to think that Dante always means both possibilities in such cases and I have, therefore rendered both.

10–11. *that haste that urges men to mar the dignity of every act:* There can be no doubt that Dante cherished his dignity. Even in moving toward salvation he preferred a slow and stately manner. On his own premises, there is obviously a taint of pride in such a disposition. When he reaches the Cornice of the Proud, he makes it clear that Pride is the sin that most weighs upon him. Dignity, of course, is closely related to Moderation, one of the Cardinal Virtues.

21 ff. *for I saw one shadow only on the ground:* The fact that Dante was still in his mortal body was evidenced in Hell by his breathing, by the way his weight made a boat settle in the water, by the fact that his foot dislodged a stone, and by the force with which he inadvertently kicked one of the damned. Now that he is once more in the light, his shadow becomes the principal means of identifying him as a living man, for souls cast no shadows. Dante is to use this device often in the Cantos that follow.

27. *It was taken to Naples from Brindisium:* Virgil died in Brindisium in 19 B.C. His bones were later exhumed and reinterred in Naples by order of the Emperor Augustus.

29–30. *the heavens which pass the light:* The heavens are the spheres of the Ptolemaic system. They are conceived as crystalline and as so clear that light passes from one to the other undiminished. Dante's figure, literally rendered, is: "whose rays do not block one another."

40–45. *You saw how some yearn:* Dante saw them in Limbo. As Virgil goes on to explain, he means "the masters of those who know." His clear implication is that if such monuments of human intellect could never penetrate the mystery of the All, it is folly for mankind to seek to explain the reasons for God's ways. *Of them and many more:* Part of Virgil's sorrow is due to the fact that he is one of the "many more."

50. *Lerici and Turbia:* Lerici lies on the shores of the Mediterranean near the river Magra, and Turbia stands a bit inland from the Mediterranean on the other side of Liguria. The tract of mountains between them is one of the most rugged in all Europe.

52. *Now who is there to say:* Virgil had traveled through Hell once before (see *Inferno,* IX, 24, note) and knew that way, but the road of Purgatory is unknown to him.

58 ff. THE CONTUMACIOUS. The section of the Mount of Purgatory that lies below the Gate (the Ante-Purgatory) is occupied by the Late-Repentant who put off their surrender to God until the end of their lives. As they made God wait, so must they now wait before they may begin their purification. These souls suffer no pain but the burning of their own frustrated desire to mount to God. They may well be compared with the souls in Limbo, except that they are all assured that they will one day rise, whereas there is no hope in Limbo.

The Contumacious, therefore, are the first class of the Late-Repentant. (Hence the slowness of their motions now. Note that such slowness, in constraining souls whose most ardent wish is to race forward to God, is a moral allegory. Purgatory, one must recall, is the way to the renunciation of sin. The soul so long curbed cannot fail to root out of itself the last laggard impulse. Such, at least, is clearly Dante's moral intention.) The present band must expiate not only personal negligence and tardiness in turning to God but disobedience to the Church from which they were excommunicated. Before they can mount to the next phase of their purification they must delay here for a period thirty times as long as the period of their disobedience.

66. *believe as you have believed:* Virgil's remark here is best taken to mean, in an extended paraphrase: "Continue as you have done [to submit yourself and your reason to the revealed fact of God without seeking to probe too deeply], for unlike these souls who put off their repentance to the moment of their deaths, you have repented early and strained every resource to win to Grace."

74. *already among the chosen:* The souls in Purgatory must suffer their purification but they are already, in effect, saved and will eventually enter Heaven.

78. *Who best knows time is most grieved by delay:* A home thrust. Who knows time better than these souls who must suffer their most grievous delay?

89–90. *to my right . . . my shadow fell upon the rock:* The sun has only recently risen. It is still, therefore, in the east. Since it threw Dante's shadow directly before him as he approached the mountain, and now throws his shadow to the right, the Poets must have moved more or less due west toward the cliff and must then have borne south.

101. *waving the backs of their hands in our direction:* To indicate the way. The gesture is Italian. We should be inclined to point.

104. *as you move on, look back:* Note that the speaker does not ask Dante to delay his journey even an instant, but only to look back while continuing on his way.

105. *over there:* In Purgatory "over there" always means "back in the world."

108. *one brow was split by a sword wound:* See also line 111: *a great slash above his breast;* Dante obviously intends the souls to be immaterial replicas of the last appearance of the mortal flesh. In future Cantos, however, he does not pursue this idea. See XXV, 34–108, note, for a discourse on the nature of aerial bodies.

112. *I am Manfred:* Manfred, King of Sicily, was the legitimized natural son of Frederick II. He was born in Sicily in 1231 and was killed at the battle of Benevento after a defeat by Charles of Anjou in

1266. (See *Inferno*, XXVIII, 16, note.) He was famous as an Epi-
curean (see *Inferno*, X, 14, note) and for his taste for physical plea-
sures rather than for godliness. In the everlasting internal wars of
Italy, Manfred often opposed the Papal States, but was too powerful
to be excommunicated while alive. He was nevertheless disobedient
to Mother Church and therefore must pass thirty times the period of
his disobedience outside the cliff. He has served 24 years to date.
Assuming that he was contumacious for half his life (17½ years),
his total delay would amount to 525 years, if not shortened by
prayer.

112–113. *grandson of the blessed Empress Constance:* Con-
stance was the mother of Frederick II. Since Manfred was not a le-
gitimate son, he identifies himself by his grandmother as a delicate
way of avoiding any reference to his illegitimacy.

115. *my sweet daughter:* Also named Constance. She married Pe-
ter of Aragon and bore him three sons. One died before full man-
hood. Of the remaining two, Frederick became King of Sicily, and
Iacapo succeeded his father to the throne of Aragon.

118. *My flesh had been twice hacked:* At the battle of Benevento.
After Manfred's defeat and death, Charles of Anjou ordered that
every soldier in his army file past the body of the dead Manfred and
place a stone upon it. Thus a great cairn was erected to the memory
of a fallen warrior.

124. *the pastor of Cosenza:* Bartolommeo Pignatelli, cardinal
and archbishop of Cosenza from 1254 to 1266. On orders from Pope
Clement IV, he disinterred the body of Manfred and had it carried
without honors (with quenched tapers) outside the kingdom of
Naples, which was then a Papal State. Thus, Clement expelled from
Church territory the body of the man he could not expel in life.

131. *the Verde:* Various streams may be identified as the Verde.
Dante clearly enough implies that Manfred's body was carried out
of the kingdom of Naples and deposited on the other side of a
boundary-river.

139. *thirty times:* There seems to be no identifiable significance
to Dante's choice of thirty (instead, say, of fifty, or a hundred, or any
other multiple).

Canto IV

------◆-◉-◆------

*The Late-Repentant
Class Two: The Indolent
Belacqua*

Listening to Manfred's discourse, Dante has lost track of time. Now, at midmorning, the Poets reach the opening in the cliff-face and begin the laborious climb. Dante soon tires and cries that he can go no farther, but Virgil urges him to pull himself a little higher yet—significantly—to the LEDGE OF THE INDOLENT, those souls whose sin was their delay in pulling themselves up the same hard path.

Seated on the ledge, Virgil explains that in the nature of the mountain, the beginning of the ascent (the First Turning from Sin to True Repentance) is always hardest. The higher one climbs from sin to repentance, the easier it becomes to climb still higher until, in the Perfection of Grace, the climb becomes effortless. But to that ultimate height, as Virgil knows, Human Reason cannot reach. It is Beatrice (Divine Love) who must guide him there.

As Virgil finishes speaking, an ironic reply comes from behind a boulder. The speaker is BELACQUA, an old friend of Dante's, and the laziest man in Florence. Because of his indolence, he put off good works and the active desire for grace until he lay dying. In life he made God wait. Now God makes him wait an equal period before he may pass through the Gate into Purgatory and begin his purification. Unless, as Belacqua adds, the prayers of the devout intercede for him.

But now Virgil points out that the sun is already at its noon-height and that Dante, unlike the Indolent, must not delay.

When any sense of ours records intense
    pleasure or pain, then the whole soul is drawn
    by such impressions into that one sense,

and seems to lose all other powers. And thus
    do I refute the error that asserts   5
    that one soul on another burns in us.

And, for this reason, when we see or hear
    whatever seizes strongly on the soul,
    time passes, and we lose it unaware.

For that which senses is one faculty;   10
    and that which keeps the soul intact, another:
    the first, as it were, bound; the second, free.

To this, my own experience bears witness,
    for while I listened to that soul and marveled,
    the Sun had climbed—without my least awareness—   15

to fifty full degrees of its noon peak
    when, at one point along the way, that band
    cried out in chorus: "Here is what you seek."

Often when grapes hang full on slope and ledge
    the peasant, with one forkful of his thorns,   20
    seals up a wider opening in his hedge

than the gap we found there in that wall of stone;
    up which—leaving that band of souls behind—
    my Guide led and I followed: we two alone.

Go up to San Leo or go down to Noli;   25
    go climb Bismantova—two legs suffice:
    here nothing but swift wings will answer wholly.

The swift wings and the feathers, I mean to say,
    of great desire led onward by that Guide
    who was my hope and light along the way.   30

Squeezed in between two walls that almost meet
　　we labor upward through the riven rock:
　　a climb that calls for both our hands and feet.

Above the cliff's last rise we reached in time
　　an open slope. "Do we go right or left?"　　　　35
　　I asked my Master, "or do we still climb?"

And he: "Take not one step to either side,
　　but follow yet, and make way up the mountain
　　till we meet someone who may serve as guide."

Higher than sight the peak soared to the sky:　　40
　　much steeper than a line drawn from mid-quadrant
　　to the center, was the slope that met my eye.

The climb had sapped my last strength when I cried:
　　"Sweet Father, turn to me: unless you pause
　　I shall be left here on the mountainside!"　　　45

He pointed to a ledge a little ahead
　　that wound around the whole face of the slope.
　　"Pull yourself that much higher, my son," he said.

His words so spurred me that I forced myself
　　to push on after him on hands and knees　　　50
　　until at last my feet were on that shelf.

There we sat, facing eastward, to survey
　　the trail we had just climbed; for oftentimes
　　a backward look comforts one on the way.

I looked down first to the low-lying shore,　　　55
　　then upward to the sun—and stopped amazed,
　　for it was from the left its arrows bore.

Virgil was quick to note the start I gave
　　when I beheld the Chariot of the Sun
　　driven between me and the North Wind's cave.　　60

"Were Castor and Pollux," he said, "in company
    of that bright mirror which sends forth its rays
    equally up and down, then you would see

the twelve-toothed cogwheel of the Zodiac
    turned till it blazed still closer to the Bears   65
    —unless it were to stray from its fixed track.

If you wish to understand why this is so,
    imagine Zion and this Mount so placed
    on earth, the one above, the other below,

that the two have one horizon though they lie   70
    in different hemispheres. Therefore, the path
    that Phaëthon could not follow in the sky

must necessarily, in passing here
    on the one side, pass there upon the other,
    as your own reasoning will have made clear."   75

And I then: "Master, I may truly vow
    I never grasped so well the very point
    on which my wits were most astray just now:

that the mid-circle of the highest Heaven,
    called the Equator, always lies between   80
    the Sun and winter, and, for the reason given,

lies as far north of this place at all times
    as the Hebrews, when they held Jerusalem,
    were wont to see it toward the warmer climes.

But—if you please—I should be glad to know   85
    how far we have yet to climb, for the peak soars
    higher to Heaven than my eye can go."

And he: "Such is this Mount that when a soul
    begins the lower slopes it most must labor;
    then less and less the more it nears its goal.   90

Thus when we reach the point where the slopes seem
    so smooth and gentle that the climb becomes
    as easy as to float a skiff downstream,

then will this road be run, and not before
    that journey's end will your repose be found.   95
    I know this much for truth and say no more."

His words were hardly out when, from nearby,
    we heard a voice say: "Maybe by that time
    you'll find you need to sit before you fly!"

We turned together at the sound, and there,   100
    close on our left, we saw a massive boulder
    of which, till then, we had not been aware.

To it we dragged ourselves, and there we found
    stretched in the shade, the way a slovenly man
    lies down to rest, some people on the ground.   105

The weariest of them, judging by his pose,
    sat hugging both knees while his head, abandoned,
    dropped down between them halfway to his toes.

"Master," I said, "look at that sorry one
    who seems so all-let-down. Were Sloth herself   110
    his sister, he could not be so far gone!"

That heap took heed, and even turned his head
    upon his thigh—enough to look at us.
    "You climb it if you're such a flash," he said.

I knew him then, and all the agony   115
    that still burned in my lungs and raced my pulse
    did not prevent my going to him. He

raising his head—just barely—when I stood by,
    drawled: "So you really know now why the sun
    steers to the left of you across the sky?"   120

His short words and his shorter acts, combined,
    made me half smile as I replied: "Belacqua,
    your fate need never again trouble my mind.

Praise be for that. But why do you remain
    crouched here? Are you waiting for a guide, perhaps? 125
    Or are you up to your old tricks again?"

"Old friend," he said, "what good is it to climb?—
    God's Bird above the Gate would never let me
    pass through to start my trials before my time.

I must wait here until the heavens wheel past   130
    as many times as they passed me in my life,
    for I delayed the good sighs till the last.

Prayer could help me, if a heart God's love
    has filled with Grace should offer it. All other
    is worthless, for it is not heard above."   135

But now the Poet already led the way
    to the slope above, saying to me: "Come now:
    the Sun has touched the very peak of day

above the sea, and night already stands
with one black foot upon Morocco's sands."   140

NOTES

1–12. THE DOCTRINE OF MULTIPLE SOULS. The original doctrine (the "error" of line 5) was set forth by Plato, who claimed that we have three souls within us, each with its specific function: the Vegetative Soul (roughly corresponding to what we might call the Somatic) which is seated in the liver, the Sensitive (*i.e.,* the Emotional) Soul which is seated in the heart, and the Intellectual Soul which is seated in the brain. Dante's emphatic concern over this point is easy enough to understand. Plato was, for him, one of the fundamental sources of the truth. Yet here, Plato was putting forth a doctrine impossible to reconcile with the Christian doctrine of the unity of the soul. (If there are several souls in a man, how shall one judgment fit them all?) Aristotle (see XXV, 52 ff.), the Church Fathers, Aquinas, and many others also found it necessary to repudiate or to modify this Platonic doctrine. The fact that Dante had seen himself as a follower of Plato in the *Vita Nuova* is one more evidence that the *Purgatorio* is intended, among other things, as a progress of the soul. Dante is correcting his earlier errors and turning his mind to greater sources.

16. *to fifty full degrees of its noon peak:* Since one degree of arc equals four minutes of time, the Sun, therefore, traverses fifteen degrees an hour. It is, therefore, three hours and twenty minutes since sunrise, at which time (Canto II) Dante saw the Angel Pilot bring in his cargo of souls. On Easter in the year 1300 the Sun rose a little before 6:00. It is now, therefore, a little after 9:00 A.M.

25–26. *San Leo:* An almost inaccessible town on a mountaintop near San Marino. *Noli:* a seacoast town accessible (in Dante's time) only from the sea or by treacherously steep steps cut into the cliffs behind the town. *Bismantova:* a village on a mountain of the same name about twenty miles south of Reggio Emilia. Dante selects three places that his contemporaries would recognize as most difficult to get to, and then says in effect that the climb to them is nothing as compared to the labor of climbing Purgatory.

30. *light:* The narrowness of the fissure would make it dark. Virgil's allegorical character as Human Reason is especially important in this context.

33. *a climb that calls for both our hands and feet:* Dante uses this same figure in describing the path that led up from the Bolgia of the Thieves (*Inferno,* XXVI, 18): "the foot could make no way without the hand."

37 ff. *Take not one step to either side:* The original contains an ambiguity that has led many commentators to understand Virgil as saying "Take not one backward step," that being the law of the mountain. In context, however, such a rendering seems doubtful. Dante had no least thought of taking a backward step. He has asked, "Do we go right or left," and Virgil replies, logically, "no least step to either side but upward only." See also *Isaiah,* xxx, 21, and *Joshua,* i, 7.

41–42. *a line drawn from mid-quadrant to the center:* Of an astrolabe. Hence 45°. Note, however, that the slope is "much steeper" than 45°.

50–51. *my feet were on that shelf:* (Literally: "the shelf was under my feet.") Dante says nothing to explain why a man climbing on "hands and knees" (Italian: *carpando*) to a ledge above him would not simply crawl onto it (especially if near exhaustion) instead of first standing on it and then sitting down. He might, perhaps, have meant that he crawled onto the ledge, then sat with his knees drawn up so that the ledge was under his feet. Perhaps.

55–75. THE POSITION OF THE SUN. Dante, habituated to the phenomena of the Northern Hemisphere, is astonished to find that the Sun is on his left (*i.e.*, north) when he faces east. Virgil points out that there is nothing surprising in that, and that as the Sun moves toward the summer solstice it will move even further north (toward "the Bears" of line 65, *i.e.*, Ursa Major and Ursa Minor, the Big and the Little Dipper) into the zodiacal sign of Gemini, the Twins (*i.e.*, Castor and Pollux). Unless, he adds with something like humor, it should depart from its fixed track.

Virgil then goes on to a more detailed statement of the case. He asks Dante to visualize the globe with the Mount of Zion and the Mount of Purgatory so placed that they are in different hemispheres but share the same celestial horizon. They are, therefore, antipodal, and since the Sun must pass between them, it follows that when it is on one side of one it must be on the other side of the other, *i.e.*, Zion must always be north of the Sun and Purgatory must always be south of it. Since the two places are antipodal, moreover, the celestial equator is always as far south of one as it is north of the other.

60. *the North Wind's cave:* Aquilon, the North Wind, rules the compass from NW to NE, *i.e.*, for 45° on either side of the North Pole.

62–63. *that bright mirror:* The Sun, reflector of God's Love. *up and down:* in two senses: first, to the upper (Northern) and lower (Southern) Hemispheres; second, up to Heaven and down to Earth.

71–72. *the path that Phaëthon could not follow:* Apollo was the charioteer of the Sun. One day Phaëthon, son of Apollo, tried to drive the chariot of his father, but lost control and the four great

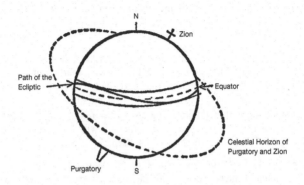

horses dragged the Sun out of its course, threatening both Heaven and Earth until Zeus killed Phaëthon with a thunderbolt and saved Creation. The Milky Way is the scar left on the sky by Phaëthon's mad course.

76–84. THE CELESTIAL EQUATOR. The passage is in Dante's most pedantic style and has given rise to several varying interpretations. I take the soundest of them to be based on Dante's *Il Convivio*, II, iv, 50–58: "And it is to be understood that each heaven below the Crystalline [*i.e.*, the *Sphere of the Fixed Stars*] has two poles that are constant in relation to that heaven itself; and the ninth [the Crystalline] has two poles that are firm and fixed and immovable in every respect; and each, the ninth like all the others, has a circle which may be called the equator of its proper heaven; the which is equally distant from one pole and the other, as one may clearly understand if he revolves an apple or some other round thing."

Hence the following extended paraphrase of lines 79–84: "The mid-circle of the Crystalline Sphere, which is called the Celestial Equator, always lies between the Sun and that hemisphere in which it is winter, and, for the reason you have just given [*i.e.*, that Purgatory and Zion are antipodal] the Celestial Equator must always lie as far to the north of this place [Purgatory] as the Hebrews [when, before the dispersion of the Jews, they looked at it from Jerusalem] were accustomed to seeing it toward the south [warmer climes]."

96. *I know this much for truth and say no more:* At that journey's end, Virgil (Human Reason) will vanish and Beatrice (Divine Love,

a compound of Mercy, Light, and Contemplation) will lead Dante. Virgil has spoken as much as Reason can know to be true.

97–135. BELACQUA. He was a Florentine who manufactured parts for musical instruments. Of him the Anonimo Fiorentino says: "He was the most indolent man who ever lived. . . . Dante was very intimate with him and used often to take him to task for his laziness." Dante's own treatment of him would certainly indicate that he is dealing with an old friend about whose indolence he has often worried.

119–120. *So you really know now . . . . :* Belacqua's words are sarcastic, perhaps by way of taking revenge for Dante's description of him to Virgil, but it is the easy and fond sarcasm of a friend, and Dante accepts Belacqua's way of speaking with a half-smile.

128. *God's Bird above the Gate:* God's Angel above the Gate Dante will come to in Canto IX. Dante refers to Angels as God's Birds in a number of passages. The gate is the entrance to Purgatory proper. There is no gate between Purgatory and Heaven as there is between Earth and Hell. Those who pass the Gate of Purgatory are already effectively in Heaven, though they must first undergo their purification.

130–132. *I must wait here:* Because Belacqua indolently put off his repentance (the good sighs) until his last breath, he in effect refused God during the days of his life. Now God makes Belacqua wait, before he may begin his approach to Heaven, for as long a period as Belacqua made Him wait.

133–135. *Prayer could help me:* See VI, 30–45.

136–140. THE TIME. It is now noon at Purgatory. It must therefore be midnight in Jerusalem. Dante believed Morocco to lie exactly 90° west of Jerusalem (in the same longitude as Spain) and 90° west of midnight is six hours earlier. Hence, it is six o'clock there and night would just be beginning.

Canto V

ANTE-PURGATORY:
THE SECOND LEDGE   *The Late-Repentant*
                          Class Three: Those Who Died
                          by Violence Without Last Rites

*The Poets continue up the mountain and Dante's shadow once
more creates excitement among the waiting souls. These are
the souls of THOSE WHO DIED BY VIOLENCE WITHOUT
LAST RITES. Since their lives were cut off, they did not have
full opportunity to repent, and therefore they are placed a
step higher than the simply Indolent.*

*These souls crowd about Dante, eager to have him bear news
of them back to the world and so to win prayers that will shorten
their delay. Virgil instructs Dante to listen to these souls, but
warns him not to interrupt his own climb to Grace. The Poets,
therefore, continue to press on while the souls cluster about
and follow them, each of them eager to tell his story and to
beg that Dante speak of them when he returns to the world.*

I was following the footsteps of my Guide,
   having already parted from those shades,
   when someone at my back pointed and cried:

"Look there! see how the Sun's shafts do not drive
   through to the left of that one lower down,   5
   and how he walks as if he were alive!"

I looked behind me to see who had spoken,
   and I saw them gazing up at me alone,
   at me, and at the light, that it was broken.

40

At which my Master said: "Why do you lag?   10
    What has so turned your mind that you look back?
    What is it to you that idle tongues will wag?

Follow my steps, though all such whisper of you:
    be as a tower of stone, its lofty crown
    unswayed by anything the winds may do.   15

For when a man lets his attention range
    toward every wisp, he loses true direction,
    sapping his mind's force with continual change."

What could I say except "I come"? I said it
    flushed with that hue that sometimes asks forgiveness   20
    for which it shows the asker to be fit.

Meanwhile across the slope a little before us
    people approached chanting the *Miserere*
    verse by verse in alternating chorus.

But when they noticed that I blocked the course   25
    of the Sun's arrows when they struck my body,
    their song changed to an "Oh! . . ." prolonged
      and hoarse.

Out of that silenced choir two spirits ran
    like messengers and, reaching us, they said:
    "We beg to know—are you a living man?"   30

My Guide replied: "You may be on your way.
    And bear back word to those who sent you here
    he does indeed still walk in mortal clay.

If, as I think, it was his shadow drew them
    to stand and stare, they know already. Tell them   35
    to honor him: that may be precious to them."

I never saw hot vapors flashing through
    the first sweet air of night, or through the clouds
    of August sunsets, faster than those two

ran up to join their band, wheeled round again,   40
   and, with the whole band following, came toward us,
   like cavalry sent forward with a loose rein.

"There are hundreds in that troop that charges so,"
   my Guide said, "and all come to beg a favor.
   Hear them, but press on, listening as you go."   45

"Pure spirit," they came crying, "you who thus
   while still inside the body you were born to
   climb to your bliss—oh pause and speak to us.

Is there no one here you recognize? Not one
   of whom you may bear tidings to the world?   50
   Wait! Won't you pause? Oh please! Why do you run?

We all are souls who died by violence,
   all sinners to our final hour, in which
   the lamp of Heaven shed its radiance

into our hearts. Thus from the brink of death,   55
   repenting all our sins, forgiving those
   who sinned against us, with our final breath

we offered up our souls at peace with Him
   who saddens us with longing to behold
   His glory on the throne of Seraphim."   60

"Oh well-born souls," I said, "I can discover
   no one among you that I recognize
   however much I search your faces over;

but if you wish some service of me, speak,
   and if the office is within my power   65
   I will perform it, by that peace I seek

in following the footsteps of this Guide,
   that peace that draws me on from world to world
   to my own good." I paused, and one replied:

"No soul among us doubts you will fulfill 70
    all you declare, without your need to swear it,
    if lack of power does not defeat your will.

I, then, who am no more than first to plead,
    beg that if ever you see that land that lies
    between Romagna and Naples, you speak my need 75

most graciously in Fano, that they to Heaven
    send holy prayers to intercede for me;
    so may my great offenses be forgiven.

I was of Fano, but the wounds that spilled
    my life's blood and my soul at once, were dealt me 80
    among the Antenori. I was killed

where I believed I had the least to fear.
    Azzo of Este, being incensed against me
    beyond all reason, had me waylaid there.

Had I turned toward La Mira when they set 85
    upon me first outside of Oriaco,
    I should be drawing breath among men yet.

I ran into the swamp, and reeds and mud
    tangled and trapped me. There I fell. And there
    I watched my veins let out a pool of blood." 90

Another spoke: "So may the Love Divine
    fulfill the wish that draws you up the mountain,
    for sweet compassion, lend your aid to mine.

I am Bonconte, once of Montefeltro.
    Because Giovanna and the rest forget me, 95
    I go among these souls with head bowed low."

And I: "What force or chance led you to stray
    so far from Campaldino that your grave
    remains to be discovered to this day?"

And he: "There flows below the Casentino   100
   a stream, the Archiana, which arises
   above the hermitage in Appennino.

There where its name ends in the Arno's flood
   I came, my throat pierced through, fleeing on foot
   and staining all my course with my life's blood.   105

There my sight failed. There with a final moan
   which was the name of Mary, speech went from me.
   I fell, and there my body lay alone.

I speak the truth. Oh speak it in my name
   to living men! God's angel took me up,   110
   and Hell's cried out: 'Why do you steal my game?

If his immortal part is your catch, brother,
   for one squeezed tear that makes me turn it loose,
   I've got another treatment for the other!'

You are familiar with the way immense   115
   watery vapors gather on the air,
   then burst as rain, as soon as they condense.

To ill will that seeks only ill, his mind
   added intelligence, and by the powers
   his nature gives, he stirred the mist and wind.   120

From Pratomagno to the spine, he spread
   a mist that filled the valley by day's end;
   then turned the skies above it dark as lead.

The saturated air changed into rain
   and down it crashed, flooding the rivulets   125
   with what the sodden earth could not retain;

the rills merged into torrents, and a flood
   swept irresistibly to the royal river.
   The Archiana, raging froth and mud,

found my remains in their last frozen rest   130
   just at its mouth, swept them into the Arno,
   and broke the cross I had formed upon my breast

in my last agony of pain and guilt.
   Along its banks and down its bed it rolled me,
   and then it bound and buried me in silt."   135

A third spoke when that second soul had done:
   "When you have found your way back to the world,
   and found your rest from this long road you run,

oh speak my name again with living breath
   to living memory. Pia am I.   140
   Siena gave me birth; Maremma, death.

As he well knows who took me as his wife
with jeweled ring before he took my life."

Notes

3. *when someone at my back pointed and cried:* Dante does not
explain how he could see a gesture made behind his back.

8–9. *at me alone, at me:* Dante feels a moment of pride at attract-
ing so much attention. He will have more to say later about Pride as
his most dangerous spiritual fault.

20. *that hue that sometimes asks forgiveness:* A typically Dan-
tean figure. The hue, of course, is red, *i.e.,* the blush. But one may
flush red with anger as well as blush with shame. Hence, the hue
only "sometimes" asks forgiveness.

22. *across:* The souls are not climbing the slope but are circling it
in their long delay. *before us:* Since the Poets are facing uphill, "be-
fore" must equal "above."

23. *Miserere:* The souls are singing the Fiftieth Psalm: "Have
mercy upon us." Each band of souls on the mountain has its particu-
lar prayer—all, that is, but the Contumacious (who have been cut
off from the offices of ritual).

24. *verse by verse in alternating chorus:* They are singing, that is to say, antiphonally, but with two choruses rather than with a single voice and a chorus as is more usual in the litany.

37–39. *hot vapors:* Dante's meteorology was built largely on a theory of the opposition of hot and wet vapors. (See *Inferno,* XXIV, 142 ff., note.) Here he describes, first, falling stars (flashing through the first sweet air of night) and, second, heat lightning (flashing through the clouds of August sunsets). He attributes both phenomena to hot or "fiery" vapors.

37–42. The figure certainly goes from the instantaneous to the merely rapid with an interesting flourish of anticlimax. One may guess that Dante set out to indicate great speed, established that in the meteorological part of the figure, and then, needing time for Virgil to make the remarks that establish the following scene, slowed down the charge from the speed of lightning to the speed of horses.

52. THE LATE-REPENTANT WHO DIED BY VIOLENCE. Like the Indolent, these souls put off repentance to their last breath, but with the partially extenuating circumstance that their lives were cut short. Had they lived out their full lives, they might have repented before the end. The benefit of the doubt is at least possible. They are, therefore, a step above the merely Indolent and a step below the Negligent Princes who, powerfully occupied by worldly affairs (with the exception of Henry III of England), had a special excuse for not turning their thoughts to Heaven sooner.

69–90. *one replied:* Jacopo del Cassero. Of a leading family of Fano, a city located in the district that lay between Romagna and the kingdom of Naples, he served as chief magistrate of Bologna from 1296 to 1297 in a manner that offended the powerful Azzo VIII of Este. In 1298, Jacopo was called to Milan to serve as chief magistrate (*podestà*) of that city. On his way there he was set upon outside the town of Oriaco (or Oriago) and killed by Azzo's hirelings after a chase in which he foundered among the reeds and mud of a nearby swamp area. Had he turned instead toward La Mira, a Paduan city, he would have found refuge. *among the Antenori:* Among the Paduans. According to legend, Padua was founded by Antenor of Troy. *incensed . . . beyond all reason:* Theologically, of course, murder is beyond all reason, but Jacopo's constant slurring references to Azzo as a traitor, and worse, would have passed as reason enough among the proud lords of that day.

94–135. Bonconte: Son of Guido da Montefeltro who is in Hell as an evil counselor (*Inferno,* XXVII). Bonconte was a leader of the Ghibellines at the battle of Campaldino, a battle in which it has been reported that Dante took part. The Florentine Guelphs defeated the Ghibellines in this battle and Bonconte was killed (June 11, 1289). The Archiana is a nearby river that rises in the Apennines and flows into the Arno (the point at which "its name ends"). Giovanna (line 95) was his wife, and neither she nor anyone else has offered prayers to shorten his time of waiting.

The nicely functioning ambiguity of line 96 must not be missed: (1) I go among these whose heads are bowed low; (2) with head bowed low in shame for such neglect I go among these.

110–114. The incident is very similar to the one Bonconte's father describes in *Inferno,* XXVII, but with opposite results. Such parallel scenes, as noted before, are very much a part of Dante's structural sense and are certainly intended to suggest moral reflection on the parallelism.

120. his nature gives: The demons are fallen but they still retain many of the powers given them by their angelic origins. Note that Dante implies the existence of no such power in those Angels found in the vestibule of Hell (those who took no sides in the Wars of Heaven).

121. From Pratomagno to the spine: The Casentino, or upper valley of the Arno, is closed in on the east by the spine of the Apennines, and on the west by the Pratomagno range.

128. the royal river: The Arno.

132. the cross I had formed upon my breast: His arms crossed in contrition and as a symbol of surrender to God.

140. Pia: She has been traditionally identified as Pia de' Tolomei (Tall-oh-MAY-yee) of Siena, who married a Guelph leader and was murdered by him. The identification is doubtful, however. The text itself must say all that is certain about her. Nor can there be much doubt that Dante's principal interest in her is poetic rather than historical. After Bonconte's fulsome account of his own dramatic importance,

Pia's gracious and courteous voice enters as a moving example of how effortlessly Dante can change and contrast tone. Note especially Pia's graciousness (despite her ardent desire to win the help of prayers) in asking nothing of Dante until he has returned and rested from his great journey.

Canto VI

ANTE-PURGATORY:
THE SECOND LEDGE   *The Late-Repentant*
                    Class Three: Those Who Died by Violence
                                              Sordello

*The Poets move along with the souls still crowding about them.
Dante promises all of them that he will bear word of them back
to the world, but he never pauses in his climb. Among that
press of souls, Dante specifically mentions seeing BENIN-
CASA DA LATERINA, GUCCIO DE' TARLATI, FEDERICO
NOVELLO, COUNT ORSO, and PIERRE DE LA BROSSE.*

*Finally free of that crowd, Dante asks Virgil how it is that
prayer may sway God's will. Virgil explains in part but once more
finishes by declaring that the whole truth is beyond him and that
Dante must refer the question to Beatrice when he meets her.*

*The Sun passes behind the mountain as they climb (mid-
afternoon of Easter Sunday). The Poets press on, and there
on the shady slope they encounter the majestic spirit of SOR-
DELLO who, like Virgil, is a Mantuan. Dante watches Sor-
dello and Virgil embrace in a transport of love for their
common birthplace and is moved to denounce Italy for setting
brothers to war on one another, to denounce the EMPEROR
ALBERT for his failure to bring unity and peace to Italy, and
finally to utter an invective against Florence as the type of the
war-torn and corrupt state.*

The loser, when a game of dice is done,
   remains behind reviewing every roll
   sadly, and sadly wiser, and alone.

The crowd leaves with the winner: one behind
   tugs at him, one ahead, one at his side—   5
   all calling their long loyalty to his mind.

Not stopping, he hands out a coin or two
   and those he has rewarded let him be.
   So he fights off the crowd and pushes through.

Such was I then, turning my face now here,   10
   now there, among that rout, and promising
   on every hand, till I at last fought clear.

There was the Aretine who came to woe
   at the murderous hand of Tacco; and the other
   who drowned while he was hunting down his foe.   15

There, hands outstretched to me as I pushed through,
   was Federico Novello; and the Pisan
   who made the good Marzucco shine so true.

I saw Count Orso; and the shade of one
   torn from its flesh, it said, by hate and envy,   20
   and not for any evil it had done—

Pierre de la Brosse, I mean: and of this word
   may the Lady of Brabant take heed while here,
   lest, there, she find herself in a worse herd.

When I had won my way free of that press   25
   of shades whose one prayer was that others pray,
   and so advance them toward their blessedness,

I said: "O my Soul's Light, it seems to me
   one of your verses most expressly states
   prayer may not alter Heaven's fixed decree: 30

yet all these souls pray only for a prayer.
   Can all their hope be vain? Or have I missed
   your true intent and read some other there?"

And he: "The sense of what I wrote is plain,
   if you bring all your wits to bear upon it.   35
   Nor is the hope of all these spirits vain.

The towering crag of Justice is not bent,
   nor is the rigor of its edict softened
   because the supplications of the fervent

and pure in heart cancel the debt of time   40
   decreed on all these souls who linger here,
   consumed with yearning to begin the climb.

The souls I wrote about were in that place
   where sin is not atoned for, and their prayers—
   they being pagan—were cut off from Grace.   45

But save all questions of such consequence
   till you meet her who will become your lamp
   between the truth and mere intelligence.

Do you understand me? I mean Beatrice.
   She will appear above here, at the summit   50
   of this same mountain, smiling in her bliss."

"My Lord," I said, "let us go faster now:
   I find the climb less tiring than at first,
   and see, the slope already throws a shadow."

"The day leads on," he said, "and we shall press   55
   as far as we yet may while the light holds,
   but the ascent is harder than you guess:

before it ends, the Sun must come around
   from its present hiding place behind the mountain
   and once more cast your shadow on the ground.   60

But see that spirit stationed all alone
   and looking down at us: he will point out
   the best road for us as we travel on."

We climbed on then. O Lombard, soul serene,
  how nobly and deliberately you watched us!   65
  how distant and majestic was your mien!

He did not speak to us as on we pressed
  but held us fixed in his unblinking eyes
  as if he were a lion at its rest.

Virgil, nonetheless, climbed to his side   70
  and begged him to point out the best ascent.
  The shade ignored the question and replied

by asking in what country we were born
  and who we were. My gentle Guide began:
  "Mantua . . ." And that shade, till then withdrawn,   75

leaped to his feet like one in sudden haste
  crying: "O Mantuan, I am Sordello
  of your own country!" And the two embraced.

Ah servile Italy, grief's hostelry,
  ah ship unpiloted in the storm's rage,   80
  no mother of provinces but of harlotry!

That noble spirit leaped up with a start
  at the mere sound of his own city's name,
  and took his fellow citizen to his heart:

while still, within you, brother wars on brother,   85
  and though one wall and moat surrounds them all,
  your living sons still gnaw at one another!

O wretched land, search all your coasts, your seas,
  the bosom of your hills—where will you find
  a single part that knows the joys of peace?   90

What does it matter that Justinian came
  to trim the bit, if no one sits the saddle?
  Without him you would have less cause for shame!

You priests who, if you heed what God decreed,
   should most seek after holiness and leave 95
   to Caesar Caesar's saddle and his steed—

see how the beast grows wild now none restrains
   its temper, nor corrects it with the spur,
   since you set meddling hands upon its reins!

O German Albert, you who turn away 100
   while she grows vicious, being masterless;
   you should have forked her long before today!

May a just judgment from the stars descend
   upon your house, a blow so weirdly clear
   that your line tremble at it to the end. 105

For you, sir, and your father, in your greed
   for the cold conquests of your northern lands,
   have let the Empire's Garden go to seed.

Come see the Montagues and Capulets,
   the Monaldi and Filippeschi, reckless man! 110
   those ruined already, these whom ruin besets.

Come, cruel Emperor, come and see your lords
   hunted and holed; come tend their wounds and see
   what fine security Santafior affords.

Come see your stricken Rome that weeps alone, 115
   widowed and miserable, and day and night
   laments: "O Caesar mine, why are you gone?"

Come see your people—everywhere the same—
   united in love; and if no pity for us
   can move you, come and blush for your good name. 120

O Supreme Jove, for mankind crucified,
   if you permit the question, I must ask it:
   are the eyes of your clear Justice turned aside?

Or is this the unfolding of a plan
   shaped in your fathomless counsels toward some good   125
   beyond all reckoning of mortal man?

For the land is a tyrant's roost, and any clod
   who comes along playing the partisan
   passes for a Marcellus with the crowd.

Florence, my Florence, may you not resent   130
   the fact that my digression has not touched you—
   thanks to your people's sober management.

Others have Justice at heart but a bow strung
   by careful counsels and not quickly drawn:
   yours shoot the word forever—from the tongue.   135

Others, offered public office, shun
   the cares of service. Yours cry out unasked:
   "I will! I'll take it on! I am the one!"

Rejoice, I say, that your great gifts endure:
   your wealth, your peacefulness, and your good sense. 140
   What truth I speak, the facts will not obscure.

Athens and Sparta when of old they drew
   the codes of law that civilized the world,
   gave only merest hints, compared to you,

of man's advance. But all time shall remember   145
   the subtlety with which the thread you spin
   in mid-October breaks before November.

How often within living recollection
   have you changed coinage, custom, law, and office,
   and hacked your own limbs off and sewed them on?   150

But if your wits and memory are not dead
   you yet will see yourself as that sick woman
   who cannot rest, though on a feather bed,

but flails as if she fenced with pain and grief.
Ah, Florence, may your cure or course be brief.   155

NOTES

13–14. *the Aretine:* Benincasa da Laterina, a justice of the city of
Arezzo. ("Aretine" means "of Arezzo.") On the charge of highway
robbery and brigandage, he passed the death sentence on the brother
of Ghino (GHEE-no) di Tacco. Soon thereafter Benincasa was
called to Rome to a Papal Judgeship. Ghino, a fierce robber-baron,
followed him there, burst in upon him in open court, cut off his head,
and escaped safely. *the other* (Aretine): Guccio (GHOO-tchoe) or
Ciacco (TCHA-coe) de' Tarlati (day Tahr-LAH-tee). He drowned in
the Arno after the battle of Montaperti, or perhaps of Campaldino.
There is some doubt as to whether he was hunter or hunted at the
time.

17. *Federico Novello:* Little is known about him except that he
was the son of Guido Novello and that he was killed in a skirmish
with a band of Aretines.

17–18. *the Pisan . . . Marzucco:* Farinata, son of Marzucco degli
Scornigiani (Score-nih-JAH-nee) of Pisa. Farinata was killed in Pisa
and Marzucco, who had become a minor friar, went to bury his body.
In one account, he preached a funeral sermon of forgiveness and
ended by kissing the hand that had murdered his son, thus "shining
so true" in Christian charity. In another account, Count Ugolino had
ordered that the body be left unburied, and Marzucco went boldly
before his enemy and won permission to bury his son, thus "shining
so true" in courage.

19. *Count Orso:* Alessandro and Napoleone degli Alberti are two
of the most infamous sinners in Hell. They lie together in the ice of
Caïna among those who were treacherous against their own kin.
Count Orso, son of Napoleone, was murdered by his cousin, the son
of Alessandro.

19–22. *Pierre de la Brosse:* Court physician and favorite of Louis
IX and later of Philip III of France. Philip had Pierre hanged in
1278. The accounts of Pierre's downfall vary. Dante clearly believes
him to have been the innocent victim of the intrigues of Queen Mary

of Brabant, "the Lady" he calls upon to repent while still on earth, for fear she may find herself in a worse herd (*i.e.,* in Hell) than that in which Pierre finds himself.

29. *one of your verses:* Dante must be referring to the *Aeneid,* VI, 376: Palinurus begs Aeneas to get him out of Hell, but the reply comes from the Sibyl: *Desine fata deum flecti sperare precando* (Do not hope to bend the fixed decree of the Gods by prayer).

54. *the slope already throws a shadow:* The Sun has declined to the west of the mountain and the Poets, on the east slope, are now in shadow. Because of the enormous height of the mountain, however, the Sun would decline behind it relatively early. It is probably about 3:00 p.m. (or a bit later) on Easter Sunday.

60. *and once more cast your shadow on the ground:* Virgil is chiding Dante for having been so proud of the attention his shadow attracted, and Dante has earned the gentle reproof (which, in one sense of course, he is giving himself). When Virgil mentioned Beatrice (line 49) Dante was suddenly afire to run up the rest of the mountain to the top. (As he was ready to climb the Mount of Joy in *Inferno,* I.) Virgil tells him that the climb is longer and harder than he supposes, for purification does not happen in a day. It is as if Virgil were saying: "Don't sound so suddenly zealous so soon after your proud strutting: you will still have a chance to astonish the souls here with that shadow of yours." Allegorically, if the Sun is taken as Divine Illumination, it will return to make Dante see the error of Pride—as it will indeed when Dante comes upon the souls of the Proud.

77. *Sordello:* A troubadour poet of the first three-quarters of the thirteenth century. He was born in Mantua, which was also Virgil's birthplace. His life is only sketchily known, but he seems to have been a person of some political consequence. Such accounts as survive also seem to indicate his considerable accomplishments as a climber into assorted bedroom windows.

Dante has given Sordello the same relative position in Purgatory and the same majestic dignity he assigns to Farinata in Hell (*Inferno,* X). There is no entirely satisfactory explanation of Dante's reasons in assigning such greatness of character to Sordello. Aside from his love poems, Sordello did write several impassioned political pieces, and Dante probably honors him for their integrity and sincerity. Great political integrity would make Sordello an especially apt guide to the souls of the Negligent Princes, the next group above, and in lines 91–137 of Canto VII, Sordello repeats exactly the sort of charges he made against the rulers of his day in *Complaint* (*Planh*) on the death of Baron Blacas, whom he represented as the figure of high chivalry dying from the world.

These correspondences may serve to explain his selection as guide to what follows, but why is he drawn so majestically? High indignation such as Sordello had shown in his *Complaint* seems always to have had a special attraction for Dante, who had his own gift for indignation. It would, moreover, honor Virgil to honor his noble fellow Mantuan. I am tempted to guess, however, that it was Dante's structural sense that ruled. Sordello is one of three majestic figures that occur at roughly equivalent points of the three kingdoms: Farinata in Hell, Sordello in Purgatory, and Cacciaguida (Dante's own ancestor) in Paradise. Since all three are political figures, it follows, too, that it is for Sordello's politics rather than for his poetry or for his amours that Dante has so ennobled him. Note too, as evidence of Dante's own character, the traits of slow dignity and hauteur for which Dante admires Sordello (*cf.* III: 10–11, and note).

91. *Justinian:* The Emperor Justinian. His reorganization and codification of Roman law trimmed the bit and adjusted the bridle of the horse (the Empire), making a unified Italy possible, but his work has gone for nothing.

94–99. *You priests . . . set meddling hands upon its reins:* Dante has already (*Inferno,* XIX, 109–111, and see note) asserted that the corruption of the Church began when it acquired wealth and power. He now charges the priests with having helped create the bloody chaos of Italian politics by meddling in temporal affairs. Thus by disregarding the Biblical injunction to render unto Caesar what is Caesar's and unto God what is God's, they have brought corruption upon the Church and destruction upon the State.

100. *German Albert:* Albert of Austria, born 1248, Emperor 1298, assassinated 1308. He was, therefore, Emperor at the purported time of Dante's journey.

At that time Italy was a part of the Holy Roman Empire though torn by internal strife between the Ghibellines (nominally the party of the Emperor though the party lines were blurred by local urgencies) and the Guelphs (nominally for independence and more often for anarchy). Many of the warring lords were, moreover, lieges of the Emperor. Dante's lament for Italy is always for her bloody internal wars, which he attributed, logically enough, to the lack of a central authority. The Emperor had that authority and could easily have brought unification and peace to Italy. But Albert and his father Rudolph (see VII, 91–96, and note) concerned themselves with affairs to the north and neither ever so much as visited Italy. Because of their negligence, Italy had all but slipped out of the Empire and the many Italian robber-barons warred on unceasingly at the very time that the northern kingdoms of the Empire were enjoying a long era of peace.

Dante goes on to specify the charges against Albert and his father more fully. They have allowed the Ghibelline lords to fall into ruinous feuds which could have been stopped by a word from the Emperor since the feuding parties were all lieges of the Emperor. Dante cites two such feuding Ghibelline pairs. The Montagues and the Capulets are the same Veronese families made familiar by *Romeo and Juliet*. The Monaldi and the Filippeschi were of Orvieto. All should have served as pillars of Empire in Italy, and all ruined themselves in their feuds.

The Emperor has, moreover, allowed robber-barons to destroy the peace of the land. Dante's reference to the district of Santafiora in the Sienese Maremma is ironic: Santafiora was a robber's roost that afforded no security whatever.

The Emperor has, further, allowed Rome, the seat and glory of his Empire, to fall into decay by withholding his authority (the strong hand of Caesar).

By such neglect (lines 118–120) he has destroyed his own people ("united in love" is a bitter irony) and his own good name.

121. *Supreme Jove:* The usage must seem strange to modern ears, but there can be no doubt that Dante is referring here to God. In Dante's view the pagan names Zeus and Jove referred always to the Christian God as (dimly) perceived by the ancients who lacked Christ's clarifying word.

129. *Marcellus:* Marcellus opposed Caesar and was forgiven by him. Dante may, therefore, mean that anyone who calls himself a local partisan may safely oppose Caesar-Emperor and win support by doing so.

130–155. INVECTIVE AGAINST FLORENCE. (*Cf. Inferno,* XXVI, 1–12.) Having bewailed the anarchy of Italy under Imperial neglect, Dante now turns to another of his invectives against his own city as the type of the bloodily self-divided and corrupt state. His praises are, of course, ironic and every semblance of a good quality ascribed to Florence should be understood to imply the opposite.

133. *Others have Justice at heart . . . :* Sense: Others have justice sincerely at heart and are ready to defend the right by arms, but they deliberate carefully, as wise men should, and are slow to draw the bow. You, Florence, have the word "justice" forever on your tongue and are forever ready to fire, but it is only the word you shoot, and from the tongue only, the deed never fulfilling the word.

136–137. *Others, offered public office, shun the cares of service:* They refuse out of conscientious misgivings because they take duty seriously, or perhaps because they are lazy, but your greedy politicians, Florence, are forever exclaiming their pious readiness to sacrifice themselves, even before they are asked—but they have no other aim than to raid the till.

140. *your wealth, your peacefulness, and your good sense:* The last two have already expired from Florence, and Dante seems to imply that the first will not last long as things are going.

145–146. *But all time shall remember the subtlety:* A mocking comparison between the stability of Athenian and Spartan law, one of the foundations of Western civilization, and the "more advanced" Florentine way of doing things in which nothing—not coinage, nor custom, nor law, nor office, nor pledged word—lives out the month.

152. *that sick woman:* Though she lies in luxury (on a feather bed) she can find no relief from what is wrong with her but flails about as if she were fencing with her pain and grief, seeking to overcome it by outmaneuvering it. The last line (155) is not in the original. It is my own addition, forced upon me by the need to rhyme.

Canto VII

ANTE-PURGATORY:
THE SECOND LEDGE
THE FLOWERING VALLEY

The Late-Repentant
Class Four:
The Negligent Rulers

Sordello, discovering Virgil's identity, pays homage to him and offers to guide the Poets as far as Peter's Gate. It is nearly sunset, however, and Sordello explains that by THE LAW OF THE ASCENT no one may go upward after sundown. He suggests that they spend the night in the nearby FLOW-ERING VALLEY in which the souls of THE NEGLIGENT RULERS wait to begin their purification. The three together climb in the failing light to the edge of the valley. In it, they observe, among others: RUDOLPH OF HAPSBURG, OTTO-CAR OF BOHEMIA, PHILIP THE BOLD OF FRANCE, HENRY OF NAVARRE, PEDRO III OF ARAGON, CHARLES I OF ANJOU, HENRY III OF ENGLAND, and WILLIAM VII, MARQUIS OF MONFERRATO.

All of the rulers, except Henry of England, were in one way or another connected with the Holy Roman Empire. Thus they were specially sanctified by the Divine Right of Kings and again sanctified for their place in the temporal hierarchy of Christ's Empire. Dante signalizes this eleva-tion by the beauty of the valley in which he places them, a flower-strewn green hollow of unearthly beauty and fra-grance. The valley is certainly a counterpart of the Citadel of the Virtuous Pagans in Limbo, but it outshines that lower splendor by as much as Divine Love outshines Human Reason.

Three or four times in brotherhood the two
    embraced and re-embraced, and then Sordello
    drew back and said: "Countryman, who are *you*?"

"Before those spirits worthy to be blessed
    had yet been given leave to climb this mountain,   5
    Octavian had laid my bones to rest.

I am Virgil, and I am lost to Heaven
    for no sin, but because I lacked the faith."
    In these words was my Master's answer given.

Just as a man who suddenly confronts   10
    something too marvelous either to believe
    or disbelieve, and so does both at once—

so did Sordello. Then his great head lowered,
    and, turning, he once more embraced my Master,
    but round the knees, as a menial does his lord.   15

"Eternal Glory of the Latin race,
    through whom our tongue made all its greatness clear!
    Of my own land the deathless pride and praise!

What grace or merit lets me see you plain?"
    he said. "And oh, if I am worthy, tell me   20
    if you come here from Hell, and from what pain."

"Through every valley of the painful kingdom
    I passed," my Lord replied. "A power from Heaven
    marked me this road, and in that power I come.

Not what I did but what I left undone,   25
    who learned too late, denies my right to share
    your hope of seeing the Eternal Sun.

There is a place below where sorrow lies
    in untormented gloom. Its lamentations
    are not the shrieks of pain, but hopeless sighs.   30

There do I dwell with souls of babes whom death
    bit off in their first innocence, before
    baptism washed them of their taint of earth.

There do I dwell with those who were not dressed
    in the Three Sacred Virtues but, unstained,   35
    recognized and practiced all the rest.

But if you know and are allowed to say,
    show us how we may reach the true beginning
    of Purgatory by the shortest way."

"We are not fixed in one place," he replied,   40
    "but roam at will up and around this slope
    far as the Gate, and I will be your guide.

But the day is fading fast, and in no case
    may one ascend at night: we will do well
    to give some thought to a good resting place.   45

Some souls are camped apart here on the right.
    If you permit, I will conduct you to them:
    I think you will find pleasure in the sight."

"What is it you say?" my Guide asked. "If one sought
    to climb at night, would others block his way?   50
    Or would he simply find that he could not?"

"Once the Sun sets," that noble soul replied,
    "you would not cross this line"—and ran his finger
    across the ground between him and my Guide.

"Nor is there anything to block the ascent   55
    except the shades of night: they of themselves
    suffice to sap the will of the most fervent.

One might, indeed, go down during the night
    and wander the whole slope, were he inclined to,
    while the horizon locks the day from sight."   60

I heard my Lord's voice, touched with wonder, say:
   "Lead us to the place of which you spoke
   where we may win some pleasure from delay."

We had not traveled very far from there
   before I saw a hollow in the slope   65
   such as one often finds in mountains here.

"There," said that spirit, "where the mountain makes
   a lap among its folds: that is the place
   where we may wait until the new day breaks."

The dell's rim sank away from left to right.   70
   A winding path, half-level and half-steep,
   led us to where the rim stood at mid-height.

Indigo, phosphorescent wood self-lit,
   gold, fine silver, white-lead, cochineal,
   fresh emerald the moment it is split—   75

all colors would seem lusterless as shade
   if placed beside the flowers and grassy banks
   that made a shining of that little glade.

Nor has glad Nature only colored there,
   but of a thousand sweet scents made a single   80
   earthless, nameless fragrance of the air.

Salve Regina!—from that green the hymn
   was raised to Heaven by a choir of souls
   hidden from outer view by the glade's rim.

"Sirs," said that Mantuan, "do not request   85
   that I conduct you there while any light
   remains before the Sun sinks to its nest.

You can observe them from this rise and follow
   their actions better, singly and en masse,
   than if you moved among them in the hollow.   90

He who sits highest with the look of one
    ashamed to move his lips when others praise,
    in life left undone what he should have done.

He was the Emperor Rudolph whose high state
    could once have stayed the death of Italy.   95
    Now, though another try, 't will be too late.

That one who comforts him ruled formerly
    the land where rise the waters that flow down
    the Moldau to the Elbe to the sea.

He was Ottocar, and more respected and feared   100
    while still in diapers than his dissipated
    son Wenceslaus is now with a full beard.

That Snubnose there who talks with head close-pressed
    to the kindly looking one, died while in flight,
    dishonoring the Lily on his crest.   105

Observe the way he beats his breast and cries.
    And how the other one has made his palm
    a bed to rest his cheek on while he sighs.

They are father and father-in-law of The Plague of
      France.
    They know his dissolute and vicious ways,   110
    and hence their grief among these holy chants.

The heavy-sinewed one beside that spirit
    with the manly nose, singing in harmony,
    bore in his life the seal of every merit.

And if that younger one who sits in place   115
    behind him, had remained king after him,
    true merit would have passed from vase to vase.

As it has not, alas, in their successors.
    Frederick and James possess the kingdoms now.
    Their father's better heritage none possesses.   120

Rare is the tree that lifts to every limb
   the sap of merit—He who gives, so wills
   that men may learn to beg their best from Him.

And what I say goes for that bignosed one
   no less than for the other who sings with him.   125
   On his account Provence and Puglia mourn.

By as much as Margaret and Beatrice
   must yield when Constance speaks her husband's
      worth,
   that much less than the tree the seedling is.

See Henry of England seated there alone,   130
   the monarch of the simple life: his branches
   came to good issue in a noble son.

The other lone one seated on the ground
   below the rest and looking up to them
   was the Marquis William Longsword, he who found   135

such grief in Allesandria, for whose pride
both Monferrato and Canavese cried."

NOTES

General Note: THE NEGLIGENT RULERS. The Negligent
Rulers are the fourth and final class of the Late-Repentant. All of the
Late-Repentant made God wait by putting off their surrender to His
will until the end. Accordingly God now makes them wait before
they may begin their ascent to Him through the purifying pains of
Purgatory-proper. The Negligent Rulers, however, had special
cause to be preoccupied by worldly affairs. Their responsibility for
their subjects was not only a duty but a duty in some measure im-
posed upon them by God's Will since kings were believed to be di-
vinely selected. Just as those who died by violence are elevated a
step above the merely indolent, so the Negligent Rulers are elevated
above their negligent subjects because their special duties made it
difficult for them to think about the welfare of their own souls.

4–6. THE FIRST SALVATION. Before Christ's redemption, the souls of the virtuous went to Limbo. In *Inferno,* IV, Dante refers to Christ's apocryphal descent into Limbo in A.D. 33. The incident is known as The Harrowing of Hell, and in it Christ was said to have taken with him to Heaven the first souls to win salvation. (Adam and Eve were among those so elevated.) From the time of the Fall until A.D. 33, therefore, Purgatory existed but was not in use. Virgil died in A.D. 19 under the Emperor Octavian.

19. *What grace or merit: I.e.,* what special grace granted me by Heaven, or what merit of my own I know not of?

33. *taint of earth:* Original sin. Unbaptized infants have not yet been taken to Christ and have not, accordingly, been cleaned of their part in Adam's guilt. They must, therefore, share the fate of the virtuous pagans (*Inferno,* IV) whom they resemble in being sinless but lacking Christ's sacrament. Infant damnation is one of the most vexed and least attractive tenets of dogmatic Christianity.

35–36. *The Three Sacred Virtues:* Faith, Hope, and Charity. These are the "revealed" or "theological" virtues. *the rest:* The Four Cardinal Virtues. They are Justice, Prudence, Temperance, and Fortitude. (See I, 23, and 31 ff., notes.)

40–60. THE LAW OF THE ASCENT. No allegory, by its nature, is containable within a paraphrase. The center of the allegory here is clearly in the fact that the Sun symbolizes Divine Illumination. Note that Dante underlines this idea by referring to God in line 27 above as "the Eternal Sun." Thus the primary meanings of the allegory may be clearly enough stated: first, that one cannot achieve true repentance and purification except in the sight of God (light of the Sun); second, that one has no difficulty in backsliding (going down the mountain) once he is out of God's sight (darkness); and third, that once out of sight of God/Sun one simply cannot find within himself the will to climb. See also note to lines 85–87, below.

Once in Heaven, it should be noted, there is no night: one is constantly in the presence and light of God, the Sun. Here is another of those harmonies of concept that mark Dante's structural power: in Heaven there is no darkness; in Hell there is no light (except the dimness of Human Reason unaided); in Purgatory—the Kingdom between—there is both light and darkness.

70–72. THE SHAPE OF THE VALLEY. The point is much disputed. I conceive the valley to lie in a U-shaped fold with the mouth of the U facing East and the sides inclining upward into the mass of the Mountain. The incline would seem to be regular. Hence, when the Poets come to the point at which the rim stands at mid-height, they are halfway up what I understand to be the southern side of the U, a position from which they can best observe the whole valley, being as it were at the fifty-yard line.

82. *Salve Regina!* The beginning of the Compline Hymn in the Roman Catholic Breviary. It is an especially apt choice as the hymn of these souls: "Hail Queen, mother of Mercy . . . to thee we sigh . . . in this valley of tears."

85–87. *"Sirs," said that Mantuan:* This is the first time Sordello's form of address includes both the Poets. Dante has not yet even been presented to him. *do not request that I conduct you there while any light remains:* See note on The Law of the Ascent. Sordello here carries it a step further: one may descend into the valley after dark (as they will in the next Canto), but no downward step may be taken while any of the Sun's light remains. Characteristically, the detail is sound both as allegory and as narrative, for the valley is in fact best observed from the rim.

91–95. THE EMPEROR RUDOLPH. Rudolph of Hapsburg, 1218–1291, crowned Emperor, 1273. He is the Father of "German Albert" (VI, 100, note) and with him shared the blame for failing to unify Italy. Dante's dream of a unified Italy was not realized until the mid-nineteenth century.

96. *Now, though another try, 't will be too late:* The other is Henry VII of Luxemburg, Emperor from 1308 to 1313. Henry, as Emperor, tried to accomplish, under circumstances that had by then made it impossible, what Rudolph and Albert had neglected to do under circumstances that assured success.

This line contains another of Dante's political "prophecies," the accuracy of which (see *Inferno*, VI, 61, note) was made possible by the fact that he was writing *as if* in 1300 but actually *as of* ten to fifteen years later. The exact dates of the composition of the *Commedia* cannot be fixed, though likely dates would be from 1308 to 1321. Clearly *Purgatory* must have been written after Henry had attempted to unify Italy and had failed, hence, after 1310.

97. *That one who comforts him:* Ottocar II, King of Bohemia (the land whose waters drain into the Moldau, to the Elbe, to the sea) from 1253 to 1278. In life he was Rudolph's enemy and a tyrant whose acts might well have reserved for him a bath in Phlegethon (*Inferno,* XII) with the Violent Against Their Neighbors. Dante may have known him only as a valiant warrior. His object in placing him here seems to be to show the reconciliation of enemies after true repentance and forgiveness.

102. *Wenceslaus:* Wenceslaus IV (the Good), born in 1270, succeeded his father as King of Bohemia in 1278. He was elected King of Poland in 1300, and died 1305. Despite a promising beginning as king, Wenceslaus was forced to cede many territories for which his warrior father would have fought to the death. Wenceslaus preferred piety to warfare, habitually hearing several masses daily. With his spirits thus restored, he seems to have found the strength for scouting various bedrooms, for he had begotten numerous illegitimate children by the time he was twenty-five. Hence Dante's charge that he was dissipated.

103. *That Snubnose:* Philip III of France (the Bold, also the Snubnose), 1245–1285, succeeded his father, Louis IX, in 1270. He did not die while actually in flight from the field of battle, but at Perpignan, to which he had retired after the French navy had been annihilated by Pedro III of Aragon.

104. *the kindly looking one:* Henry (the Fat) of Navarre, reigned 1270–1274. He died reportedly "suffocated by the fat of his own body." In life he was quite other than kindly, and might have made excellent Hell-bait, but Dante obviously credits him with having breathed a true repentance from somewhere among the folds of his "suffocating fat."

109. *The Plague of France:* Philip IV (the Fair) of France, born 1268, crowned 1285, died 1314. Second son of Philip III, he married Juana, daughter of Henry of Navarre. It is his misrule and his vicious life that unite (line 103: their heads "close pressed") his father and father-in-law.

Philip IV was for Dante the archetype of the evil ruler, in much the same way that Boniface VIII (whom Philip humiliated and drove to an early death) was the archetype of the evil Pope. Internally, Philip ruined whole provinces by his extortions and currency frauds. He systematically jailed Italian merchants (for ransom) on false charges, cruelly robbed the Jews, and suppressed the Knights Templars in order to confiscate their properties. Externally, he played a disastrous hand in Italian politics. Soon after he had eliminated Boniface VIII, he succeeded in placing one of his puppet cardinals on the Papal Throne as Clement V. Under Clement V the Papal Seat was transferred to Avignon. (*Inferno,* XIX, refers to Clement's intrigue with Philip and makes clear that a place in Hell is awaiting Clement.) In XX and XXXII, below, Dante inveighs against Philip, and again in *Paradiso,* XIX.

112–113. *The heavy-sinewed one . . . that spirit with the manly nose:* Another pair of former enemies reconciled. The first is Pedro III of Aragon, 1236–1285, King of Aragon, 1276, and (after the bloody Sicilian Vespers of 1282 in which all the French were massacred) King of Sicily. He married Manfred's "good Constance" (III, 143). Dante's phrasing in these lines obviously suggests that the first spirit is virile, whereas the second is virile only in the nose.

That second spirit, Pedro's equal only in the nose, is Charles I of Anjou, 1220–1285, crowned King of Sicily and Puglia (Apulia) in 1265. It was Charles who destroyed Manfred at Benevento in 1265 and who was overthrown in the Sicilian Vespers. Dante inveighs against his misrule in XX and again in *Paradiso,* VIII, 73 ff. Once again Dante's intent in presenting the soul of such a man in Purgatory must have been to show that no amount of wickedness will damn a man if he achieves true repentance.

115. *that younger one:* Alfonso III (the Magnificent), 1271–1291, crowned King of Aragon, 1286. He left no heirs and his rule passed to his degenerate younger brothers, the throne of Aragon to James, and that of Sicily to Frederick, both of whom were ruling in 1300, hence the "now" of line 119. Thus the meaning of lines 119–120 is that the younger sons have the material heritage of their father, Pedro, but that no one (now that Alfonso is dead) possesses his better heritage (*i.e.,* his merit).

124–129. A difficult passage. Dante refers again to Charles and Pedro, still developing the theme of the degeneracy of sons. The theme applies not only to Pedro in the degeneracy of James and of Frederick, but to Charles as well. Dante's meaning is that the son, Charles the Lame, is as inferior to his father, Charles I, as Charles I is to Pedro. Hence their kingdoms mourn. But Dante carries the figure through a very complicated comparison, which may be read: "The seedling [Charles II] is inferior to the tree [Charles I] by as much as Constance [widow of Pedro III] may praise her husband above the husband of Margaret and Beatrice [they were the two wives of Charles I]."

130. *Henry of England:* Henry III, 1216–1278. A pious but pallid king. His son, Edward I, however (who was ruling in 1300), crowned a glorious reign with an enduring reform of English law. Hence Henry's "branches came to a good issue in a noble son."

Henry is seated alone in part, perhaps, because he had no connection with the Holy Roman Empire, but much more importantly because he is unique in this company. Henry attended so many masses daily that he never got around to governing his kingdom. His sin, therefore, could not have been neglect of God, but rather neglect of his divinely-imposed duties to rule his kingdom well. His presence in this company adds an interesting dimension to Dante's concept, for Henry's sin is the reverse of the general pattern here. Dante's Aristotelian mind could not cherish any excess: the Good is the Golden Mean, to wander from the mean in either direction is equally culpable.

133–137. THE MARQUIS WILLIAM. William VII (Longsword), Marquis of Monferrato, 1245–1292. A lesser prince than the others, hence he sits below and looks up to them. As Imperial Vicar to Italy he headed a coalition of Ghibelline towns. In 1290 the Republic of Asti fomented a rebellion in Alessandria, a town held by William. William, attempting to put down the rebellion, was captured, locked in an iron cage, and exposed to public ridicule. He died in the cage, and even in death his body was shockingly abused by the Alessandrians. William's son moved against Alessandria to avenge his father, but the Alessandrians defeated him and invaded Monferrato and Canavese, the two districts of William's fief. Their invasion left the citizens with ample reasons for tears.

Canto VIII

ANTE-PURGATORY:
THE FLOWERING VALLEY   *The Negligent Rulers*
Nightfall, Easter Sunday
The Guardian Angels
The Serpent

As the light fades, Dante, Virgil, and Sordello stand on the bank and watch the souls below gather and sing the COM-PLINE HYMN, asking for protection in the night. In response to the hymn TWO GREEN ANGELS descend from Heaven and take their posts, one on each side of the valley. Full dark-ness now settles, and the Poets may make their DESCENT INTO THE VALLEY.

Dante immediately finds a soul he knows, JUDGE NINO DE' VISCONTI, and has a long conversation with him in which both bemoan the infidelity of widows who remarry.

When Judge Nino has finished speaking, Dante looks at the South Pole and sees that THREE STARS (the Three Theo-logical Virtues) have replaced THE FOUR STARS (the Four Cardinal Virtues) he had seen at dawn.

As he is discussing them with Virgil THE SERPENT ap-pears and is immediately routed by the Angels, who return to their posts. Dante then has a conversation with CONRAD MALASPINA, whom Judge Nino had summoned when he found out Dante was a living man. Dante owes a debt of grat-itude to the Malaspina House for its hospitality to him in his exile, and he takes this opportunity to praise the house and to have Conrad prophesy that Dante shall live to know more about it.

It was the hour that turns the memories
   of sailing men their first day out, to home,
   and friends they sailed from on that morning's breeze;

that thrills the traveler newly on his way
   with love and yearning when he hears afar   5
   the bell that seems to mourn the dying day—

when I began, for lack of any sound,
   to count my hearing vain: and watched a spirit
   who signaled for attention all around.

Raising his hands, he joined his palms in prayer   10
   and turned his rapt eyes east, as if to say:
   "I have no thought except that Thou art there."

"Te lucis ante" swelled from him so sweetly,
   with such devotion and so pure a tone,
   my senses lost the sense of self completely.   15

Then all the others with a golden peal
   joined in the hymn and sang it to the end,
   their eyes devoutly raised to Heaven's wheel.

Reader, if you seek truth, sharpen your eyes,
   for here the veil of allegory thins   20
   and may be pierced by any man who tries.

I saw that host of kings, its supplication
   sung to a close, stand still and pale and humble,
   eyes raised to Heaven as if in expectation.

I saw two angels issue and descend   25
   from Heaven's height, bearing two flaming swords
   without a point, snapped off to a stub end.

Green as a leaf is at its first unfurling,
   their robes; and green the wings that beat and blew
   the flowing folds back, fluttering and whirling.   30

One landed just above me, and one flew
   to the other bank. Thus, in the silent valley,
   the people were contained between the two.

I could see clearly that their hair was gold,
   but my eyes drew back bedazzled from their faces,   35
   defeated by more light than they could hold.

"They are from Mary's bosom," Sordello said,
   "and come to guard the valley from the Serpent
   that in a moment now will show its head."

And I, not knowing where it would appear,   40
   turned so I stood behind those trusted shoulders
   and pressed against them icy-cold with fear.

Once more Sordello spoke: "Now let us go
   to where the great souls are, and speak to them.
   The sight of you will please them much, I know."   45

It was, I think, but three steps to the base
   of the little bank; and there I saw a shade
   who stared at me as if he knew my face.

The air was closing on its darkling hour,
   yet not so fast but what it let me see,   50
   at that close range, what it had veiled before.

I took a step toward him; he, one toward me—
   Noble Judge Nin! how it rejoiced my soul
   to see you safe for all eternity!

No welcome was left unsaid on either side.   55
   Then he inquired: "How long since did you come
   to the mountain's foot over that widest tide?"

"Oh," I replied, "I came by the pits of woe—
   this morning. I am still in my first life,
   though I gain the other on the road I go."   60

He and Sordello, when they heard me thus
   answer the question, suddenly drew back
   as if surprised by something marvelous.

One turned to Virgil, and one turned aside
   to a shade who sat nearby. "Conrad! Get up!   65
   See what the grace of God has willed!" he cried.

And then to me: "By all the thankful praise
   you owe to Him who hides His primal cause
   so deep that none may ever know His ways—

when you have once more crossed the enormous tide,   70
   tell my Giovanna to cry out my name
   there where the innocent are gratified.

I do not think her mother cares for me
   since she put off the weeds and the white veil
   that she will once more long for presently.   75

She shows all men how long love's fire will burn
   within a woman's heart when sight and touch
   do not rekindle it at every turn.

Nor will the Milanese viper she must bear
   upon her tomb do her such honor in it   80
   as would Gallura's cock emblazoned there."

So spoke he; and his features bore the seal
   of that considered anger a good man
   reaches in reason and may rightly feel.

I looked up at the Heavens next, and eyed   85
   that center point at which the stars are slowest,
   as a wheel is next the axle. And my Guide:

"My son, what is it that you stare at so?"
   And I: "At those three stars there in whose light
   the polar regions here are all aglow."   90

And he to me: "Below the rim of space
   now ride the four bright stars you saw this morning,
   and these three have arisen in their place."

Sordello started as my Guide said this;
   and clutching him, he pointed arm and finger,   95
   crying: "Our Adversary! There he is!"

Straight through the valley's unprotected side
   a serpent came, perhaps the very one
   that gave the bitter food for which Eve cried.

Through the sweet grass and flowers the long sneak drew, 100
   turning its head around from time to time
   to lick itself as preening beasts will do.

I did not see and cannot tell you here
   how the celestial falcons took to flight;
   but I did see that both were in the air.   105

Hearing their green wings beating through the night,
   the serpent fled. The angels wheeled and climbed
   back to their posts again in equal flight.

The shade the Judge had summoned with his cry
   had not moved from his side; through all that fray   110
   he stared at me without blinking an eye.

"So may the lamp that leads to what you seek
   find oil enough," he said, "in your own will
   to light your way to the enameled peak;

if you can say for certain how things stand   115
   in Val di Magra or those parts, please do,
   for I was once a great lord in that land.

Conrad Malaspina I was—the grandson
   and not the Elder. Here I purify
   the love I bore for those who were my own."   120

"Oh," I replied, "I never have been near
   the lands you held; but is there in all Europe
   a hamlet ignorant of the name you bear?

The glories of your noble house proclaim
   its lords abroad, proclaim the lands that bear them;   125
   and he who does not know them knows their fame.

I swear to you—so may my present course
   lead me on high—your honored house has never
   put by its strict sword and its easy purse.

Usage and nature have so formed your race   130
   that, though the Guilty Head pervert all else,
   it still shuns ill to walk the path of grace."

And he: "Go now, for the Sun shall not complete
   its seventh rest in that great bed the Ram
   bestrides and covers with its four spread feet,   135

before this testimony you have given
   shall be nailed to the center of your head
   with stouter nails, and more securely driven,

than ever hearsay was. And this shall be
certain as fate is in its fixed decree."   140

NOTES

7–9. The original passage is hard to interpret. I think it is best
taken as another of Dante's extraordinary accounts of how his
senses work. (*Cf. Inferno,* XX, 10, and XXXI, 14–15, and notes
thereto.) Dante's descriptions of how his senses work seem ever to
call forth his pedantry. His basic idea here seems to be most nearly
related to that with which he opens Canto IV—that the soul, under
intense stimulus, is absorbed into one sense at a time. Up to this
point he has been absorbed in listening to the spirits sing *Salve
Regina!* and to Sordello's account of the spirits. Now both have
fallen still, and Dante gives what amounts to a sort of physiological

report of his reactions, stating that bit by bit he emerges from his absorption in the sense of hearing, now useless for lack of anything to hear, and resettles his attention in his sense of sight. (*Cf.* also lines 13–15, below.)

13. *Te lucis ante:* The beginning of the Compline Hymn, *Te lucis ante terminum* ("To Thee before the light is done"). The hymn is a prayer for protection against the evils that walk the dark. Like all of Dante's hymn choices, it is fitted to the situation, the vision that follows being precisely in answer to the hymn's plea.

15. *my senses lost the sense of self completely:* (Lit.: "It made me from myself pass from all awareness.") Here, too, I think the key to the proper interpretation lies in the opening lines of Canto IV.

26–27. THE BROKEN SWORDS. Symbols, well used, can seldom be narrowed to a single meaning that excludes other possibilities. The swords may symbolize God's Justice, and the broken points that it is tempered with Mercy. They may equally symbolize that the Angel Guardians are for defense only and not for offense. There is also a possible reference to the legend that the guardian angels broke their swords when Christ entered Paradise, thereby symbolizing that they would no longer exclude with the whole sword, *i.e.,* completely.

34–36. In line 36, Dante clearly meant one of his characteristic comments on the behavior of *all* of our senses. A more literal rendering of this tercet would be:

I could distinctly see their golden hair,
> but my eyes drew back defeated from their faces,
> like a sense perceiving more than it can bear.

I have preferred the less literal rendering because it seems to manage a better effect as English poetry.

46. *three steps:* I am inclined to think Dante intended only to show that the bank was not very high, but three is an important number and any of its symbolic possibilities could be argued here.

51. *before:* Then Dante was standing on the bank.

53. *Judge Nin:* Nino de' Visconti da Pisa, nephew of Count Ugolino (see *Inferno,* XXXIII) was Justiciary of Gallura in Sardinia,

then a Pisan possession. It was he who ordered the hanging of Friar
Gomita (see *Inferno,* XXII, 82, note). He should be thought of as
more nearly a viceroy for his uncle than as a judge in the modern
sense. Dante knew him intimately. Lines 53–54 should be taken not
as an implication that Dante knew of any great sin for which Nino
should have been damned, but rather as a simple rejoicing that a
man so deeply involved in worldly affairs had yet managed not to
lose his soul to worldliness. Nino died in 1296.

68–69. *Cf.* III, 34–39.

70. *enormous tide:* Figuratively, the enormous tide between life
and death. Literally, the sea between the mouth of the Tiber and the
shores of Purgatory, the longest sea-route on earth as Dante con-
ceived it.

71. *my Giovanna:* His daughter.

72–81. JUDGE NINO'S REPROACH OF HIS WIFE, BEA-
TRICE. Nino Visconti's widow was Beatrice, daughter of Opizzo
da Esti (*Inferno,* XII, 111). She put off the weeds and white veil
(the mourning costume of Dante's time) first in being betrothed to Al-
berto Scotti, Lord of Piacenza, and then in jilting him to marry
Galeazzo Visconti of Milan, all under the pressure of her family's
insistence and for political motives. Nino makes no allowance for
the pressures that must have been brought to bear upon Beatrice,
and Dante (see below) endorses his sentiments with the same lack of
reservation.

Nino proceeds to prophesy (it had already happened between
1300 and the time of the writing) that Beatrice will one day wish she
had remained a widow, for the jilted Scotti took his revenge by ruin-
ing Visconti, and Beatrice had to share his poverty. Nino carries his
reproach to eternity in saying that even her burial will be less honor-
able than it would have been had she remained true. (It was the cus-
tom for the tombs of ladies to be marked with their husbands' coats
of arms.) "The Milan" (I hope that form will do for "Milanese," *i.e.,*
"of Milan," and in any case it will have to) is Galeazzo Visconti,
whose arms contained a viper eating a child. That viper on her tomb,
says Nino, will do her less honor than would the cock of Gallura
from Nino's arms. A piece of family pride, the arms of Gallura were
more ancient than those of the Visconti of Milan and Nino looks
upon Galeazzo as an upstart.

In 1328 Beatrice's son (she was then a widow for the second time) was made Lord of Milan and her fortunes thereafter (she died in 1334) rode high once again—a turn of events Dante could not have prophesied at the time of the writing, and which, in fact, he did not live to see.

73. *her mother:* Nino's wife. But note that he refers to her not as "my wife" but as "her mother."

83. *considered anger: Cf. Inferno,* VIII, 43, and note.

85–87. *I looked up . . . next:* Students regularly take this line to mean that Dante is avoiding Nino's eyes. It is simply one of Dante's fast transitions. Nino's remarks are closed, Dante has emphatically approved them, and with no time wasted, he passes on to the next thing of interest—the South Pole, whose stars he has never before seen except for a glimpse at dawn.

90. *the polar regions here:* "Here," equals "on this side of the Equator." The stars are important symbols and will recur. At dawn, on the shore (at the beginning of the Ante-Purgatory) Dante had seen four stars representing the Four Cardinal Virtues. Now, just before beginning the True Purgatory, he sees three evening stars which may be taken as the Three Theological Virtues. In Canto XXIX, just before the appearance of Beatrice in the Earthly Paradise, Dante sees all seven together in the form of Heavenly Nymphs.

106. *hearing their green wings:* How even the Serpent can register with his hearing the color of the wings remains an unanswered question. This sort of figure is one of Dante's mannerisms. *Cf.* his first description of Virgil in *Inferno,* I, where Virgil is described as appearing (visual) hoarse (auditory) with long silence. Some critics have labeled both these passages as master ambiguities. Perhaps so.

107–108. *climbed back to their posts again:* Dante does not specify whether to the bank (their watch posts) or to Heaven (their original posts). I think he meant watch posts, for the souls' prayer (which the Angels answer) is for night-long protection. In Purgatory, only the souls below the Gate (Ante-Purgatory) are subject to temptation, and that, it would seem, of only the most perfunctory sort. In any case it is certain that they will not yield to temptation, for they are saved. The Serpent, therefore, is best taken as a formal masque-like allegory, like the Heavenly Pageant Dante will encounter at the top of the mountain.

109–111. *The shade the Judge had summoned with his cry:* Conrad. See line 65. *stared at me without blinking an eye:* Another Dantean peculiarity. If Dante was staring at the Angels and the Serpent, he could not know this detail.

112–113. *The lamp:* The light of Divine Grace must be merited (*i.e.,* find oil within the soul). The summit of Purgatory (the Earthly Paradise) is an "enameled" plateau. Dante uses the same word to describe the Citadel of Limbo (*Inferno,* IV, 115). Sense: "So may you find within your soul all the merit you need to win to the summit. . . ."

118. *Conrad Malaspina:* Very little is known about this Conrad except that he was the son of Frederick I, Marchese di Villafranca, and the grandson of Conrad I. The house of Malaspina, on the other hand, was honorably known, though scarcely as well as Dante declares below. In his praise of the Malaspina family, Dante is paying a debt of gratitude for the honor and hospitality with which it received him after his exile from Florence.

119–120. *Here I purify . . . :* Various interpretations of these lines have been offered. I think Conrad means that for love of friends and kin he remained so occupied in worldly affairs that he neglected God. Now in Purgatory he purifies and offers to God the love that formerly led him to be negligent.

129. *strict sword . . . easy purse:* Valor . . . liberality.

131. *the Guilty Head:* Certainly the primary meaning is the Devil. The corrupt Papacy and the negligent Emperor may be secondary meanings.

133–134. *the Sun shall not complete its seventh rest:* The Sun will not have completed its seventh transit of Aries (the Ram), *i.e.,* the seven years will not pass, before Dante will know from his own experience the truth of what he has here uttered as hearsay (of the virtue and liberality of the Malaspina family). *that great bed the Ram bestrides:* That portion of the zodiac which falls under the sign of Aries. Aries is often depicted with his four feet spread wide.

Canto IX

THE GATE OF PURGATORY   *The Angel Guardian*

Dawn is approaching. Dante has a dream of A GOLDEN EA-
GLE that descends from the height of Heaven and carries
him up to the Sphere of Fire. He wakes to find he has been
transported in his sleep, that it was LUCIA who bore him,
laying him down beside an enormous wall, through an open-
ing in which he and Virgil may approach THE GATE OF
PURGATORY.

Having explained these matters, Virgil leads Dante to the
Gate and its ANGEL GUARDIAN. The Angel is seated on the
topmost of THREE STEPS that symbolize the three parts of a
perfect ACT OF CONFESSION. Dante prostrates himself at
the feet of the Angel, who cuts SEVEN P's in Dante's forehead
with the point of a blazing sword. He then allows the Poets to
enter. As the Gates open with a sound of thunder, the moun-
tain resounds with a great HYMN OF PRAISE.

Now pale upon the balcony of the East
   ancient Tithonus' concubine appeared,
   but lately from her lover's arms released.

Across her brow, their radiance like a veil,
   a scroll of gems was set, worked in the shape   5
   of the cold beast whose sting is in his tail.

And now already, where we were, the night
   had taken two steps upward, while the third
   thrust down its wings in the first stroke of flight;

when I, by Adam's weight of flesh defeated,   10
    was overcome by sleep, and sank to rest
    across the grass on which we five were seated.

At that new hour when the first dawn light grows
    and the little swallow starts her mournful cry,
    perhaps in memory of her former woes;   15

and when the mind, escaped from its submission
    to flesh and to the chains of waking thought,
    becomes almost prophetic in its vision;

in a dream I saw a soaring eagle hold
    the shining height of Heaven, poised to strike,   20
    yet motionless on widespread wings of gold.

He seemed to hover where old history
    records that Ganymede rose from his friends,
    borne off to the supreme consistory.

I thought to myself: "Perhaps his habit is   25
    to strike at this one spot; perhaps he scorns
    to take his prey from any place but this."

Then from his easy wheel in Heaven's spire,
    terrible as a lightning bolt, he struck
    and snatched me up high as the Sphere of Fire.   30

It seemed that we were swept in a great blaze,
    and the imaginary fire so scorched me
    my sleep broke and I wakened in a daze.

Achilles must have roused exactly thus—
    glancing about with unadjusted eyes,   35
    now here, now there, not knowing where he was—

when Thetis stole him sleeping, still a boy,
    and fled with him from Chiron's care to Scyros,
    whence the Greeks later lured him off to Troy.

I sat up with a start; and as sleep fled   40
   out of my face, I turned the deathly white
   of one whose blood is turned to ice by dread.

There at my side my Comfort sat—alone.
   The Sun stood two hours high, and more. I sat
   facing the sea. The flowering glen was gone.   45

"Don't be afraid," he said. "From here our course
   leads us to joy, you may be sure. Now, therefore,
   hold nothing back, but strive with all your force.

You are now at Purgatory. See the great
   encircling rampart there ahead. And see   50
   that opening—it contains the Golden Gate.

A while back, in the dawn before the day,
   while still your soul was locked in sleep inside you,
   across the flowers that made the valley gay,

a Lady came. 'I am Lucia,' she said.   55
   'Let me take up this sleeping man and bear him
   that he may wake to see his hope ahead.'

Sordello and the others stayed. She bent
   and took you up. And as the light grew full,
   she led, I followed, up the sweet ascent.   60

Here she put you down. Then with a sweep
   of her sweet eyes she marked that open entrance.
   Then she was gone; and with her went your sleep."

As one who finds his doubt dispelled, sheds fear
   and feels it change into new confidence   65
   as bit by bit he sees the truth shine clear—

so did I change; and seeing my face brim
   with happiness, my Guide set off at once
   to climb the slope, and I moved after him.

Reader, you know to what exalted height   70
   I raised my theme. Small wonder if I now
   summon still greater art to what I write.

As we drew near the height, we reached a place
   from which—inside what I had first believed
   to be an open breach in the rock face—   75

I saw a great gate fixed in place above
   three steps, each its own color; and a guard
   who did not say a word and did not move.

Slow bit by bit, raising my lids with care,
   I made him out seated on the top step,   80
   his face more radiant than my eyes could bear.

He held a drawn sword, and the eye of day
   beat such a fire back from it, that each time
   I tried to look, I had to look away.

I heard him call: "What is your business here?   85
   Answer from where you stand. Where is your Guide?
   Take care you do not find your coming dear."

"A little while ago," my Teacher said,
   "a Heavenly Lady, well versed in these matters,
   told us: 'Go there. That is the Gate ahead.' "   90

"And may she still assist you, once inside,
   to your souls' good! Come forward to our three steps,"
   the courteous keeper of the gate replied.

We came to the first step: white marble gleaming
   so polished and so smooth that in its mirror   95
   I saw my true reflection past all seeming.

The second was stained darker than blue-black
   and of a rough-grained and a fire-flaked stone,
   its length and breadth crisscrossed by many a crack.

The third and topmost was of porphyry, 100
 or so it seemed, but of a red as flaming
 as blood that spurts out of an artery.

The Angel of the Lord had both feet on
 this final step and sat upon the sill
 which seemed made of some adamantine stone. 105

With great good will my Master guided me
 up the three steps and whispered in my ear:
 "Now beg him humbly that he turn the key."

Devoutly prostrate at his holy feet,
 I begged in mercy's name to be let in, 110
 but first three times upon my breast I beat.

Seven *P*'s, the seven scars of sin,
 his sword point cut into my brow. He said:
 "Scrub off these wounds when you have passed
  within."

Color of ashes, of parched earth one sees 115
 deep in an excavation, were his vestments,
 and from beneath them he drew out two keys.

One was of gold, one silver. He applied
 the white one to the gate first, then the yellow,
 and did with them what left me satisfied. 120

"Whenever either of these keys is put
 improperly in the lock and fails to turn it,"
 the Angel said to us, "the door stays shut.

One is more precious. The other is so wrought
 as to require the greater skill and genius, 125
 for it is that one which unties the knot.

They are from Peter, and he bade me be
 more eager to let in than to keep out
 whoever cast himself prostrate before me."

Then opening the sacred portals wide: 130
  "Enter. But first be warned: do not look back
  or you will find yourself once more outside."

The Tarpeian rock-face, in that fatal hour
  that robbed it of Metellus, and then the treasure,
  did not give off so loud and harsh a roar   135

as did the pivots of the holy gate—
  which were of resonant and hard-forged metal—
  when they turned under their enormous weight.

At the first thunderous roll I turned half-round,
  for it seemed to me I heard a chorus singing   140
  Te deum laudamus mixed with that sweet sound.

I stood there and the strains that reached my ears
  left on my soul exactly that impression
  a man receives who goes to church and hears

the choir and organ ringing out their chords   145
and now does, now does not, make out the words.

NOTES

1–9. There is no wholly satisfactory explanation of this complex
opening description. Dante seems to be saying that the third hour of
darkness is beginning (hence, if sunset occurred at 6:00 it is now a
bit after 8:00 P.M.) and that the aurora of the rising moon is appear-
ing above the horizon.

He describes the Moon as the concubine of Tithonus. Tithonus,
however, married the daughter of the Sun, Aurora (dawn), and it
was she who begged Jove to give her husband immortality while
forgetting to ask perpetual youth for him. Thus Tithonus lived but
grew older and older beside his ageless bride. (In one legend he was
later changed into a grasshopper.) Despite his advanced years, how-
ever, he seems here to be philandering with the Moon as his concu-
bine. Dante describes the Moon as rising from Tithonus' bed and
standing on the balcony of the East (the horizon) with the constella-

tion Scorpio gemmed on her forehead, that "cold [-blooded] beast whose sting is in his tail" being the scorpion.

Having given Tithonus a double life, Dante now adds a mixed metaphor in which the "steps" of the night have "wings." Two of the steps (hours) have flown, and the third has just completed the first downstroke of its wings (*i.e.,* has just begun its flight).

15. *former woes:* Tereus, the husband of Procne, raped her sister Philomela, and cut out her tongue so that she could not accuse him. Philomela managed to communicate the truth to Procne by means of her weaving. The two sisters thereupon took revenge by killing Itys, son of Procne and Tereus, and serving up his flesh to his father. Tereus, learning the truth, was about to kill the sisters when all were turned into birds. Ovid (*Metamorphoses,* VI, 424 ff.) has Tereus changed into a hoopoe, and probably (though the text leaves some doubt) Procne into a swallow and Philomela into a nightingale. Dante clearly takes the swallow to be Philomela.

18. *prophetic in its vision: (Cf. Inferno,* XXVI, 7.) It was an ancient belief that the dreams that came toward dawn were prophetic.

19–33. DANTE'S DREAM. Each of Dante's three nights on the Mount of Purgatory ends with a dream that comes just before dawn. The present dream is relatively simple in its symbolism, and as we learn shortly after Dante's awakening, it parallels his ascent of the mountain in the arms of Lucia. The dream is told, however, with such complexities of allusion that every reference must be carefully weighed.

To summarize the symbolism in the simplest terms, the Golden Eagle may best be rendered in its attributes. It comes from highest Heaven (from God), its feathers are pure gold (Love? God's splendor?), its wings are outspread (the open arms of Divine Love?), and it appears poised to descend in an instant (as is Divine Grace). The Eagle snatches Dante up to the Sphere of Fire (the presence of God? the beginning of Purgatorial purification? both?), and both are so consumed by the fire that Dante, in his unpurified state, cannot bear it.

On another level, of course, the Eagle is Lucia (Divine Light), who has descended from Heaven, and who bears the sleeping Dante from the Flowering Valley to the beginning of the true Purgatory. Note that Lucia is an anagram for *acuila,* "eagle."

On a third level, the dream simultaneously connects with the earlier reference to Ganymede, also snatched up by the eagle of God, but the two experiences are contrasted as much as they are compared. Ganymede was carried up by Jove's eagle, Dante by Lucia. Ganymede was out hunting in the company of his worldly associates; Dante was laboring for grace, had renounced worldliness, and was in the company of great souls who were themselves awaiting purification. Ganymede was carried to Olympus; Dante to the beginning of a purification which, though he was still too unworthy to endure it, would in time make him a perfect servant of the true God. Thus, his experience is in the same pattern as Ganymede's, but surpasses it as Faith surpasses Human Reason, and as Beatrice surpasses Virgil.

23. *Ganymede:* Son of Tros, the mythical founder of Troy, was reputedly the most beautiful of mortals, so beautiful that Jove sent an eagle (or perhaps went himself in the form of an eagle) to snatch up the boy and bring him to Heaven, where he became cup-bearer to the gods. The fact that Dante himself is about to begin the ascent of Purgatory proper (and hence to Heaven) inevitably suggests an allegory of the soul in the history of Ganymede. God calls to Himself what is most beautiful in man.

The fact that Dante always thought of the Trojans as an especially chosen people is also relevant (*cf. Inferno,* II, 13–30, and note). Ganymede was the son of the founder of Troy; Troy, in Dante's Virgilian view, founded Rome. And through the Church of Rome men's souls were enabled to mount to Heaven.

24. *consistory:* Here, the council of the gods on Olympus. Dante uses the same term to describe Paradise.

30. *Sphere of Fire:* The four elemental substances are earth, water, fire, and air. In Dante's cosmography, the Sphere of Fire was located above the Sphere of Air and just under the Sphere of the Moon. Hence the eagle bore him to the top of the atmosphere. The Sphere of Fire, however, may also be taken as another symbol for God.

34–39. ACHILLES' WAKING. It had been prophesied that Achilles would be killed at Troy. Upon the outbreak of the Trojan War, his mother, Thetis, stole him while he was sleeping from the care of the centaur Chiron who was his tutor (see *Inferno,* XII, 71 ff.)

and fled with him to Scyros, where she hid him disguised as a girl. He was found there and lured away by Ulysses and Diomede, who burn for that sin (among others) in Malebolge (see *Inferno,* XXVI, 56–63, and note). Thus Achilles, like Dante, was borne off in his sleep and awoke to find himself in a strange place.

51. *that opening:* The Gate, as the Poets will find, is closed and guarded. Dante (here and in line 62, below) can only mean "the opening in which the gate was set" and not "an open entrance." At this distance, they do not see the Gate itself but only the gap in the otherwise solid wall.

55. *Lucia* (Loo-TCHEE-ya): Symbolizes Divine Light, Divine Grace. (See *Inferno,* II, 97, and note.)

77. *three steps:* (See also lines 94–102, below.) The entrance into Purgatory involves the ritual of the Roman Catholic confessional with the Angel serving as the confessor. The three steps are the three acts of the perfect confession: candid confession (mirroring the whole man), mournful contrition, and burning gratitude for God's mercy. The Angel Guardian, as the priestly confessor, does not move or speak as the Poets approach, because he can admit to purification only those who ask for admission.

86. *Where is your Guide?:* It must follow from the Angel's question that souls ready to enter Purgatory are led up the mountain by another Angel. Dante and Virgil are arriving in an irregular way, as they did to the shore below, where they were asked essentially the same question by Cato. Note, too, that Virgil answers for the Poets, as he did to Cato. The allegory may be that right thinking answers for a man, at least to start with, though the actual entrance into the state of Grace requires an act of Faith and of Submission.

90. *told us:* Lucia spoke only with her eyes, and what Virgil is quoting is her look. What he is quoting is, in essence, correct, but it does seem he could have been a bit more accurate in his first actual conversation with an Angel.

94–96. *the first step:* Contrition of the heart. White for purity, shining for hope, and flawless for perfection. It is not only the mirror of the soul, but it is that mirror in which the soul sees itself as it truly is and not in its outward seeming.

97–99. *the second:* Contrition of the mouth, *i.e.,* confession. The color of a bruise for the shame that envelops the soul as it confesses, rough-grained and fire-flaked for the pain the confessant must endure, and cracked for the imperfection (sin) the soul confesses.

100–102. *the third:* Satisfaction by works. Red for the ardor that leads to good works. Porphyry is, of course, a purple stone, but Dante does not say the stone was porphyry; only that it resembled it, though red in color.

"Artery" here is, of course, an anachronism, the circulation of the blood having yet to be discovered in Dante's time. Dante uses the word *vena* (vein), but it seems to me the anachronism will be less confusing to a modern reader than would be the idea of bright red and spurting venous blood.

103–105. The Angel, as noted, represents the confessor, and, more exactly, the Church Confessant. Thus the Church is founded on adamant and rests its feet on Good Works.

112. *Seven P's:* P is for the Latin *peccatum.* Thus there is one *P* for each of the Seven Deadly Sins for which the sinners suffer on the seven ledges above: Pride, Envy, Wrath, Acedia (Sloth), Avarice (Hoarding and Prodigality), Gluttony, and Lust.

Dante has just completed the act of confession and the Angel confessor marks him to indicate that even in a shriven soul there remain traces of the seven sins which can be removed only by suffering.

115–117. *Color of ashes, of parched earth:* The colors of humility which befit the office of the confessor. *two keys:* (*Cf.* the Papal Seal, which is a crown above two crossed keys, and also *Inferno,* XXVII, 99–102.) The keys symbolize the power of the confessor (the Church, and hence the Pope) to grant or to withhold absolution. In the present context they may further be interpreted as the two parts of the confessor's office of admission: the gold key may be taken to represent his ordained authority, the silver key as the learning and reflection with which he must weigh the guilt before assigning penance and offering absolution.

126. *unties the knot:* Another mixed metaphor. The soul-searched judgment of the confessor (the silver key) decides who may and who may not receive absolution, and in resolving that problem the

door is opened, provided that the gold key of ordained authority has already been turned.

133–138. *The Tarpeian rock-face:* The public treasury of Rome was kept in the great scarp of Tarpeia on the Campidoglio. The tribune Metellus was its custodian when Caesar, returned to Rome after crossing the Rubicon, moved to seize the treasury. Metellus opposed him but was driven away and the great gates were opened. Lucan (*Pharsalia,* III, 154–156 and 165–168) describes the scene and the roar that echoed from the rock-face as the gates were forced open.

139–141. The thunder of the opening of the Gates notifies the souls within that a new soul has entered, and they burst into the hymn "We Praise Thee, O God." (Contrast these first sounds of Purgatory with the first sounds of Hell—*Inferno,* III, 22–24.) Despite the thunderous roar right next to him, Dante seems to hear with his "allegorical ear" what certainly could not have registered upon his physical ear.

This seeming incongruity has long troubled me. I owe Professor MacAllister a glad thanks for what is certainly the essential clarification. The whole *Purgatorio,* he points out, is built upon the structure of a Mass. The Mass moreover is happening not on the mountain but in church with Dante devoutly following its well-known steps. I have not yet had time to digest Professor MacAllister's suggestion, but it strikes me immediately as a true insight and promises another illuminating way of reading the *Purgatorio.*

Canto X

The gate closes behind them and the Poets begin the ascent to
THE FIRST CORNICE through a tortuous passage that Dante
describes as a NEEDLE'S EYE. They reach the Cornice about
9:00 or 10:00 of Monday morning.

At first the Cornice seems deserted. Dante's eye is caught
by a series of three marvelously wrought bas-reliefs in the
marble of the inner cliff-face. Three panels depict three
scenes that serve as THE WHIP OF PRIDE, exemplifying to
each sinner as he enters how far greater souls have put by
far greater reasons for pride in order to pursue the grace of
humility.

As Dante stands in admiration before the carvings, Virgil
calls his attention to a band of souls approaching from the
left, and Dante turns for his first sight of the souls of THE
PROUD, who crawl agonizingly round and round the Cor-
nice under the crushing weight of enormous slabs of rock.
Their punishment is so simple and so terrible that Dante can
scarcely bear to describe it. He cries out in anguish to the
proud of this world to take heed of the nature of their sin and
of its unbearable punishment.

When we had crossed the threshold of that gate
   so seldom used because man's perverse love
   so often makes the crooked path seem straight,

I knew by the sound that it had closed again;
    and had I looked back, to what water ever 5
    could I have gone to wash away that stain?

We climbed the rock along a narrow crack
    through which a zigzag pathway pitched and slid
    just as a wave swells full and then falls back.

"This calls for careful judgment," said my Guide. 10
    "Avoid the places where the rock swells up
    and weave among the troughs from side to side."

Our steps became so difficult and few,
    the waning moon had reached its western bed
    and sunk to rest before we could work through 15

that needle's eye. But when we had won clear
    to an open space above, at which the mountain
    steps back to form a ledge, we halted there;

I tired, and both of us confused for lack
    of any sign or guide. The ledge was level, 20
    and lonelier even than a desert track.

From brink to cliff-face measured three men's height,
    and the Cornice did not vary in its width
    as far as I could see to left or right.

Our feet had not yet moved a step up there, 25
    when I made out that all the inner cliff
    which rose without a foothold anywhere

was white and flawless marble and adorned
    with sculptured scenes beside which Polyclitus',
    and even Nature's, best works would be scorned. 30

The Angel who came down from God to man
    with the decree of peace the centuries wept for,
    which opened Heaven, ending the long ban,

stood carved before us with such force and love,
   with such a living grace in his whole pose,   35
   the image seemed about to speak and move.

One could have sworn an *Ave!* sounded clear,
   for she who turned the key that opened to us
   the Perfect Love, was also figured there;

and all her flowing gesture seemed to say—   40
   impressed there as distinctly as a seal
   impresses wax—*Ecce ancilla Dei.*

"Do not give all your thoughts to this one part,"
   my gentle Master said. (I was then standing
   on that side of him where man has his heart.)   45

I turned my eyes a little to the right
   (the side on which he stood who had thus urged me)
   and there, at Mary's back, carved in that white

and flawless wall, I saw another scene,
   and I crossed in front of Virgil and drew near it   50
   the better to make out what it might mean.

Emerging from the marble were portrayed
   the cart, the oxen, and the Ark from which
   the sacrilegious learned to be afraid.

Seven choirs moved there before it, bringing   55
   confusion to my senses; with my hearing
   I thought "No," with my sight, "Yes, they are singing."

In the same way, the smokes the censers poured
   were shown so faithfully that eyes and nose
   disputed yes and no in happy discord.   60

And there before the Holy Vessel, dancing
   with girt-up robes, the humble Psalmist moved,
   less than a king, and more, in his wild prancing.

Facing him, portrayed with a vexed frown
   of mingled sadness and contempt, Michal   65
   stood at a palace window looking down.

I moved a little further to the right,
   the better to observe another panel
   that shone at Michal's back, dazzling and white.

Here was portrayed from glorious history   70
   that Roman Prince whose passion to do justice
   moved Gregory to his great victory.

I speak of Trajan, blessed Emperor.
   And at his bridle was portrayed a widow
   in tears wept from the long grief of the poor.   75

Filling the space on both sides and behind
   were mounted knights on whose great golden banners
   the eagles seemed to flutter in the wind.

The widow knelt and by consummate art
   appeared to say: "My Lord, avenge my son   80
   for he is slain and I am sick at heart."

And he to answer: "Justice shall be done;
   wait only my return." And she: "My Lord"—
   speaking from the great grief that urged her on—

"If you do not?" And he: "Who wears my crown   85
   will right your wrong." And she: "Can the good deed
   another does grace him who shuns his own?"

And he, then: "Be assured. For it is clear
   this duty is to do before I go.
   Justice halts me, pity binds me here."   90

The Maker who can never see or know
   anything new, produced that "visible speaking":
   new to us, because not found below.

As I stood relishing the art and thought
  of those high images—dear in themselves,   95
  and dearer yet as works His hand had wrought—

the Poet said: "Look there: they seem to crawl
  but those are people coming on our left:
  they can tell us where to climb the wall."

My eyes, always intent to look ahead   100
  to some new thing, finding delight in learning,
  lost little time in doing as he said.

Reader, I would not have you be afraid,
  nor turn from your intention to repent
  through hearing how God wills the debt be paid.   105

Do not think of the torments: think, I say,
  of what comes after them: think that at worst
  they cannot last beyond the Judgment Day.

"Master," I said, "those do not seem to me
  people approaching us; nor do I know—   110
  they so confuse my sight—what they may be."

And he to me: "Their painful circumstance
  doubles them to the very earth: my own eyes
  debated what they saw there at first glance.

Look hard and you will see the people pressed   115
  under the moving boulders there. Already
  you can make out how each one beats his breast."

O you proud Christians, wretched souls and small,
  who by the dim lights of your twisted minds
  believe you prosper even as you fall—   120

can you not see that we are worms, each one
  born to become the Angelic butterfly
  that flies defenseless to the Judgment Throne?

What have your souls to boast of and be proud?
   You are no more than insects, incomplete   125
   as any grub until it burst the shroud.

Sometimes at roof or ceiling-beam one sees
   a human figure set there as a corbel,
   carved with its chest crushed in by its own knees,

so cramped that what one sees imagined there   130
   makes his bones ache in fact—just such a sense
   grew on me as I watched those souls with care.

True, those who crawled along that painful track
   were more or less distorted, each one bent
   according to the burden on his back;   135

yet even the most patient, wracked and sore,
   seemed to be groaning: "I can bear no more!"

NOTES

2. *perverse love:* All human actions, in Dante's view, are moti-
vated by love: right love produces good actions and perverse love
produces bad. Virgil discusses this concept in detail in XVII, 103 ff.

7–12. THE NEEDLE'S EYE. "It is easier for a camel to pass
through the eye of a needle than for a rich man to enter into the king-
dom of God." (*Matthew,* xix, 24, and *Mark,* xx, 25. See also *Luke,*
xvii, 25.) I understand Dante to mean here that there shall be no pas-
sage to purification without the ardor of the spirit that strips a man of
worldliness. Once again, as in the first climb at the very foot of the
mountain, the beginning is the most difficult part of the ascent.

14. *waning moon:* The Moon had been full on the night before
Good Friday (*Inferno,* XX, 127). It is now four and a half days later.
In two and a half more days it will be a half moon.

15. *sunk to rest:* The Moon rose sometime after 8:00 P.M., per-
haps closer to 9:00, as described at the beginning of Canto X. It
would set about twelve hours later. But Dante says it has *already* set.

It is, therefore, sometime after 8:00 A.M. But to assume that it has just set would make it only two hours after sunrise, and would mark the hour of Dante's awakening outside the Gate. The passage, moreover, was a slow one. Something between 9:00 and 10:00 A.M. would, therefore, seem to be a reasonable time for Dante's emergence on the first ledge. See XII, 80–81, note.

22–24. The turns of Dante's style and the natural tendency of Italian to use more syllables than does English in stating a similar thought sometimes make it desirable to render six lines of Dante into three of English. I have so rendered it here. A literal translation of the original would read: "From its edge where it borders the void, to the foot of the high bank which rises again, would measure three times a human body; and as far as my eyes could extend their flight either to the left or to the right side, this Cornice seemed to me to be that [wide]."

26 ff. THE WHIP AND THE REIN. At the entrance to each Cornice, Dante presents high examples of the virtue opposite the sin punished on that Cornice. Their purpose is clearly to whip the souls on to emulation. The form in which these examples are presented varies from Cornice to Cornice, but the examples are usually three, and the first of them is always taken from the life of the Virgin.

At the end of the passage of each Cornice, also in various forms, Dante presents examples of the terrible price one must pay for succumbing to each particular sin. The opening exhortations designed to drive the souls on to emulation may be called the Whip of each sin; the closing examples, or admonitions, may be called the Rein, serving to check the impulse toward that sin. See XIII, 39–40.

29. *Polyclitus:* Greek sculptor of the late fifth century B.C., contemporary with Phidias. His name seems to have been the word for artistic perfection during the late Middle Ages and early Renaissance, probably because he is often mentioned by Aristotle.

31–90. THE WHIP OF PRIDE. It consists of three bas-relief panels carved on the inner cliff-face, each panel portraying a scene of great humility, humility being, of course, the virtue opposite pride.

The first panel (lines 31–42) depicts the Annunciation. The angel Gabriel appears to Mary, bringing the word of her great election, and Mary, untouched by pride, answers in her great hour, *Ecce an-*

cilla Dei, "Behold the handmaiden of God." (*Luke,* i, 38.) *the key:* Christ.

The second panel (lines 49–66) depicts King David putting aside all the offices of majesty to dance in humility and total abandonment before the Lord (see *II Samuel,* vi, 14) on bringing the Ark to Jerusalem from the house of the Gittite, Obed-edom. Dante has confused, or deliberately blended, two scenes into one. The first journey of the Ark began with an ox-drawn cart and it was then that Uzzah (an example of overweening pride) was struck dead for laying unsanctified hands upon the Ark, a sacrilegious act. (See *II Samuel,* vi, 6–7.) David laid up the Ark in the house of the Gittite and returned for it three months later, on which occasion it was carried to Jerusalem by the Levites. It was on the second journey that David put by his majesty to dance before the Lord. Michal, daughter of King Saul, and David's first wife, looked on scornfully and was punished for her arrogance by sterility: "therefore Michal the daughter of Saul had no child unto the day of her death." (*II Samuel,* vi, 23.)

The third panel (lines 70–90) depicts the Emperor Trajan halting his royal cavalry en route to battle and dismounting in order to secure justice for a poor woman. Dante places Trajan in *Paradiso,* XX, his soul according to legend having been summoned back to earth and baptized by St. Gregory.

100 ff. THE PUNISHMENT OF THE PROUD. The simple and terrible penance of these souls is that each must crawl round and round the Cornice bearing enormous slabs of rock that press him down, each according to the degree of his sin. The higher a soul tried to raise itself in its pride, the more it is crushed to earth. For pride is a weight of worldliness and bears down the spirit, and therefore it is crushed under the rock of the earth. It is, moreover, the primal sin and the father of all other sins, for the proud man seeks to set himself up as God, and therefore his soul, here, is crushed agonizingly into the very dust until it has suffered itself clean and may rise free of the weight it has placed upon itself.

Canto XI

*As the souls of the Proud creep near, the Poets hear them re-
cite a long and humble prayer based on the Paternoster. When
the prayer is ended, Virgil asks one of the souls, hidden from
view under its enormous burden, the way to the ascent. The sin-
ner, who identifies himself as OMBERTO ALDOBRANDESCO,
instructs the Poets to follow along in the direction the souls
are crawling. He recites his history in brief, and it becomes
clear that Dante means him to exemplify PRIDE OF BIRTH.
The conversation between Dante and Omberto is overheard
by ODERISI D'AGOBBIO, who turns in pain and speaks to
Dante, explaining his sin of PRIDE OF TALENT, the avidity of
the artist for pre-eminence. Oderisi also points out the soul that
struggles along just ahead of him as PROVENZANO SALVANI,
once war lord of Siena, who is being punished for PRIDE OF
TEMPORAL POWER, though he has been advanced toward
his purification in recognition of a single ACT OF GREAT HU-
MILITY performed in order to save the life of a friend.*

    *Oderisi concludes with a DARK PROPHECY OF DANTE'S
EXILE from Florence.*

*Our Father in Heaven, not by Heaven bounded
   but there indwelling for the greater love
   Thou bear'st Thy first works in the realm first-founded,*

hallowed be Thy name, hallowed Thy Power   5
   *by every creature as its nature grants it
   to praise Thy quickening breath in its brief hour.*

Let come to us the sweet peace of Thy reign,
   for if it come not we cannot ourselves
   attain to it however much we strain.

And as Thine Angels kneeling at the throne   10
   offer their wills to Thee, singing Hosannah,
   so teach all men to offer up their own.

Give us this day Thy manna, Lord, we pray,
   for if he have it not, though man most strive
   through these harsh wastes, his speed is his delay.   15

As we forgive our trespassers the ill
   we have endured, do Thou forgive, not weighing
   our merits, but the mercy of Thy will.

Our strength is as a reed bent to the ground:
   do not Thou test us with the Adversary,   20
   but deliver us from him who sets us round.

This last petition, Lord, with grateful mind,
   we pray not for ourselves who have no need,
   but for the souls of those we left behind.

—So praying godspeed for themselves and us,   25
   those souls were crawling by under such burdens
   as we at times may dream of. Laden thus,

unequally tormented, weary, bent,
   they circled the First Cornice round and round,
   purging away the world's foul sediment.   30

If they forever speak our good above,
   what can be done for their good here below
   by those whose will is rooted in God's love?

Surely, we should help those souls grow clear
   of time's deep stain, that each at last may issue   35
   spotless and weightless to his starry sphere.

"Ah, so may Justice and pity soon remove
    the load you bear, that you may spread your wings
    and rise rejoicing to the Perfect Love—

help us to reach the stairs the shortest way,   40
    and should there be more than one passage, show us
    the one least difficult to climb, I pray;

for my companion, who is burdened still
    with Adam's flesh, grows weak in the ascent,
    though to climb ever higher is all his will."   45

I heard some words in answer to my Lord's,
    but could not tell which of those souls had spoken,
    nor from beneath which stone. These were the words:

"Your way is to the right, along with ours.
    If you will come with us, you will discover   50
    a pass within a living person's powers.

And were I not prevented by the stone
    that masters my stiff neck and makes me keep
    my head bowed to the dust as I move on,

I would look up, hoping to recognize   55
    this living and still nameless man with you,
    and pray to find compassion in his eyes.

I was Italian. A Tuscan of great fame—
    Guglielmo Aldobrandesco—was my father.
    I do not know if you have heard the name.   60

My ancient lineage and the hardihood
    my forebears showed in war went to my head.
    With no thought that we all share the one blood

of Mother Eve, I scorned all others so
    I died for it; as all Siena knows,   65
    and every child in Campagnatico.

I am Omberto, and my haughty ways
    were not my ruin alone, but brought my house
    and all my followers to evil days.

Here until God be pleased to raise my head   70
    I bear this weight. Because I did not do so
    among the living, I must among the dead."

I had bowed low, better to know his state,
    when one among them—not he who was speaking—
    twisted around beneath his crushing weight,   75

saw me, knew me, and cried out. And so
    he kept his eyes upon me with great effort
    as I moved with those souls, my head bowed low.

"Aren't you Od'risi?" I said. "He who was known
    as the honor of Agobbio, and of that art   80
    Parisians call *illumination*?"

"Brother," he said, "what pages truly shine
    are Franco Bolognese's. The real honor
    is all his now, and only partly mine.

While I was living, I know very well,   85
    I never would have granted him first place,
    so great was my heart's yearning to excel.

Here pride is paid for. Nor would I have been
    among these souls, had I not turned to God
    while I still had in me the power to sin.   90

O gifted men, vainglorious for first place,
    how short a time the laurel crown stays green
    unless the age that follows lacks all grace!

Once Cimabue thought to hold the field
    in painting, and now Giotto has the cry   95
    so that the other's fame, grown dim, must yield.

So from one Guido has another shorn
  poetic glory, and perhaps the man
  who will un-nest both is already born.

A breath of wind is all there is to fame   100
  here upon earth: it blows this way and that,
  and when it changes quarter it changes name.

Though loosed from flesh in old age, will you have
  in, say, a thousand years, more reputation
  than if you went from child's play to the grave?   105

What, to eternity, is a thousand years?
  Not so much as the blinking of an eye
  to the turning of the slowest of the spheres.

All Tuscany once sounded with the fame
  of this one who goes hobbling on before me;   110
  now, one hears scarce a whisper of his name,

even in Siena, where he was in power
  when he destroyed the rage of Florence (then,
  as much a shrew as she is, now, a whore).

The fame of man is like the green of grass: 115
  it comes, it goes; and He by whom it springs
  bright from earth's plenty makes it fade and pass."

And I to him: "These truths bend my soul low
  from swollen pride to sweet humility.
  But who is he of whom you spoke just now?"   120

"That's Provenzan Salvani, and the stone
  is on him," he replied, "for his presumption
  in making all Siena his alone.

So he goes on and has gone since his death,
  without a pause. Such coin must one pay here   125
  for being too presumptuous on earth."

And I: "But if the souls that do not mend
   their sinful ways until the brink of life
   must wait below before they can ascend

(unless the prayers of those whom God holds dear   130
   come to their aid) the period of their lives—
   how was he given license to be here?"

"At the peak of his life's glory," said the ghost,
   "in the Campo of Siena, willingly,
   and putting by all pride, he took his post;   135

and there, to free his dear friend from the pains
   he suffered in the dungeons of King Charles,
   stood firm, although he trembled in his veins.

I say no more; and though you well may feel
   I speak in riddles, it will not be long   140
   before your neighbors' actions will reveal

all you need know to fathom what I say.
—It was this good work spared him his delay."

Notes

1–24. THE PRAYER OF THE PROUD. The sinners on each
Cornice of Purgatory recite a prayer appropriate to their particular
penance. The prayer spoken by the souls under the stones is, of
course, an extended form of the Lord's Prayer, and Dante's choice
of it must be understood by its relevance to the sin of Pride.

The Lord's Prayer is so basic to Christian practice, and so much
the possession of every Christian child, that its very nature as a
primer of the creed must explain its first relevance here. If Pride is
seen as a blind and arrogant assertion of secondary things (self,
power, family name, talent, etc.), it follows that such a wrong em-
phasis on what is secondary can only be arrived at by ignoring what
is primary. It is in these terms, I believe, that Dante's intent can
be best grasped. The proud must begin over again as children, learn-
ing the first expression of the first principles of faith. It is exactly

relevant that the first child's prayer is also the most central to Christian belief. Note, moreover, that every petition of the prayer is for the grace of humility and subservience to God's will, and that the last petition is for the good of others.

1–3. *Our Father . . . not by Heaven bounded:* God lives in Heaven by choice, not in confinement. He is drawn to Heaven by the greater love (greater than His love for man) He bears His first works (the Angels) in His first realm (Heaven).

6. *Thy quickening breath:* The breath of life.

21. *but deliver us from him:* In the original form, the Lord's Prayer reads, "Deliver us from the Evil One."

22–24. *This last petition:* The last petition is for deliverance from the Evil One. It is obviously not needed by the souls in Purgatory proper, since they are no longer subject to temptation, but is offered up (a happy instance of concern for others) for the souls of those left behind on earth, and perhaps also in Ante-Purgatory.

25. *us:* Refers not to the Poets but to all mankind.

28. *unequally tormented:* As Dante has already indicated (X, 134–135) the burdens of the sinners varied according to the degree of their sin.

30. *the world's foul sediment:* The traces of pride and worldliness surviving in each soul.

33. *by those . . . God's love:* No other prayer helps. *Cf.* Belacqua, IV, 130–135.

43. *for my companion, who is burdened still:* Virgil's famous tact hardly shines brilliantly in begging these souls, bowed as they are under their enormous loads, to help Dante so heavily burdened with his own flesh.

47. *could not tell which of those souls had spoken:* It must be remembered that Dante and Virgil are standing above the souls, who are bent to the ground under slabs of stone that must, in some cases at least, completely hide them from sight.

53. *stiff neck:* A recurring Biblical figure for pride and obstinacy. *Cf. Acts,* vii, 51: "Ye stiffnecked and uncircumcised in heart and

ears." (An interesting piece of language.) See also *Exodus,* xxxii, 9, and xxxiii, 3, 5.

58–72. THE ALDOBRANDESCHI. Guglielmo Aldobrandesco (Gool-YELL-mo Ahl-doe-brahnd-ESS-coe) was a powerful Ghibelline of the Sienese Maremma, and Count of Santafiora, the district Dante has already cited as a lawless robber-barony. Little is known of Omberto, and such accounts as there are contradict one another, though all agree that he was excessively proud of his lineage. The Aldobrandeschi were in constant conflict with Siena. In 1259, according to varying accounts, the Sienese either besieged the Aldobrandeschi castle in Campagnatico (Cahm-pahn-YAH-tee-coe), killing Omberto in battle, or their agents crept in and strangled Omberto in bed. Since Dante refers to it (line 66) as an event known to every child, he was probably following the account in which Omberto, though with very few men at his disposal, scorned his enemies, refused to surrender, killed many Sienese, and even made a mad charge into the thick of the enemy's forces, where he was killed after giving a bloody account of himself. Omberto's words seem to indicate that his main motive in this action was utter contempt for those who opposed him. Thus (lines 64–65) his scorn was so great that he died for it.

Omberto's death broke the power of the Aldobrandeschi, their rule passing to the Sienese. Thus (lines 67–69) his pride destroyed not only Omberto but all of his line and its adherents.

60. *I do not know if you have heard the name:* One of those Dantean touches that must not be missed. As Omberto goes on to say, he was, while alive, overweeningly proud of his father's fame. The proud mention of him may, thus, be taken as a relapse into his besetting sin. He immediately covers it with a deliberate act of modesty, as if to say, "You probably never heard of him." The fact is that everyone in Italy would have known of Guglielmo Aldobrandesco.

73. *I had bowed low, better to know his state:* I think Dante intends an ambiguity here. He had bowed low physically better to hear Omberto, and he had bowed low in the spirit of humility better to experience the state of those who purify themselves of pride by making themselves humble. Line 78 reinforces this second meaning.

79. *Od'risi:* Oderisi d'Agobbio. Agobbio or Gubbio is a small city in Umbria, and was known to the Romans as Eugubium.

Oderisi was a famous illuminator of manuscripts and a miniaturist. He is reputed to have illuminated many Vatican manuscripts on Papal commission. He probably died in Rome in 1299, though the record is not certain.

As Omberto typifies pride of lineage, Oderisi typifies the pride of the artist avid for reputation. Dante's praise of him may be a test to see how a Proud one so recently dead (within the year) would respond.

83. *Franco Bolognese* (Bo-lo-NYEA-zeh): Oderisi's student. He was alive in 1300 (hence the "now" of line 84). A few mentions of his name and some disputed traces of his work still exist, but the words Dante puts into Oderisi's mouth will have to explain themselves, there being no other record.

Note especially that Dante cites little-known artists working in what is generally considered to be a minor art. He could, of course, have demonstrated artistic pride in artists of much greater stature, but his point is certainly the more strongly made when he presents great pride swelling in little men.

86–87. *I never would have granted him first place:* Oderisi may mean that in his lifetime he so desired to excel that he would have labored for greater mastery and so have wrested first place from his student. In context, however, the far more likely meaning is that he was then too proud to admit what he now, in his new-found humility, well knows.

88–90. *Nor would I have been among these souls:* Oderisi would still have been in Ante-Purgatory enduring his delay had he waited for a deathbed repentance. *while I still had in me the power to sin:* While I was yet alive.

91–93. The difficulty of Dante's condensed way of speaking is here compounded by his easy way with mixed metaphors. Sense: "O talented men [of arts, crafts, government, and every human attainment], what a vanity it is to seek to be known as foremost in your field! How short a while the laurel crown stays green, unless the age that succeeds you is graceless [*i.e.,* lacks the talent to produce rivals who will excel you]."

94. *Cimabue:* Giovanni dei Cimabui (Joe-VAH-nee day Tcheem-ah-BOO-ee), 1240?–1308. He was esteemed by his Florentine con-

temporaries as the master painter. His particular innovation was in liberating painting from strict Byzantine domination in favor of a more natural style. If he is no longer hailed as a supreme master, succeeding ages have generally been aware of his genius.

95. *Giotto* (DJAW-toe): A shepherd boy who became Cimabue's pupil and who went on to excel his teacher, becoming the true father of the Renaissance tradition of painting from nature. He was probably a friend of Dante's. The most familiar portrait of Dante is one commonly, but uncertainly, attributed to Giotto.

97–99. THE TWO GUIDOS. The first is Guido (GWEE-doe) Cavalcanti (1250?–1300), a fellow poet whom Dante saluted in the *Vita Nuova* as "he whom I call first among my friends." (See also *Inferno,* X, 52 ff. for a different feeling toward him.) The other Guido, whose poetic glory was shorn by Cavalcanti, is generally taken to be Guido Guinizelli (Gwee-nee-TZELL-ee) of Bologna (died approx. 1275–1276).

Dante may mean himself by "the man who will un-nest them both," or he may be making a general statement. Good arguments can support either interpretation. If it is argued that Dante, his head bowed in humility and observing the terrible penance of the proud, would not be praising himself, it can as forcibly be shown that Dante has already (*Inferno,* X, 52 ff.) asserted his poetical supremacy to Guido, ascribing it modestly to the fact that Guido did not give his whole devotion to the high models Dante took for his own.

108. *the turning of the slowest of the spheres:* The Ptolemaic cosmography attributed to the Sphere of the Fixed Stars a west-to-east rotation of 1 degree per 100 years, hence 36,000 years for one revolution. (See *Il Convivio,* II, 6, lines 140–143.)

110. *this one:* Provenzano Salvani, the Ghibelline chief of Siena at the battle of Montaperti (see *Inferno,* X, 85–87, 91–93, and note to 32–51). After the defeat of the Florentine forces, he led the cry for the destruction of Florence. In 1269 the Florentines defeated the Sienese at Colle di Val d'Elsa, and Salvani, taken prisoner, was beheaded on the field of battle.

116. *He:* God is constantly identified with the Sun in Dante. Here the identification is especially apt.

127–132. *But . . . how was he given license to be here?:* Salvani died, as noted, in 1269. He has, therefore, been dead thirty-one years. Dante assumes that he put off repentance till the end. Normally, therefore, he would have had to wait in Ante-Purgatory for a period equal to his lifetime, and though his exact age at death is not known, his normal delay would still have years to run. Dante asks the cause of this exception and Oderisi tells of an incident of great self-abasement that won special grace for Salvani. See below.

133–138. The incident here referred to is variously told, but the gist of it remains the same in all accounts. A friend of Salvani's was captured, probably by Charles of Anjou at Tagliacozza, and held for a great ransom to be paid within a month, failing which the friend would be executed. Salvani, despite his great pride, posted himself in the Piazza del Campo in Siena and begged alms to raise his friend's ransom. Whether beggars do especially well in Siena, or whether Salvani's action was the sort of thing we now call a "promotional campaign," the sum was made up and the friend freed.

Note how the law is still, as in Hell, an eye for an eye and a tooth for a tooth, but now in reverse: as ye merited, so shall ye be rewarded— with the additional boons that may be procured by the prayers of the pure in heart.

139–142. *I say no more:* Still another of the dark prophecies of impending exile Dante hears throughout his journey. (His "neighbors" are, of course, the Florentines. Their "actions" will be to exile him, thus forcing him to beg as did Salvani. Then only will he understand what it means to tremble in his veins.) Dante left Florence in 1301 and a decree of banishment was read against him in 1302. He never returned.

It is especially appropriate that Dante should be reminded of his banishment to beggary at just this point. Dante, as he makes clear later, was especially concerned about Pride as his own besetting sin. The reminder of his banishment serves aptly to humble him.

Canto XII

The Rein of Pride
The Angel of Humility

Virgil instructs Dante to arise from where he has been walk-
ing bent beside Oderisi and to move on. Dante follows obedi-
ently, and soon Virgil points out to him THE REIN OF
PRIDE carved in thirteen scenes into the stone beneath their
feet. The scenes portray dreadful examples of the destruction
that follows upon great pride.

The Poets pass on and find THE ANGEL OF HUMILITY
approaching to welcome them. The Angel strikes Dante's
forehead with his wings and, though Dante does not discover
it till later, THE FIRST P instantly disappears without a
trace, symbolizing the purification from the sin of Pride. The
Poets pass on, up a narrow ASCENT TO THE SECOND
CORNICE, but though the way is narrow, Dante finds it much
easier than the first, since steps have been cut into it, and
since he is lighter by the weight of the first P. As they climb
they hear the First Beatitude, Beati pauperes spiritu, *ring out*
behind them, sung by the Angel of Humility.

As oxen go in yoke—step matched, head bowed—
    I moved along beside that laden soul
    as long as the sweet pedagogue allowed.

But when he said: "Leave him his weary trail:
    here each must speed his boat as best he can   5
    urging it onward with both oars and sail"—

I drew myself again to the position
   required for walking: thus my body rose,
   but my thoughts were still bent double in contrition.

I was following my Guide, and we had put   10
   those laden souls behind us far enough
   to make it clear that we were light of foot,

when he said, without turning back his head:
   "Look down. You will find solace on the way
   in studying what pavement your feet tread."   15

In order that some memory survive
   of those who die, their slabs are often carved
   to show us how they looked while yet alive.

And often at the sight a thought will stir
   the passer-by to weep for what has been—   20
   though only the compassionate feel that spur.

Just so, but with a far more life-like grace—
   they being divinely wrought—stone figures covered
   the track that jutted from the mountain's face.

Mark there, on one side, him who had been given   25
   a nobler form than any other creature.
   He plunged like lightning from the peak of Heaven.

Mark, on the other, lying on the earth,
   stricken by the celestial thunderbolt,
   Briareus, heavy with the chill of death.   30

Mark there, still armed, ranged at their father's side,
   Thymbraeus, Mars, and Pallas looking down
   at the Giants' severed limbs strewn far and wide.

Mark Nimrod at the foot of his great tower,
   bemused, confounded, staring at his people   35
   who shared at Shinar his mad dream of power.

Ah, Niobe! with what eyes wrung with pain
   I saw your likeness sculptured on that road
   between your seven and seven children slain!

Ah, Saul! how still you seemed to me, run through   40
   with your own sword, dead upon Mount Gilboa,
   which never after that felt rain nor dew.

Ah, mad Arachne! so I saw you there—
   already half turned spider—on the shreds
   of what you wove to be your own despair.   45

Ah, Rehoboam! your image in that place
   no longer menaces; a chariot bears it
   in panic flight, though no one gives it chase.

Now see Alcmaeon, there on the hard pavement,
   standing above her mother when she learned   50
   the full cost of the fatal ornament.

Now see there how his own sons fell upon
   Sennacherib at prayer within the temple,
   and how they left him dead when they were done.

Now see Tomyris bloody with her kill   55
   after the ruin she wrought, saying to Cyrus:
   "Your thirst was all for blood. Now drink your fill."

Now see how the Assyrians broke and ran
   from Israel after Holofernes' murder;
   and showed the slaughtered remnants of the man.   60

Mark Troy there in its ashes overthrown.
   Ah, Ilion! how lowly and how lost!
   Now see your hollow shell upon that stone!

What brush could paint, or etching-stylus draw
   such lineaments and shadings? At such skill   65
   the subtlest genius would have stared in awe.

The dead seemed dead, the living alive. A witness
   to the event itself saw it no better
   than I did, looking down there at its likeness.

Now swell with pride and cut your reckless swath   70
   with head held high, you sons of Eve, and never
   bow down to see the evil in your path!

We had, I found, gone round more of the mount,
   and the Sun had run more of its daily course,
   than my bound soul had taken into account;   75

when Virgil, ever watchful, ever leading,
   commanded: "Lift your head. This is no time
   to be shut up in your own thoughts, unheeding.

Look there and see an Angel on his way
   to welcome us; and see—the sixth handmaiden   80
   returns now from her service to the day.

That he may gladly send us up the mountain,
   let reverence grace your gestures and your look.
   Remember, this day will not dawn again."

I was well used to his warnings to abjure   85
   all that delayed me from my good: on that point
   nothing he said to me could be obscure.

Toward us, dressed in white, and with a face
   serenely tremulous as the Morning Star,
   the glorious being came, radiant with Grace.   90

First his arms and then his wings spread wide.
   "Come," he said, "the stars are near, and now
   the way is easy up the mountainside.

Few, all too few, come answering to this call.
   O sons of man, born to ascend on high,   95
   how can so slight a wind-puff make you fall?"

Straight to where the rock was cut he led.
   There he struck my forehead with his wings,
   then promised us safe journeying ahead.

When a man has climbed the first slope toward the crown   100
   on which is built the church that overhangs
   at the Rubaconte, the well-managed town,

the abrupt ascent is softened on his right
   by steps cut in the rock in other days,
   before the stave and ledger had grown light—   105

just so the bank here, plunging like a slide
   from the Round above, has been made easier,
   though towering cliffs squeeze us from either side.

We set out on the climb, and on the way
   Beati pauperes spiritu rang out,   110
   more sweetly sung than any words could say.

Ah, what a difference between these trails
   and those of Hell: here every entrance fills
   with joyous song, and there with savage wails!

We were going up the holy steps, and though   115
   the climb was steep, I seemed to feel much lighter
   than I had felt on level ground below.

"Master," I said, "tell me what heaviness
   has been removed from me that I can climb
   yet seem to feel almost no weariness."   120

He answered: "When the *P*'s that still remain,
   though fading, on your brow, are wiped away
   as the first was, without a trace of stain—

then will your feet be filled with good desire:
   not only will they feel no more fatigue   125
   but all their joy will be in mounting higher."

A man with some strange thing lodged on his hat
　　will stroll, not knowing, till the stares of others
　　set him to wonder what they're staring at:

whereat his hand seeks out and verifies　　　　　　　130
　　what he suspected, thus performing for him
　　the office he could not serve with his eyes—

just so, I put my right hand to my brow,
　　fingers outspread, and found six letters only
　　of those that had been carved there down below　　135

by the Angel with the keys to every grace;
at which a smile shone on my Master's face.

NOTES

3. *the sweet pedagogue:* Virgil.

5–6. *boat . . . oars and sail:* Virgil may simply be saying something equivalent to "every man must do his utmost." More likely, however, each item mentioned had some allegorical significance in Dante's mind. Thus *boat* might equal "the will to grace"; *oars,* "the individual's own efforts"; and *sail,* "assistance from the prayers of others."

12. *light of foot:* Dante intends eagerness, of course. But one must remember that weight is always equated to sin. (See *Inferno,* XXXII, 73, note.) Every step toward purification makes the soul lighter.

17. *slabs:* Dante specifically means a kind of gravestone rare in the United States but common in Europe and usually found in churches where the dead are sometimes buried under the pavement, their gravestones being set flush with the pavement and forming part of it.

25–63. THE REIN OF PRIDE. The Whip of Pride consisted of examples of great humility designed to whip the soul on to emulation. Now as the Poets leave the First Cornice, their souls made humble, they find set before them as a final lesson, examples of great Pride and of the downfall to which it brings men. Their

thoughts are reined in and brought under God's control by a final re-
minder of what disasters they have escaped.

The present rein is elaborately conceived and consists of thirteen
bas-reliefs cut into the pavement over which the souls pass. Dante's
description of the first four panels begins with "Mark," of the next
four, with "Ah!" and of the next four, with "Now see." In Italian
these phrases are: *Vedea . . . O! . . . Mostrava.* Acrostically (*V* being
equal to *U* in Latin), this combination reads: *UOM, i.e.,* "man." The
tercet describing the thirteenth panel repeats the three phrases in or-
der at the beginning of each of the three lines. The pattern in the
original reads, therefore: *UUUU, OOOO, MMMM, UOM.*

This elaborate structure is clearly intended to show not only that
Pride is the first and heaviest of man's sins, but that it is so character-
istic of him that PRIDE and MAN are practically synonymous.

25. *him:* Satan.

30. *Briareus:* One of the Titans (Giants) who now guard the cen-
tral well of Hell. (See *Inferno,* XXXI, 97–99, and note.) He stormed
Olympus and tried to unseat Jupiter (as Satan tried to unseat God)
but was felled by a thunderbolt.

31–33. *their father:* Jupiter. *Thymbraeus:* Apollo, so called after
his temple at Thymbra. *Pallas:* Minerva. The scene portrays another
repulse of the Titans in their effort to storm Heaven, this time at
Phlegra in Thessaly.

34–36. *Nimrod:* (See *Inferno,* XXXI, 77, note.) The first king of
Babylon and builder of the Tower of Babel at Shinar. ". . . the Lord
scattered them abroad from thence upon the face of all the earth; and
they left off to build the city. Therefore is the name of it called Ba-
bel; because the Lord did there confound the language of all the
earth." (*Genesis,* xi, 8–9.)

37–39. *Niobe:* Had seven sons and seven daughters. In her pride,
she mocked Latona, concubine of Jupiter, for having only one son
(Apollo) and one daughter (Diana). Thereupon, Apollo took his bow
and killed all the sons; Diana, hers, and killed all the daughters.
Dante follows Ovid's version of this happy little legend on the so-
laces of religion (*Metamorphoses,* VI, 146–312).

40. *Saul:* The proud first king of Israel. Defeated by the Philistines
on Mount Gilboa, he fell on his own sword to avoid capture (*I Samuel,*

xxxi, 4–5). David, mourning the death of Saul, cursed Mount Gilboa: "Ye mountains of Gilboa, let there be no dew, neither let there be rain upon you, nor fields of offerings." (*II Samuel*, i, 21.)

43. *Arachne:* Her story runs much like that of the Pierides (I, 11, note). So proud was Arachne of her weaving that she boasted that it was superior to Minerva's. Minerva in disguise challenged her to a contest. Arachne presumed to disparage the gods in her tapestry and was changed into a spider by Minerva, who had portrayed the glory of the gods.

46–48. *Rehoboam:* The arrogant king of Israel who would not lighten the taxes of the ten tribes. He sent Adoram to collect the taxes, and when Adoram was stoned to death, Rehoboam fled in panic from Jerusalem, though no one pursued him (see *I Kings*, xii, 1–18).

49–51. *Alcmaeon:* Son of Amphiareus, the Soothsayer (*Inferno*, XX, 34, note). Through his arts, Amphiareus foresaw that he would die at Thebes, and to avoid having to go there he hid in a place known only to Eriphyle, his wife. Eriphyle accepted a gold necklace as a bribe for revealing his hiding place, whereupon Amphiareus instructed his son, Alcmaeon, to avenge him. The panel, therefore, would represent Alcmaeon killing his mother, her downfall being the result of vanity, which is, of course, a form of pride. The ornament (certainly a further moral) was, moreover, predestined to be fatal. It had been made by Vulcan and it bore a charm that brought to grief whoever owned it. (Dante would certainly have thought of Vanity as precisely such an ornament.)

52–54. *Sennacherib:* King of Assyria. He was defeated by the inferior forces of Hezekiah of Judah. Praying to his gods after his defeat, he was murdered by two of his sons. (See *Isaiah*, xxxvii, 37–38, and *II Kings*, xix, 37.)

Dante's moral seems to be that Sennacherib's downfall was the result of his arrogant faith in a false god. Sennacherib with a mighty host blasphemed God. Hezekiah, with an inferior force, prayed humbly to the God of Israel and won the battle. Sennacherib, not yet sufficiently humbled, went back to his false god and met death in the act of prayer, but the true God made Hezekiah rejoice.

55–57. *Tomyris . . . Cyrus:* Cyrus (560–529 B.C.), Emperor of the Persians, showed his contempt for Tomyris, the Scythian queen, by killing her son. Tomyris gathered her armies and defeated Cyrus in a battle in which he was killed. She then had Cyrus' head cut off and threw it into an urn full of human blood, commanding the head of the bloodthirsty tyrant to drink its fill. (History does not record where Tomyris got an urnful of human blood.)

58–60. *Holofernes:* He laid siege to Bethulia as general of the army of Nebuchadnezzar. The city, cut off from water, was about to surrender when Judith, a beautiful widow, made her way to Holofernes' tent to spend the night with him. While he slept, she cut off his head and took it back to the city, where it was mounted on the wall. Holofernes' fate threw the Assyrians into a panic and they fled, pursued by the Jews.

75. *bound soul:* See IV, 1–18, and especially 10–12.

80–81. *the sixth handmaiden:* The figure here conceives of the twelve hours of the light as twelve handmaidens serving the day. The sixth handmaiden is, therefore, the sixth hour of light, hence, noon, sunrise being at six o'clock. If the Poets emerged from the Needle's Eye about 10:00 A.M. or a bit before, they have been on the First Cornice about two hours.

89. *the Morning Star:* Venus. Note that the Angel Boatman of Canto II was first seen as a ruddy glow and compared to Mars.

90. *the glorious being:* The Angel of Humility.

92. *now:* Now that the soul has been purged of the heaviness of Pride. The Angel is about to remove the first *P.*

96. *so slight a wind-puff:* The Angel of Humility is specifically concerned with Pride. In that context, the feeble wind seems best interpreted as the vanity of earthly ambition as compared to the eternal good of the soul.

100–105. The church is San Miniato, built on a rise across the Arno from Florence. The Rubaconte (now Ponte alle Grazie) is the bridge that leads most directly to San Miniato. An old account explains: "Issuing from the gate [in the city walls] to go to San Miniato, one finds at first, only one road by which to climb. Then the road forks. And the one on the climber's right hand has the stairs."

"Well managed" is, of course, ironic when applied to Florentine affairs. The "stave" was formerly an official measure, primarily for salt, which was taxed. One of the Chiaramontesi family, as head of the Salt Tax Department, had given rise to a famous scandal by auditing the salt in with a full stave and auditing it out with a lightened one, thus shaving a certain quantity from each transaction. The "ledger" had grown light when two officials ripped out a page to remove evidence of graft. The exact date of these events are disputed, but both took place in Dante's time and both were widely known. The matter of the lightened stave even became the subject for a mocking popular ditty.

110. *Beati pauperes spiritu:* "Blessed are the poor in spirit: for theirs is the kingdom of Heaven." (*Matthew,* v, 3.) Each time Dante leaves one of the Cornices, he hears sung one of the Beatitudes from the Sermon on the Mount. Dante does not specify in this instance that it is the Angel who sings. At each subsequent ascent, however, the beatitude is sung by the Angel who has allowed the Poets to pass. It should be clear that Dante is not likely to break so firm a part of his pattern without special reason. One must conclude, therefore, that it is the Angel who sings.

Canto XIII

THE SECOND CORNICE   *The Envious*
            The Whip of Envy

*The Poets reach THE SECOND CORNICE and find the blue-
black rock unadorned by carvings. There are no souls in sight
to guide them and Virgil, therefore, turns toward the Sun as
his Guide, BEARING RIGHT around the Cornice.*

*As they walk on, Dante hears voices crying out examples
of great love of others (CARITAS), the virtue opposed to
Envy. These voices are THE WHIP OF ENVY.*

*A short way beyond, Dante comes upon the souls of THE
ENVIOUS and describes THEIR PUNISHMENT. The Cor-
nice on which they sit is the color of a bruise, for every other
man's good fortune bruised the souls of the Envious. They of-
fended with their eyes, envying all the good they saw of oth-
ers, and therefore their eyes are wired shut. So blinded, they
sit supporting one another, as they never did in life, and all of
them lean for support against the blue-black cliff (God's De-
cree). They are dressed in haircloth, the further to subdue
their souls, and they intone endlessly THE LITANY OF THE
SAINTS.*

*Among them Dante encounters SAPÌA OF SIENA and has
her relate her story. When she questions him in turn, Dante
confesses his fear of HIS OWN BESETTING SIN, which is
Pride.*

We climbed the stairs and stood, now, on the track
    where, for a second time, the mount that heals
    all who ascend it, had been terraced back.

The terrace circles the entire ascent
   in much the same way as the one below,   5
   save that the arc it cuts is sooner bent.

There were no spirits and no carvings there.
   Bare was the cliff-face, bare the level path.
   The rock of both was livid, dark and bare.

"Were we to wait till someone came this way   10
   who might direct us," Virgil said to me,
   "I fear that would involve a long delay."

Then he looked up and stared straight at the Sun;
   and then, using his right side as a pivot,
   he swung his left around; then he moved on.   15

"O Blessed Lamp, we face the road ahead
   placing our faith in you: lead us the way
   that we should go in this new place," he said.

"You are the warmth of the world, you are its light;
   if other cause do not urge otherwise,   20
   your rays alone should serve to lead us right."

We moved on with a will, and in a while
   we had already gone so far up there
   as would be reckoned, here on earth, a mile;

when we began to hear in the air above   25
   invisible spirits who flew toward us speaking
   sweet invitations to the feast of love.

The first voice that flew past rang to the sky
   "Vinum non habent." And from far behind us
   we heard it fade repeating the same cry.   30

Even before we heard it cry its last
   far round the slope, another voice rang out:
   "I am Orestes!"—and it, too, sped past.

"Sweet Father," I began, "what are these cries?"—
   and even as I asked, I heard a third   35
   bodiless voice say: "Love your enemies."

And my good Master then: "This circle purges
   the guilt of Envious spirits, and for these
   who failed in Love, Love is the lash that scourges.

The Rein must cry the opposite of Love: 40
   you will hear it, I expect, before you reach
   the pass of absolution that leads above.

But now look carefully across the air
   ahead of us, and you will see some people
   seated against the inner cliff up there."   45

I opened my eyes wider: further on
   I saw a group of spirits dressed in cloaks
   exactly the same color as the stone.

As we drew nearer I heard prayers and plaints.
   "O Mary, pray for us," I heard them cry;   50
   and to Michael, and to Peter, and all Saints.

I cannot think there walks the earth today
   a man so hard that he would not be moved
   by what I saw next on that ashen way.

For when I drew near and could see the whole   55
   penance imposed upon those praying people,
   my eyes milked a great anguish from my soul.

Their cloaks were made of haircloth, coarse and stiff.
   Each soul supported another with his shoulder,
   and all leaned for support against the cliff.   60

The impoverished blind who sit all in a row
   during Indulgences to beg their bread
   lean with their heads together exactly so,

the better to win the pity they beseech,
   not only with their cries, but with their look   65
   of fainting grief, which pleads as loud as speech.

Just as the Sun does not reach to their sight,
   so to those shades of which I spoke just now
   God's rays refuse to offer their delight;

for each soul has its eyelids pierced and sewn   70
   with iron wires, as men sew new-caught falcons,
   sealing their eyes to make them settle down.

Somehow it seemed to me a shameful act
   to stare at others and remain unseen.
   I turned to Virgil. He, with perfect tact,   75

knew what the mute was laboring to say
   and did not wait my question. "Speak," he said,
   "but count your words and see they do not stray."

Virgil was walking by me down the ledge
   on the side from which—because no parapet   80
   circled the cliff—one might plunge off the edge.

On the other side those spirits kept their places
   absorbed in prayer, while through the ghastly stitches
   tears forced their way and flowed down from their
      faces.

I turned to them and said: "O souls afire   85
   with hope of seeing Heaven's Light, and thus
   already certain of your heart's desire—

so may High Grace soon wash away the scum
   that clogs your consciousness, that memory's stream
   may flow without a stain in joys to come—   90

tell me if there is any Latin soul
   among you here: I dearly wish to know,
   and telling me may help him to his goal."

—"We are all citizens of one sublime
  and final city, brother; you mean to ask   95
  who lived in Italy in his pilgrim-time."

These are the words I heard a spirit say
  from somewhere further on. I moved up, therefore,
  in order to direct my voice that way.

I saw one shade who seemed to have in mind   100
  what I had said.—How could I tell? She sat
  chin raised, the waiting gesture of the blind.

"O soul self-humbled for the climb to Grace,"
  I said, "if it was you who spoke, I beg you,
  make yourself known either by name or place."   105

"I was Sienese," she answered. "On this shelf
  I weep away my world-guilt with these others
  in prayers to Him that he vouchsafe Himself.

Sapìa was I, though sapient I was not;
  I found more joy in the bad luck of others   110
  than in the good that fell to my own lot.

If this confession rings false to your ears,
  hear my tale out; then see if I was mad.
  —In the descending arc of my own years,

the blood of my own land was being spilled   115
  in battle outside Colle's walls, and I
  prayed God to do what He already willed.

So were they turned—their forces overthrown—
  to the bitter paths of flight; and as I watched
  I felt such joy as I had never known;   120

such that I raised my face, flushed with false power,
  and screamed to God: 'Now I no longer fear you'—
  like a blackbird when the sun comes out an hour.

Not till my final hour had all but set
   did I turn back to God, longing for peace.   125
   Penance would not yet have reduced my debt

had not Pier Pettinaio in saintly love
   grieved for my soul and offered holy prayers
   that interceded for me there above.

But who are you that you come here to seek   130
   such news of us; and have your eyes unsewn,
   as I believe; and breathe yet when you speak?"

"My eyes," I said, "will yet be taken from me
   upon this ledge, but not for very long:
   little they sinned through being turned in envy.   135

My soul is gripped by a far greater fear
   of the torment here below, for even now
   I seem to feel the burden those souls bear."

And she: "Then who has led you to this Round,
   if you think to go below again?" And I: 140
   "He who is with me and who makes no sound.

And I still live: if you would have me move
   my mortal feet down there in your behalf,
   ask what you will, O soul blessed by God's love."

"Oh," she replied, "this is a thing so rare   145
   it surely means that God has loved you greatly;
   from time to time, then, help me with a prayer.

I beg by all you most desire to win
   that if you walk again on Tuscan soil
   you will restore my name among my kin.   150

You will find them in that foolish mob whose dream
   is Talamone now, and who will lose there
   more than they did once in their silly scheme

to find the lost Diana. Though on that coast
it is the admirals who will lose the most."   155

NOTES

6. *the arc it cuts is sooner bent:* As the mountain tapers, the circumference of each succeeding circle shrinks; its arc, therefore, is "sooner bent."

9. *livid:* I have found this word to be so frequently misunderstood that it seems well to remind readers that Latin *livious* means "ashen blue-black, the color of a bruise." The color is symbolic of Envy, the fortune of all others bruising the souls of the Envious. There are no carvings on this ledge, only the first ledge is so carved, and carvings would in any case be lost on these blind shades.

13–15. Having contemplated the Divine Light for a while, Virgil executes a sort of military right-face, swinging his left side around on the pivot of his right heel, and then moves toward the Sun. He has learned the rule of the Mountain, which is, to follow the Light of God. In the first twenty-seven Cantos of the *Purgatorio* (up to the time Virgil disappears), there are two pilgrims. In the *Inferno,* only Dante was the pilgrim. There, Virgil was an experienced guide. Dante's rather strange way of describing Virgil's action is almost certainly meant to indicate how utterly Virgil gives himself to the Sun's (God's) guidance.

It is shortly after noon (see XII, 80–81); the Sun is a little beyond the mid-point from east to west, and, of course, to the north of the Poets. They have, therefore, entered the Second Cornice at a point just a bit north of east.

19–21. VIRGIL'S ADDRESS TO THE SUN. Virgil seems to be confusing the allegorical and the literal function of the Sun in this apostrophe. How could the Sun as Divine Illumination fail to lead men right? Virgil can only mean, "Since no other guide is available to us, let us walk toward the [literal] Sun." Yet his words seem clearly to take the Sun in more than its literal significance.

25 ff. THE WHIP OF ENVY. Since the Envious have their eyes wired shut, it is appropriate that the Whip of Envy be oral rather than visual. The Whip, accordingly, consists of three disembodied voices

that cry out the key lines from scenes that exemplify great Charity (*i.e., Caritas,* the love of others). Thus "sweet invitations to the feast of love" (line 27) may be read in two senses. The feast may be in contemplating these high examples, and it may as readily be taken to mean the feast of Divine Love these sinners will share in the sight of God when they have been purified.

29. *Vinum non habent:* "They have no wine." These words were spoken by Mary at the Wedding Feast in Cana of Galilee (*John,* ii, 1–10). Mary, instead of envying those about her, thought only of their happiness, and noting that there was not enough wine, she turned to Jesus and spoke her loving dismay. Thereupon Jesus turned the water into wine, his first miracle. Note that it was in response to an act of *Caritas* that the first miracle took place.

Structurally, it may be well to note again, that the first incident in each Whip is drawn from the life of Mary.

33. *I am Orestes:* The second lesson in love of others clearly reflects *John,* xv, 13: "Greater love hath no man than this, that a man lay down his life for his friends."

Orestes and Pylades were famous for the depth of their friendship. Cicero (*De Amicitia,* VII, 24) relates the incident in which, Orestes having been condemned to death, Pylades pretended to be Orestes in order to die in his friend's place. Orestes then came forward asserting his own identity, and thereupon both friends argued "I am Orestes," each trying to save the other.

36. *Love your enemies:* These words were spoken by Jesus in the Sermon on the Mount (*cf.* the Mount of Purgatory). "Love your enemies, bless them that curse you, do good to them that hate you, and pray for them which despitefully use you, and persecute you." (*Matthew,* v, 44.) Dante specifies that the first two voices were loud, but in their special dignity the words of Christ are not rung out; they are "said."

So the third lesson in love: not only to love others, and to love friends, but to love those who offer injury. When the Envious have suffered their souls to this understanding, they will be free to ascend to the next ledge.

37–42. It must be remembered that Virgil is not speaking here from experience. His earlier journey (see *Inferno,* IX, 19–24) was only as far as Judecca. Virgil, in his capacity as Human Reason, is deducing what probably lies ahead by analogy to what has gone before, and from his understanding of the nature of Envy.

46. *I opened my eyes wider:* Another example of Dante's characteristically strange way of describing how his senses work.

50. *I heard them cry:* They are chanting the Litany of the Saints, hence invoking those who were most free of Envy. Note, moreover, that they are chanting "pray for *us*" rather than "pray for *me*," as they might have prayed on earth in their Envy.

57. *my eyes milked a great anguish from my soul:* The line literally rendered would be: "Through my eyes I was milked of heavy grief," a strange and daring figure.

58. *haircloth:* A coarse, heavy fabric made of goat hair. Even today peasants wear haircloth capes in heavy weather, but in the Middle Ages, and beyond, haircloth was worn against the skin as a penance, and to discipline the flesh. Such hair shirts were not only intolerably itchy; they actually rubbed the flesh open, causing running sores. In an age, moreover, that was very slightly given to soap and water, such hair shirts offered an attractive habitat to all sorts of bodily vermin that were certain to increase the odor of sanctity, even to the point of the gangrenous. I am told, and have no wish to verify, that hair shirts are still worn today by some penitential and unventilated souls.

59–60. *each soul supported another:* As they had failed to do in life. *and all leaned for support against the cliff:* The cliff is probably best taken as God's Decree: their punishment, which is also their purification, sustains them.

61–66. The figure here is based on the behavior of blind beggars at church doors, and particularly at the doors of those churches which offer special Indulgences (Pardons for Sin) during certain feast days. English readers, long devoted to the illustrations of Doré, will do well to visualize Dante's scenes in terms of Dante's own details rather than in terms of Doré's romantic misconceptions.

71–72. *sew new-caught falcons:* Since diurnal birds sit still in the dark, the eyelids of newly caught falcons were sewn shut by their trainers to make them sit still, partly, as I understand it, to keep them from battering themselves against the cage, and partly to break them for their later training. In hunting, the birds were normally carried hooded to the point of release.

76. *the mute:* Dante himself.

81. *one might plunge off the edge:* Allegorically, therefore, Dante places Human Reason between him and a fall.

86. *Heaven's Light:* God.

88–90. Dante is alluding here to the River Lethe, the same stream along whose banks he climbed from Hell. At the top of Purgatory, the finally purified souls are washed in Lethe, and it removes from them the very memory of sin. Thus Dante is uttering a wish for the more rapid advancement of these souls, a sentiment all of them would take in good part.

93. *and telling me may help him to his goal:* Dante is making use here of one of those narrator's devices in which the reader will understand the remark made, more fully than will the characters to whom it is addressed. We know that Dante is alive and that he may therefore win prayers for these souls on earth. The souls addressed, however, know only that an unknown voice is making a vague but attractive offer.

94 ff. SAPÌA OF SIENA. Dante speaks briefly and to the point, as Virgil instructed him, but Sapìa responds with a long and rambling narrative, to understand which one must recall the story of Provenzano Salvani (Canto XI). Sapìa was Salvani's paternal aunt. As the wife of another nobleman, she resented Salvani's rise to great power. When Salvani attacked the Florentines at Colle in 1269, she stationed herself at a palace window to watch the battle, and when she saw Salvani defeated and beheaded on the field, she is reported to have cried: "Now God, do what you will with me, and do me any harm you can, for after this I shall live happily and die content."

According to another account, she had been exiled from Siena (hence her resentment) and was living at Colle at the time of the battle.

The dates of her birth and death are unknown, but she seems to have been about sixty at the time of the Battle of Colle, and Dante makes clear that she died before Pier Pettinaio, whose death occurred in 1289.

94–95. *one sublime and final city:* Heaven, The New Jerusalem.

96. *his pilgrim-time:* His time on earth. As any concordance to the Bible will show, "pilgrim" for "wayfarer through life" and "pilgrimage" for "man's time on earth" are common Biblical usages.

103. *self-humbled for the climb to Grace:* A poor compromise rendering of *che per salir ti dome* (literally: "who master yourself in order to ascend"). The idea not to be missed here touches upon *the* essence of Purgatory: that the souls purify themselves. Just as Hell is the state of things the damned truly desire (see *Inferno,* III, 123, note), so the souls in Purgatory *will* their purifying pains upon themselves, and nothing but their own will keeps them from ascending, for they themselves decide when they are worthy to move up.

105. *either by name or place:* I.e., "Let me know who you are or from what city you came."

109. *Sapìa was I, though sapient I was not:* The pun is based, of course, upon the fact that the name "Sapìa" is derived from Latin *sapiens.*

114. *the descending arc of my own years:* The figure seems to envision life as a semicircle. Since Dante has already made clear (*Inferno,* I, 1) that thirty-five is the mid-point, the arc would rise on one side of thirty-five and descend on the other. Since Sapìa was actually about sixty at the time she refers to, the figure may be taken to mean simply "my declining years."

117. *prayed God to do what He already willed:* Sapìa's prayer that the Sienese be defeated was granted, and at the time she took the defeat as the answer to her prayer. Now, however, she sees that her prayer was answered by accident: she had simply happened to pray for what God had already willed should happen.

123. *like a blackbird:* The occasional warm, sunny days that occur in Italy in January and February are called in Tuscany and Lombardy "the days of the blackbird." The European blackbird is reputed by Italians to dread cold. When the winter sun shines brightly, however, it immediately perks up and acts as if it owned the world. But as soon as the cold returns, it huddles shivering and miserable.

126. *Penance would not yet have reduced my debt:* As one of the Negligent who put off repentance till her final hour, Sapìa would

still be waiting below but for the prayers of Pier Pettinaio. Her presently accomplished penance, therefore, would not yet have begun to reduce her debt of pain.

127. *Pier Pettinaio* (Peh-tin-EYE-oh): Literally, Peter Combseller. He came to Siena as a boy from the country, became a Sienese citizen, and grew into a local legend of piety, later being honored by an annual feast day such as is normally reserved for saints. He operated a small shop in which he sold combs, hence his name. The legend of his piety is general among Sienese writers, but the incidents they cite from his life seem at least as daft as they are saintly. He was, however, much given to public prayer and to elaborate ideas of honesty, and as Dante might say, either tendency would be more than enough to distinguish him from the rest of the Sienese.

131–132. *and have your eyes unsewn:* Sapìa could certainly tell from Dante's words that he was not one of the Envious, but his very freedom in walking around would have been enough to tell her he was not blind. *and breathe yet when you speak:* The blind are well known for the sharpness of their hearing; even a slight aspiration on Dante's part would reveal him to Sapìa. How the spirits managed to talk without breathing is a matter Dante would, of course, refer to God's Will.

Throughout this Cornice, Dante's description of the behavior of the blind is marvelously acute: the way they turn their heads, the way they talk (in the next Canto) about a man who is standing in front of them as if he were not there, the way they put their heads together to speak to one another—all bear evidence to Dante's powers of observation.

142–143. *if you would have me move:* If you would like me to bestir myself to solicit prayers for you when I return to Earth.

150. *restore my name:* In her final years Sapìa performed a number of good works for Siena, but there are several reports that she was generally contemned as a traitor.

151–155. A complicated passage of local reference certainly put into Sapìa's mouth by Dante as a Florentine jibe at the Sienese ("that foolish mob"). Dante (who fears the Ledge of Pride just below him) may have to carry his stone a bit further for his addiction to such touches, but his poem is certainly the livelier for them.

Talamone is a point on Italy's west coast about eighty miles almost due south of Siena. The Sienese, lacking a port, and wanting to compete with Genoa, bought the site in 1303 and invested heavily in building and dredging operations. The scheme, not nearly as unreasonable as Dante would have it seem, failed because of malarial conditions and because the hoped-for port silted in almost as fast as it could be dredged.

The Diana was another project intermittently undertaken by the Sienese over a long period. Siena was water-poor, but the magnificent flow at certain wells suggested to the Sienese the presence of an underground river which they christened the Diana, and which they dug for at great expense. All efforts had failed up to Dante's time and the failures were used as a standing joke against the Sienese as overambitious crackpots trying to make themselves better than they were. The Sienese, however (and largely out of hard necessity), continued their expensive digging and did, sometime later, locate a substantial underground flow. There is still a Well of Diana in a convent in Siena.

A third difficulty in this passage is in the meaning of "admirals." Some of the old commentators report "admiral" was the term for what we should call "contractor" or "engineer in charge of construction." (*Cf.* British-English "navvy," derived from "navigator.") Or it may be that Dante meant that "port-admirals" (*i.e.,* "port-masters" or "harbor-masters") supervised the work. If these are proper interpretations, then the "admirals" would "lose the most" because they would die of malaria. If, however, Dante means "admirals" as "ships' captains," they would lose the most if they tried to use the port, or if they waited until the Sienese finished it. Dante may, of course, have intended all three possibilities at once.

Canto XIV

*Dante's conversation with Sapìa of Siena is overheard by two
spirits who sit side by side against the inner cliff-face. They
are GUIDO DEL DUCA and RINIERI DA CALBOLI.*

*Dante enters into conversation with them, and Guido de-
nounces the inhabitants of the cities of the Valley of the Arno.
He then prophesies the slaughter that Rinieri's grandson,
FULCIERI, shall visit upon Florence. And he prophesies
also that Fulcieri's actions will have a bearing on Dante's
approaching exile from Florence. Guido concludes with a
lament for the past glories of Romagna as compared to its
present degeneracy.*

*Leaving the two spirits in tears, Dante and Virgil move on,
and they have hardly left when Dante is struck with terror by
two bodiless voices that break upon them like thunder. The
voices are THE REIN OF ENVY. The first is THE VOICE OF
CAIN lamenting that he is forever cut off from mankind. The
second is THE VOICE OF AGLAUROS, who was changed to
stone as a consequence of her envy of her sister.*

*Virgil concludes the Canto with a denunciation of mankind's
stubborn refusal to heed the glory of the Heavens and to pre-
pare for eternal Grace.*

"Who do you think that is? He roams our hill
    before death gives him wings, and he's left free
    to shut his eyes or open them at will."

"I don't know, but I know he's not alone.
    Ask him—you're nearer—but put in a way   5
    that won't offend him. Take a careful tone."

Thus, on my right, and leaning head to head,
    two of those spirits were discussing me.
    Then they turned up their faces, and one said:

"O soul that though locked fast within the flesh   10
    still makes its way toward Heaven's blessedness,
    in charity, give comfort to our wish:

tell us your name and city, for your climb
    fills us with awe at such a gift of grace
    as never has been seen up to this time."   15

And I: "In Falterona lies the source
    of a brook that grows and winds through Tuscany
    till a hundred miles will not contain its course.

From its banks I bring this flesh. As for my name—
    to tell you who I am would serve no purpose: 20
    I have as yet won very little fame."

And the first spirit: "If I rightly weigh
    your words upon the balance of my mind,
    it is the Arno you intend to say."

And the other to him: "Why is he so careful   25
    to avoid the river's name? He speaks as men do
    when they refer to things too foul or fearful."

To which the shade he had addressed replied:
    "That I don't know; but it would be a mercy
    if even the name of such a valley died.   30

From its source high in the great range that outsoars
    almost all others (from whose chain Pelorus
    was cut away), to the point where it restores

in endless soft surrender what the Sun
    draws from the deep to fall again as rain,   35
    that every rill and river may flow on,

men run from virtue as if from a foe
    or poisonous snake. Either the land is cursed,
    or long-corrupted custom drives them so.

And curse or custom so transform all men   40
    who live there in that miserable valley,
    one would believe they fed in Circe's pen.

It sets its first weak course among sour swine,
    indecent beasts more fit to grub and grunt
    for acorns than to sit to bread and wine.   45

It finds next, as it flows down and fills out,
    a pack of curs, their snarl worse than their bite;
    and in contempt it turns aside its snout.

Down, down it flows, and as the dogs grow fewer
    the wolves grow thicker on the widening banks   50
    of that accursed and God-forsaken sewer.

It drops through darkened gorges, then, to find
    the foxes in their lairs, so full of fraud
    they fear no trap set by a mortal mind.

Nor will I, though this man hear what I say,   55
    hold back the prophecy revealed to me;
    for well may he recall it on his way.

I see your grandson riding to the chase.
    He hunts the wolves that prowl by the fierce river.
    He has become the terror of that place.   60

He sells their living flesh, then—shame on shame—
    the old beast slaughters them himself, for sport.
    Many will die, and with them, his good name.

He comes from that sad wood covered with gore,
    and leaves it in such ruin, a thousand years   65
    will not serve to restock its groves once more."

Just as a man to whom bad chance announces
    a dreadful ill, distorts his face in grief,
    no matter from what quarter the hurt pounces—

just so that shade, who had half turned his head   70
    better to listen, showed his shock and pain
    when he had registered what the other said.

So moved by one's words and the other's face,
    I longed to know their names. I asked them, therefore,
    phrasing my plea with prayers to win their grace;   75

at which the spokesman of the two replied:
    "You beg me of my good grace that I grant you
    what I have asked of you and been denied;

but God has willed His favor to shine forth
    so greatly in you, I cannot be meager: 80
    Guido del Duca was my name on earth.

The fires of envy raged so in my blood
    that I turned livid if I chanced to see
    another man rejoice in his own good.

This seed I sowed; this sad straw I reap here.   85
    O humankind, why do you set your hearts
    on what it is forbidden you to share?

This is Rinier, the honor and the pride
    of the house of the Calboli, of which no one
    inherited his merit when he died.   90

Nor in that war-torn land whose boundary-lines
    the sea and the Reno draw to the east and west,
    and, north and south, the Po and the Apennines,

is his the only house that seems to be
    bred bare of those accomplishments and merits   95
    which are the good and truth of chivalry.

For the land has lost the good of hoe and plow,
    and poisonous thorns so choke it that long years
    of cultivation would scarce clear it now.

Where is Mainardi? Have you lost the seed   100
    of Lizio? Traversaro? di Carpigna?
    O Romagnoles changed to a bastard breed!

When will a Fabbro evermore take root
    in all Bologna? or in Faenza, a Fosco?—
    who was his little plant's most noble shoot.   105

O Tuscan, can I speak without a tear
    of Ugolino d'Azzo and Guido da Prata,
    who shared our time on earth? and with them there

Federico di Tignoso and his train?
    the house of the Traversari and the Anastagi,   110
    both heirless now? or, dry-eyed, think again

of knights and ladies, of the court and field
    that bonded us in love and courtesy
    where now all hearts are savagely self-sealed?

O Brettinoro, why do you delay?   115
    Your lords and many more have fled your guilt;
    and why, like them, will you not melt away?

Bagnacaval does well to have no heirs;
    and Castrocaro badly, and Conio worse
    in bothering to breed such Counts as theirs.   120

The Pagani will do well enough, all told,
    when once their fiend is gone, but not so well
    their name will ever again shine as pure gold.

O Ugolin de' Fantolini, your name
   remains secure, since you have none to bear it   125
   and, in degeneracy, bring it to shame.

But leave me, Tuscan, I am more inclined
   to spell my grief in tears now than in words;
   for speaking thus has wrung my heart and mind."

We knew those dear souls heard us go away.   130
   Their silence, therefore, served as our assurance
   that, leaving them, we had not gone astray.

We had scarce left those spirits to their prayer,
   when suddenly a voice that ripped like lightning
   struck at us with a cry that split the air: 135

"All men are my destroyers!" It rolled past
   as thunder rolls away into the sky
   if the cloud bursts to rain in the first blast.

Our ears were scarcely settled from that burst
   when lo, the second broke, with such a crash   140
   it seemed the following thunder of the first:

"I am Aglauros who was turned to stone!"
   Whereat, to cower in Virgil's arms, I took
   a step to my right instead of going on.

The air had fallen still on every hand   145
   when Virgil said: "That was the iron bit
   that ought to hold men hard to God's command.

But still you gulp the Hellbait hook and all
   and the Old Adversary reels you in.
   Small good to you is either curb or call.   150

The Heavens cry to you, and all around
   your stubborn souls wheel their eternal glory,
   and yet you keep your eyes fixed on the ground.

And for each turning from the joys of Love
the All-Discerning flails you from above."   155

NOTES

16. Falterona: One of the major peaks of the Tuscan Apennines.
It is northeast of Florence and both the Arno and the Tiber spring
from its sides.

18. a hundred miles: "Hundred" is used here as a large round
number; the Arno with all its windings has a course of at least a hun-
dred and fifty miles.

22–24. If I rightly weigh: The first spirit is Guido (see below). He
does most of the talking here and hereafter. Dante has answered in
words that run like a riddle, and Guido, knowing that Falterona
gives rise to both the Arno and the Tiber, has to weigh out his own
conclusion. He would have decided that Dante meant the Arno be-
cause the Tiber is so much longer that "a hundred miles" would be
out of all reason for its length.

31–36. The gist of these lines may be stated as: "From the Arno's
source to the point at which it enters the sea." *the great range:* The
Apennines. *Pelorus:* A mountain in Sicily, part of the Apennine sys-
tem, but cut off from the rest of the chain by the Straits of Messina.

42. they fed in Circe's pen: Circe changed men into beasts of var-
ious kinds. Guido goes on to specify four species of beasts into
which the Arno transforms the people along its course: the swine of
the Casentine, the curs of Arezzo, the wolves of Florence, and the
foxes of Pisa.
    Dante's riddle-like answer to a simple question, though it appears
to be mere ornamentation at first, serves to introduce the whole dis-
cussion of the degeneracy of the city-states of the Arno Valley.

43. its first weak course: In the Upper Casentine the Arno is not
yet swollen by any tributaries.

46–48. a pack of curs: The Aretines. *turns aside its snout:* The
Arno flows from the Upper Casentine straight toward Arezzo but at
a point a few miles north of the town it swings east without entering

the town proper. Note how Dante's phrasing gives the river itself bestial characteristics, beast scorning beast.

53–57. For the sense of this difficult passage one must remember that Guido (not yet identified) is speaking to Rinieri (not yet identified) and not to Dante. Guido is about to reveal a prophecy concerning the evil actions of Rinieri's grandson, and further concerning Dante's banishment from Florence. The prophecy will grieve Rinieri, but it will be well for Dante to hear it and ponder it. The sense then: "Though it grieve you to hear me say this, especially in front of others, I still must say it, and it will in fact be well for this man to think about it as he moves on." Note that Guido obviously knows who Dante is, though Dante has refused to identify himself by name.

These lines imply strongly, and lines 67 ff. confirm, that Rinieri does not share Guido's prophetic powers, at least at this point. I know of nothing in Dante that will explain why one soul in a given category should be more prophetic than another, but it can certainly be assumed that the prophetic vision comes in flashes now to one soul, now to another.

58–66. *your grandson:* Rinieri's grandson (Dante calls him *nipote,* which may mean either "nephew" or "grandson") was Fulcieri da Calboli (Ful-CHYEH-ree dah KAHL-boe-lee), who in 1302 became *podestà* (chief magistrate) of Florence.

In Dante's time many of the city-states of Italy were so torn by internal strife that they could not hope to agree on one of their own citizens as *podestà.* The practice grew, therefore, of electing a (presumably neutral) outsider to administer impartial justice for a given term. Fulcieri (either bribed by the Black Guelphs, or put into office in the first place as part of their plot) arrested and put to painful death many leaders of the White Guelphs (Dante's party) as well as some of the few remaining and powerless Ghibellines. The leaders disposed of, he proceeded murderously against the Whites in general. The "wolves" he hunts (line 59) are, of course, the White Florentines; the "sad wood" (line 64) is, of course, Florence. "The old beast" is Fulcieri, who, after selling them alive, piles shame on shame by killing them himself for sport.

69. *no matter from what quarter the hurt pounces:* I have no satisfactory explanation of this line. Dante seems to stress the unexpectedness of the news. "Pounces" in the original is *l'assanni (i.e.,*

"seizes him by the teeth"). But what the source of the bad news has to do with the man's reaction to it, in this case at least, remains unexplained, though one may, of course, conjecture at will.

81. *Guido del Duca:* Little is known about him. He was a Ghibelline of Brettinoro, a member of the prominent Onesti family of Ravenna. He served in various judicial posts in Romagna from 1195 on, and is known to have been alive in 1229.

85. *This seed:* Envy. *this sad straw:* His present pains. "Be not deceived; God is not mocked: for whatsoever a man soweth, that shall he also reap." (*Galatians,* vi, 7.)

87. *on what it is forbidden you to share:* These words puzzle Dante and remain in his mind. In the next Canto he asks Virgil what they mean. For Virgil's reply see XV, 46–57, and 64–81. See also note on Dante's Doctrine of Wealth (p. 152), and *Inferno,* VII, 68, note on Dame Fortune.

88. *Rinier:* Rinieri dei Paolucci da Calboli di Forlì. (Rih-NYEH-ree DAY-ee Pah-oh-LOO-tchee da KAHL-boe-lee dee For-LEE.) A Guelph leader, *podestà* of Faenza in 1247, and later of other cities. In 1292 he was re-elected *podestà* of Faenza, but he and his supporters were expelled by the Ghibellines in 1294. In 1296 Rinieri seized Faenza while the Ghibellines were away paying a social war on Bologna. Those courtesies concluded, they returned in force, and Rinieri was killed in the homecoming festivities.

91–96. To avoid a tangle of scholarly references and disputes I have simplified the text here and taken six lines to render three of Dante's, into what I hope is a reasonably clear exposition. The war-torn land is Romagna. The Reno is a river that bounds Romagna on the west. The sea on the east is the Adriatic.

100–102. All the persons mentioned here were leaders of Romagna during the last decades of the twelfth century and into the first three quarters of the thirteenth. All are cited as examples of knightly grace, bravery, largesse, and sound counsel. *Romagnoles:* People of Romagna (Roe-MAH-nyah). Dante's phrasing unmistakably suggests here the opening lines of Ariosto's *Orlando Furioso.*

103–105. Dante is carrying out the agricultural metaphor begun in lines 97–99. *Fabbro:* Fabbro de' Lambertazzi, leader of all Romagna's Ghibellines, died in 1259. *Fosco:* Bernardin di Fosco, son of a small landholder (hence his family tree was "a little plant"), rose to high estate through great merit and served as *podestà* of Pisa in 1248 and of Siena in 1249. Both men are cited for the same virtues exemplified by Mainardi and the others listed in lines 100–114.

The first part of Guido's denunciation of Romagna cites the glories of its past. All those mentioned here by Duca were prominent leaders of Romagna, and all were alive during some part of Guido's lifetime. He laments their passing as the passing of chivalric virtue.

110. *the house of the Traversari:* Guido has cited Pier Traversaro among the best lords of the land. Here he extends his praise to the whole house, along with his lament that it is an expiring line. *the Anastagi* (Ah-nah-STAH-djee): of Ravenna. Another great house left without heirs.

115–117. *Brettinoro:* (Now Bertinoro.) A small town between Forlì and Cesena, it was Guido's birthplace. Some of the details of this passage may be variously interpreted, but the general sense is clear enough: "Since the best of your people have fled you to escape the contagion of your guilt, why don't you just do away with yourself?" *Your lords:* Your ruling house. *and many more:* and many more of your citizens.

118–120. The towns here mentioned are small fortified towns of Romagna. In Guido's view, their ruling houses have bred down to degenerate stock. In 1300 the Malvacini di Bagnacavallo (Mahl-vah-TCHEE-nee dee Bah-nya-kah-VAH-loe) had no male heirs and the line was doomed to extinction.

121–123. The Pagani ruled over various holdings in Romagna, Faenza and Imola among them. The "fiend" of the Pagani was Count Maginardo (see *Inferno,* XXVII, 47–49, and note). Maginardo died in 1302, and after him his sons ruled well, but never well enough to remove the stain left on the family name by Maginardo's misrule.

124. *Ugolin de' Fantolini:* Of Faenza. A lord of great good reputation. He died in 1278 leaving two sons and two daughters, but both sons had died without issue by 1286.

130–132. *We knew those dear souls heard us . . . :* A good example of Dante's characteristic sparseness and precision. The souls, well disposed toward the Poets, could hear in which direction they walked away. Had the Poets turned the wrong way (left), the souls would have spoken up. Since nothing was said, the Poets knew they were headed the right way—and each pair knew that the other knew.

134–141. Dante's theory of electric storms (see *Inferno,* XXIV, 145–149, and note at end of that Canto) is likely to confuse modern readers. His basic theory is that fiery vapors (lightning) try to shatter watery vapors (clouds), bringing them down as rain. (So line 138, *if the cloud bursts . . .*)

136–144. THE REIN OF ENVY. Like the Whip, the Rein consists of bodiless voices racing through the air.

The first voice is that of Cain crying to God at his punishment: "Everyone that findeth me shall slay me." (*Genesis,* iv, 14.) Thus the first crash resounds with the cry of the first man punished for envy.

The second voice is of Aglauros, daughter of Cecrops, King of Athens. Her sisters were Herse and Pandrace. Mercury fell in love with the beautiful Herse and bribed Aglauros to arrange for him an assignation with her sister. Aglauros took the bribe, but in envy that her sister should lie with a god, she turned Mercury away when he arrived for his appointment. Mercury, enraged, turned her to stone.

Thus the doom brought on by envy cries in the voice of brother sinning against brother and sister sinning against sister.

146–150. VIRGIL'S REPLY. As mixed metaphors go, this one ranks high even for Dante. "You [mankind] ought to be bridled [like a horse] but instead you swallow the hook [like a fish] and are not saved by either curb [bridle] or call [the original word is *richiamo,* signifying the whistle used to call a falcon back from the hunt]."

Canto XV

THE SECOND CORNICE   *The Envious*
THE ASCENT   *The Angel of Caritas*
THE THIRD CORNICE   *The Wrathful*
                 The Whip of Wrath

It is 3:00 P.M. and the Poets are walking straight into the Sun
when an even greater radiance blinds Dante and he finds
himself in the presence of THE ANGEL OF CARITAS who
passes the Poets on to the ledge above. As they ascend, they
hear the Angel sing THE FIFTH BEATITUDE.

As soon as the Poets enter THE THIRD CORNICE, Dante is
entranced by THREE VISIONS which constitute THE WHIP
OF WRATH, extolling the virtue of MEEKNESS toward kin,
toward friends, and toward enemies.

These events consume three hours. It is, therefore, 6:00
P.M. of THE SECOND DAY IN PURGATORY when the Poets,
moving forward, observe an enormous CLOUD OF SMOKE
ahead of them.

Of that bright Sphere that, like a child at play,
   skips endlessly, as much as lies between
   the third hour's end and the first light of day

remained yet of the Sun's course toward the night.
   Thus, it was Vespers there upon the mountain   5
   and midnight here in Italy, where I write.

The Sun's late rays struck us full in the face,
   for in our circling course around the mountain
   we now were heading toward his resting place.

Suddenly, then, I felt my brow weighed down   10
    by a much greater splendor than the first.
    I was left dazzled by some cause unknown

and raised my hands and joined them in the air
    above my brows, making a sunshade of them
    which, so to speak, blunted the piercing glare.   15

When a ray strikes glass or water, its reflection
    leaps upward from the surface once again
    at the same angle but opposite direction

from which it strikes, and in an equal space
    spreads equally from a plumb-line to mid-point,   20
    as trial and theory show to be the case.

Just so, it seemed to me, reflected light
    struck me from up ahead, so dazzlingly
    I had to shut my eyes to spare my sight.

"Dear Father, what is that great blaze ahead   25
    from which I cannot shade my eyes enough,
    and which is still approaching us?" I said.

"Do not be astonished," answered my sweet Friend,
    "if those of the Heavenly Family still blind you.
    He has been sent to bid us to ascend.   30

Soon now, such sights will not aggrieve your sense
    but fill you with a joy as great as any
    Nature has fitted you to experience."

We stand before the Blessed Angel now.
    With joyous voice he cries: "Enter. The stair   35
    is far less steep than were the two below."

We had gone past him and were climbing on
    when *Blessed are the merciful* hymned out
    behind us, and *Rejoice you who have won.*

My Guide and I were going up the stair— 40
   we two alone—and I, thinking to profit
   from his wise words as we were climbing there,

questioned him thus: "What deep intent lay hidden
   in what the spirit from Romagna said?
   He spoke of 'sharing' and said it was 'forbidden.' " 45

And he: "He knows the sad cost of his own
   besetting sin: small wonder he reviles it
   in hope that you may have less to atone.

It is because you focus on the prize
   of worldly goods, which every sharing lessens 50
   that Envy pumps the bellows for your sighs.

But if, in true love for the Highest Sphere,
   your longing were turned upward, then your hearts
   would never be consumed by such a fear;

for the more there are there who say 'ours'—not 'mine'— 55
   by that much is each richer, and the brighter
   within that cloister burns the Love Divine."

"I am left hungrier being thus fed,
   and my mind is more in doubt being thus answered,
   than if I had not asked at all," I said. 60

"How can each one of many who divide
   a single good have more of it, so shared,
   than if a few had kept it?" He replied:

"Because within the habit of mankind
   you set your whole intent on earthly things, 65
   the true light falls as darkness on your mind.

The infinite and inexpressible Grace
   which is in Heaven, gives itself to Love
   as a sunbeam gives itself to a bright surface.

As much light as it finds there, it bestows;   70
    thus, as the blaze of Love is spread more widely,
    the greater the Eternal Glory grows.

As mirror reflects mirror, so, above,
    the more there are who join their souls, the more
    Love learns perfection, and the more they love.   75

And if this answer does not yet appease
    your hunger, you will soon see Beatrice,
    and this, and every wish, shall find surcease.

Only strive hard that soon no trace may show
    of the five scars which true contrition heals—   80
    as the first two have faded from your brow."

I was about to say, "I am satisfied,"
    when suddenly we came to the next Round,
    and my eyes' avidity left me tongue-tied.

Here suddenly, in an ecstatic trance,   85
    I find myself caught up into a vision.
    I see a crowded temple, and in the entrance

a lady by herself, her eyes aglow
    with the sweet grace of a mother, saying gently:
    "My son, my son, why do you treat us so?   90

Your father and I were seeking you in tears."
    So saying, she falls silent, and as quickly
    as it first came, the vision disappears.

Another lady now appears, her cheeks
    bathed in those waters that are born of grief   95
    when grief is born of anger. Now she speaks:

"O Pisistratus, if you are true Lord
    of the city for whose name the Gods debated,
    and whence all learning shone forth afterward,

avenge yourself on the presumptuous one 100
   who dared embrace our daughter." And her master,
   sweetly forbearing, in a placid tone,

and smiling gently at her, answers thus:
   "What shall we do to those that wish us harm
   if we take vengeance upon those that love us?" 105

Then there appears a wild and murderous spill
   of people hate-incensed, stoning a boy,
   and roaring to each other's wrath: "Kill! Kill!"

I see the boy sink to the ground, his death
   already heavy on him, but his eyes, 110
   like gates of Heaven, open through such wrath;

and even in his last extremity
   he prays God to forgive his murderers,
   turning to Him the look that unlocks pity.

When finally my soul could see and feel 115
   things which were true outside it, I understood
   my not-false errors had been dreams, though real.

My Guide, who watched me as I moved along
   like one just wakened and still sleep-stunned, said:
   "You barely seem to keep your feet—what's wrong? 120

You've stumbled on now for a good half-league
   with eyes half-shut and legs too-wide, like one
   groggy with wine or dropping with fatigue."

"O my sweet Father, if you wish to know,
   listen, and I shall tell you what I saw," 125
   I answered, "when my legs were stricken so."

"Were you to wear a hundred masks," he said,
   "to hide your face, it would lie open to me
   so that your slightest thought might yet be read.

These visions warn your soul on no account   130
  still to refuse the water of that peace
  which flows to man from the Eternal Fount.

I did not ask 'what's wrong' as a man might
  who sees with eyes alone, and when the body
  is lying senseless has no other sight;   135

but rather to put strength into your stride:
  for so must laggards be spurred on to use
  their reawakening senses as a guide."

Through the last vesper-hour we traveled on,
  looking ahead as far as eye could see   140
  against the level rays of the late sun.

And there ahead of us against the light
  we saw come billowing in our direction
  by slow degrees, a smoke as black as night.

Nor was there refuge from it anywhere.   145
It took our sight from us, and the pure air.

NOTES

1–6. *that bright Sphere that . . . skips endlessly:* Despite the fact that Dante says "Sphere" rather than "great circle" or "zone," the reference here is best taken to be to the zodiac, which dips above and below the horizon and may, therefore, be said to "skip endlessly." Dante uses the word *scherza*, which may signify any kind of play. *as much as lies between:* Three full hours (from the end of the third hour of the day, *i.e.*, 9:00 A.M., back to the dawn, *i.e.*, 6:00 A.M.). Since one hour equals 15°, "as much as" must equal 45°. If the Sun has 45° remaining of its daily course, it is three hours short of sunset, hence 3:00 P.M. *it was Vespers there . . . and midnight here:* Purgatory is antipodal to Jerusalem. If it is 3:00 P.M. in Purgatory, it is 3:00 A.M. in Jerusalem. But by Dante's reckoning, Italy is taken as lying exactly 45° west of Jerusalem. As above, 45° converts to three hours, and since Italy is to the west (hence in an earlier time zone), it must be midnight there.

16–21. *a ray . . . its reflection:* In the old didactic tradition, Dante is describing the reflection of a beam of light.

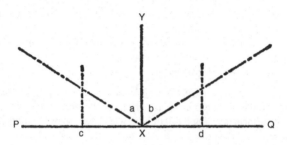

Angle *a* equals angle *b.* *YX* is a "plumb-line to mid-point." If from any two points on line *PQ* equally distant from *X* (*c* and *d,* for example) perpendiculars are raised to intersect that ray of light and its reflection, they will intersect an amount of reflection equal to the amount of ray.

Allegorically, this process of reflection may best be taken for the perfection of outgoing love, which the Angel—as the true opposite of the Envious—represents.

34. *the Blessed Angel:* Since the Angel of each Cornice represents the virtue opposite the sin there punished, this would be the Angel of *Caritas, i.e.,* of Love of Others.

38–39. *Blessed are the merciful:* The Fifth Beatitude. See *Matthew,* v, 7. It is probably the Angel who sings this Beatitude and the spirits of the Envious who reply: *Rejoice you who have won.* The words are chosen from no particular text, but their sentiment is that which concludes the Beatitudes, a rejoicing in the triumph over sin. See *Matthew,* v. 12.

48. *you:* You living men. Mankind in general.

51. *that Envy pumps the bellows for your sighs:* A Dantean figure. Envy seems to change the breast into a bellows which does nothing but pump out sighs of envious desire.

52–57. *the Highest Sphere:* The Empyrean. *such a fear:* that someone else will get the material good one cherishes. *that cloister:* Heaven.

64 ff. DANTE'S DOCTRINE OF WEALTH. Virgil is propounding a favorite Dantean doctrine. Since there is a limit to material wealth, everything that one man possesses lessens what others may possess. Those, therefore, who are avid for the goods of the world must live in fear that it will be taken by others, and therefore Envy drives them to lament everyone else's material gains. The treasure of Heaven, however, grows greater in being shared.

67. *The infinite and inexpressible Grace:* God's love. It shines forth to the souls of those who love Him as a sunbeam shines upon a bright surface, dazzling it full of light without in any way diminishing the source but rather, by giving, increasing the total of light.

76–77. *appease your hunger:* The phrasing here responds to the phrasing of line 58: "I am left hungrier being thus fed."

84. *my eyes' avidity left me tongue-tied:* The avidity of my eyes [to observe new sights] left me [so busy staring at all about me that I was] tongue-tied. *Cf.,* the opening lines of Canto IV, and Dante's discussion of how one sense may so absorb the soul that all others fail.

85–114. THE WHIP OF WRATH. Consists of three visions that seize upon the souls on their way to enter the cloud of smoke.

The first (lines 85–93) is, as always, from the life of Mary. It is based on *Luke,* ii, 41–52. When the Nazarenes started back from Jerusalem after Passover, Jesus did not leave with them, but stayed behind without informing either Joseph or Mary. They, thinking he must be in some other part of the caravan, had traveled a whole day before they learned the truth. They turned back to search for him and spent three days combing Jerusalem before they found him in the Temple disputing with the learned men. Mary, despite the anxieties and exertions to which Jesus had put her, remonstrates without wrath.

The second (lines 94–105) is of an incident from the life of Pisistratus, Tyrant of Athens from 560–527 B.C., the usurper who ruled so wisely and gently that the Athenians forgave his usurpation. A young man who loved the daughter of Pisistratus and wished to marry her, but who had not won the parents' consent, embraced her in public in a moment of high spirits. The wife of Pisistratus, seething with wrath, demands a bloody vengeance for what she takes to be an act of dishonor, but Pisistratus turns away wrath with a soft answer. (Valerius Maximus, *Facta et Dicta,* VI, i.)

The third (lines 106–114) is of the martyrdom of St. Stephen. (*Acts,* vii, 58.) Dante is in error in making Stephen a boy at the time of his death.

Thus the Whip once more presents three degrees of the virtue opposed to the sin being punished, and thus the Wrathful are whipped on by high examples of Meekness toward kin, toward friends, and toward enemies.

98. *for whose name the Gods debated:* The legend is that Neptune and Athena both wished the new city to bear their names. Ovid (*Metamorphoses,* VI, 70–82) describes the resultant contest, which Athena won.

131. *still to refuse:* Dante has already recognized that his own besetting sin is Pride, and Pride is clearly related to Wrath. He seems to have had so strong a sense of his own rightness that any indignity or error could arouse his anger. Boccaccio says that everyone in Romagna was sure Dante would throw stones even at women and children if he heard them insult his principles. His mistreatment by the Florentines, moreover, must have left him with some substantial hunger for revenge. Thus these examples of high meekness have special point for him, and Virgil (his own reason) tells him so.

132. *the Eternal Fount:* Jeremiah, ii, 13, and xvii, 13, refers to God as "the fountain of living waters."

133–138. *lying senseless:* Virgil means "so caught up in a trance that the soul is beyond the reach of the senses." In extension, he is saying: "I do not ask in a material way, seeing things only with the physical senses, but rather in terms of your newly awakened spiritual understanding of your faults, and to urge you to act upon that new understanding."

In a second sense, of course, Dante is analyzing himself. If he is to move higher up the mountain he must put by all his Wrath, all his sense of outraged righteousness, all his desire for vindication and vengeance. But he knows it will not be easy for him truly to forgive his enemies, for he knows how deeply Wrath is rooted in his nature.

It requires, therefore, a special urging to act truly upon the three visions he has seen. (Contrast, for example, how lightly Dante was able to dismiss Envy as a personal concern of his soul.)

139–141. It is nearing 6:00 P.M., the last hour of Vespers. Note that about three hours ago (lines 1–6 above), the Poets were on the ledge below and were walking straight into the Sun. Now, having climbed the stairway and having walked half a league (about a mile and a half) and a bit more, at a very slow pace (lines 121–123), they are still walking straight into the Sun. The fact that they could walk so far without a turning that would leave the Sun on their right certainly indicates that these first Cornices circle very slowly, being conceived on an enormous scale.

Canto XVI

The Wrathful
Marco Lombardo

*The Poets enter the acrid and blinding smoke in which THE
WRATHFUL suffer their purification. As Wrath is a corrosive
state of the spirit, so the smoke stings and smarts. As Wrath ob-
scures the true light of God, so the smoke plunges all into dark-
ness. Within it, Dante hears souls singing THE LITANY OF THE
LAMB OF GOD. The Lamb, of course, is the symbol of the
MEEKNESS of Divine Love. As such, it is the opposite of Wrath.
A further purification is implicit in the fact that the souls all sing
as if with one voice, for Wrath is the sin that soonest breeds divi-
sion among men, and only Spiritual Concord can reunite them.*

*MARCO LOMBARDO hears Dante speak and calls to him.
Invited by Dante, Marco accompanies the Poets to the edge of
the smoke, discoursing on the causes of the modern world's
corruption, which he locates in the usurpation of temporal
power and wealth by the Church. As Marco concludes, a light
begins to appear through the smoke. Marco explains that it is
the radiance of the Angel who waits ahead. He then turns back,
for he is not yet fit to show himself to the Angel of the Lord.*

No gloom of Hell, nor of a night allowed
   no planet under its impoverished sky,
   the deepest dark that may be drawn by cloud,

ever drew such a veil across my face,
   nor one whose texture rasped my senses so,   5
   as did the smoke that wrapped us in that place.

The sting was more than open eyes could stand.
   My wise and faithful Guide drew near me, therefore,
   and let me grasp his shoulder with my hand.

Just as a blind man—lest he lose his road   10
   or tumble headlong and be hurt or killed—
   walks at his guide's back when he goes abroad,

so moved I through that foul and acrid air,
   led by my sweet Friend's voice, which kept repeating:
   "Take care. Do not let go of me. Take care."   15

And I heard other voices. They seemed to pray
   for peace and pardon to the Lamb of God
   which, of Its mercy, takes our sins away.

They offered up three prayers, and every one
   began with *Agnus Dei,* and each word   20
   and measure rose in perfect unison.

"Master, do I hear spirits on this path?"
   I said. And he to me: "You do indeed,
   and they are loosening the knot of Wrath."

"And who are you, then, that you cleave our smoke,   25
   yet speak of us as if you still kept time
   by kalends?"—without warning, someone spoke

these words to me; at which my Lord and Guide
   said: "Answer. And inquire respectfully
   if one may find a way up on this side."   30

And I: "O spirit growing pure and free
   to go once more in beauty to your Maker—
   you will hear wonders if you follow me."

"As far as is permitted me," he said,
   "I will. And if the smoke divide our eyes,   35
   our ears shall serve to join us in their stead."

So I began: "I make my way above
    still in these swathings death dissolves. I came here
    through the Infernal grief. Now, since God's love

incloses me in Grace so bounteous   40
    that he permits me to behold His court
    by means wholly unknown to modern use—

pray tell me who you were before you died,
    and if I go the right way to the pass
    that leads above. Your words shall be our guide."   45

"I was a Lombard. Marco was my name.
    I knew the ways of the world, and loved that good
    at which the bows of men no longer aim.

You are headed the right way to reach the stair
    that leads above," he added. And: "I pray you   50
    to pray for me when you have mounted there."

And I: "On my faith I vow it. But a doubt
    has formed within me and has swelled so large
    I shall explode unless I speak it out.

It was a simple doubt at first, but now   55
    it doubles and grows sure as I compare
    your words with what was said to me below.

The world, as you have said, is truly bare
    of every trace of good; swollen with evil;
    by evil overshadowed everywhere.   60

But wherein lies the fault? I beg to know
    that I may see the truth and so teach others.
    Some see it in the stars; some, here below."

A deep sigh wrung by grief, almost a moan
    escaped as a long "Ah!" Then he said: "Brother,   65
    the world is blind and you are its true son.

Mankind sees in the heavens alone the source
   of all things, good and evil; as if by Law
   they shaped all mortal actions in their course.

If that were truly so, then all Free Will   70
   would be destroyed, and there would be no justice
   in giving bliss for virtue, pain for evil.

The spheres *do* start your impulses along.
   I do not say *all,* but suppose I did—
   the light of reason still tells right from wrong;   75

and Free Will also, which, though it be strained
   in the first battles with the heavens, still
   can conquer all if it is well sustained.

You are free subjects of a more immense
   nature and power which grants you intellect   80
   to free you from the heavens' influence.

If, therefore, men today turn from God's laws,
   the fault is in yourselves to seek and find;
   and I shall truly explicate the cause:

from the hand of God, whose love shines like a ray   85
   upon it, even before birth, comes forth
   the simple soul which, like a child at play,

cries, laughs, and ignorant of every measure
   but the glad impulse of its joyous Maker,
   turns eagerly to all that gives it pleasure.   90

It tastes small pleasures first. To these it clings,
   deceived, and seeks no others, unless someone
   curb it, or guide its love to higher things.

Men, therefore, need restraint by law, and need
   a monarch over them who sees at least   95
   the towers of The True City. Laws, indeed,

there are, but who puts nations to their proof?
   No one. The shepherd who now leads mankind
   can chew the cud, but lacks the cloven hoof.

The people, then, seeing their guide devour   100
   those worldly things to which their hunger turns
   graze where he grazes, and ask nothing more.

The bad state of the modern world is due—
   as you may see, then—to bad leadership;
   and not to natural corruption in you.   105

Rome used to shine in two suns when her rod
   made the world good, and each showed her its way:
   one to the ordered world, and one to God.

Now one declining sun puts out the other.
   The sword and crook are one, and only evil   110
   can follow from them when they are together;

for neither fears the other, being one.
   Look closely at the ear, if still you doubt me,
   for by the seed it bears is the plant known.

Honor and Courtesy once made their home   115
   in the land the Po and the Adige water—
   till Frederick came to loggerheads with Rome.

Now any man who has good cause to fear
   the sound of truth or honest company
   may cross it safely—he will find none there.   120

True, three old men are left in whom the past
   reproves the present. How time drags for them
   till God remove them to their joy at last—

Conrad da Palazzo, the good Gherard',
   and Guido da Castel, who is better named,   125
   in the fashion of the French, 'The Honest Lombard.'

Say, then, that since the Church has sought to be
    two governments at once, she sinks in muck,
    befouling both her power and ministry."

"O Marco mine," I said, "you reason well!   130
    And now I know why Levi's sons alone
    could not inherit wealth in Israel.

But who is this Gherard' in whom you say
    the past survives untarnished to reprove
    the savage breed of this degenerate day?"   135

"Your question seeks to test me," said Lombardo,
    "or else to trick me. How can you speak Tuscan
    and still seem to know nothing of Gherardo?

Just what his surname is, I do not know—
    unless he might be known as Gaia's father.   140
    Godspeed: this is as far as I may go.

See there across the smoke, like dawn's first rays,
    the light swell like a glory and a guide.
    The Angel of this place gives forth that blaze,

and it is not fit he see me." Thus he spoke,   145
and said no more, but turned back through the smoke.

NOTES

    2. *no planet:* Dante, it must be remembered, considered the Moon (like the Sun) to be a planet.

    15. *Take care. Do not let go of me. Take care:* Virgil's warning is especially apt at this point. Wrath is a bitter and a smoky passion that blinds the wrathful soul to reason. The Italian idiom *a perso i lumi degli occhii* (literally, "he has lost the lamps of his eyes") means that a man has lost his reason. Thus Virgil is warning Dante, allegorically, not to lose his Guiding Reason in the blind immoderations of Wrath.

19–20. *Agnus Dei:* The Litany of the Mass includes three prayers, each of which begins with *Agnus Dei*—"Lamb of God which taketh away the sins of the world." The first two add "have mercy upon us." The third adds "give us peace."

21. *in perfect unison:* Wrath is a discord that divides men. So, as part of their purification, these souls learn to unite in perfect concord.

27. *kalends:* The kalends were the first day of each Roman month. To reckon time by kalends, therefore, is to use mortal measures which are meaningless in the eternity of the dead.

27. *someone spoke:* Marco Lombardo, or Marco the Lombard. Nothing is definitely known of him, not even his exact name, for his own identification of himself may mean either "I am a man of Lombardy named Marco," or "I am Marco of the Lombardi family."

38. *these swathings death dissolves:* Mortal flesh. That Dante is alive and that he came by way of Hell are the wonders he promised to reveal to Marco in line 33. (Here, too, one may argue that he is comparing his eternal journey with the voyages of Marco Polo.)

51. *mounted there:* To Heaven, not to the next Cornice.

57. *what was said to me below:* Dante must surely mean what was said by Guido del Duca. Lombardo's theme certainly continues from what Guido had said.

63. *Some see it in the stars; some, here below:* The movements of the stars and planets, as surviving astrologists still believe, determine man's fate and compel his actions. *here below:* Despite the fact that Dante is in Purgatory, his words here must mean "in the world."

66. *and you are its true son: I.e.,* "you have inherited its blindness."

70–72. The problem of Free Will is one of the knottiest in Christian theology. Dante is arguing that if a man's actions were entirely determined by the stars, he would have no control over what he does, and that he could not, therefore, justly be given eternal rewards for his virtues nor punishment for his sins.

98–99. *The shepherd who now leads mankind:* The Pope. In 1300 the Pope was Boniface VIII, Dante's supreme symbol of clerical corruption. *can chew the cud, but lacks the cloven hoof . . . :* Another mixed metaphor: the shepherd is presented as himself a sheep. Almost all commentators agree that chewing the cud signified spiritual reflection, and that the cloven hoof signifies the ability to distinguish between good and evil. *Cf.* Aquinas: *discrezionem boni et mali.*

105. *in you:* In mankind.

116. *the land the Po and the Adige water:* Lombardy.

117. *till Frederick came to loggerheads with Rome:* Frederick II engaged in a long and disastrous conflict with, successively, Popes Honorius III, Gregory IX, and Innocent IV.

121–122. *in whom the past reproves the present:* Their merit as survivors from a better age of honor and courtesy is a living reproof to the debased new age.

124. *Conrad* (Corrado) *da Palazzo:* A nobleman of Brescia (BRESH-ah). He held various high offices in Florence, Siena, and Piacenza between 1276 and 1289. According to one old commentator, there was a report that during a battle in which Conrad served as standard-bearer, both his arms were hacked off, but that he held the standard up by hugging it with his stumps until he died. The report is unconfirmed.

124. *Gherard':* Gherardo da Cammino, Captain-General of Treviso from 1283 till his death in 1306. Dante cites him as the type of the true noble in *Il Convivio,* IV, 16, 114–123.

125. *Guido da Castel* (Castello): A nobleman of Reggio, famous for his graciousness and liberality. Dante himself had been received by Guido with great honor.

126. *in the fashion of the French, "The Honest Lombard":* The French called all Italians "Lombards" and believed all of them to be shrewd and unscrupulous usurers. To be thus called "honest" by them would be to win praise from the least likely source. (Dante's word is "simple"—*i.e.,* not shrewd and unscrupulous—but "honest" is closer in English to what Dante intended.)

127. *Say, then:* Dante has asked to be shown the truth that he may teach it to others. Here, Marco is summing up with Dante's request in mind. "Say [to them] then [to sum up the whole thing]."

131. *why Levi's sons alone:* The Levites, the priests of Israel, were forbidden to inherit wealth, for the Lord was their inheritance, and except for their houses, they were commanded to depend on the tithes and offerings of the people. (See *Numbers,* xviii, 20; *Joshua,* xiii, 14; and *Deuteronomy,* xviii, 2.) Dante has returned once more to his basic charge against the Church—that in massing wealth and power it lost spirituality and grew corrupt. (See *Inferno,* XIX, 109–111.)

139. *Just what his surname is, I do not know:* Whoever Marco may be, it seems unlikely that he, in his turn, could speak Tuscan, know so much about Gherardo, and not know him as one of the famous da Cammino family. Dante probably has Marco phrase things in this way in order to bring in a reference to the daughter, Gaia (GUY-yah). Gaia seems to have left two reputations behind her, one for chastity, and one for sexual abandon. Dante has been developing the theme of the degeneration of the descendants of great and good men. It seems likely, therefore, that he thought of Gaia as a wanton, hence, as one more example of the degenerate age in which the daughter of great virtue flits through easy beds.

Canto XVII

THE FOURTH CORNICE   *The Wrathful*
         The Rein of Wrath

THE ASCENT   *The Angel of Meekness*

*The Poets emerge from the smoke and Dante is immediately
enrapt by the visions that make up THE REIN OF WRATH. In
succession he beholds THE DESTRUCTION CAUSED BY
WRATH to PROCNE, to HAMAN, and to QUEEN AMATA.
Dante emerges from his trance to hear THE ANGEL OF
MEEKNESS calling to him to show him the ascent, and the
Poets mount at once as the Beatitude,* Blessed are the Peace-
makers, *is sounded behind them.*

    *They reach the top of the Ascent just as night falls, and
though they might normally continue along the level way
Dante feels his body so weighed down that he has to pause
and rest.*

    *As the Poets rest, Virgil gives Dante a DISCOURSE ON
LOVE, demonstrating to him that all actions spring from
either NATURAL or SPIRITUAL LOVE, and that it is the var-
ious PERVERSIONS OF LOVE that lead to the sins that are
punished in Purgatory.*

Reader, if you have ever been closed in
   by mountain mist that left you with no eyes
   to see with, save as moles do, through the skin,

think how those dense damp vapors thinned away
   slow bit by bit till through them the Sun's ball   5
   was once more dimly visible—thus you may,

and without strain, imagine from your own
   recalled experience how I came again
   to see the Sun, which now was almost down.

Thus, matching steps with my true Guide once more,   10
   I passed beyond the cloud into those rays
   which lay already dead on the low shore.

O Fantasy, which can entrance us so
   that we at times stand and are not aware
   though in our ears a thousand trumpets blow!—   15

what moves you since our senses lie dead then?
   —A light that forms in Heaven of itself,
   or of His will who sends its rays to men.

A vision grew within me of the wrong
   she did who for her cruelty was changed   20
   into that bird which most delights in song;

and my imagination was so shut
   into itself that what I saw revealed
   could never have come to me from without.

Next, down like rain, a figure crucified   25
   fell into my high fantasy, his face
   fierce and contemptuous even as he died.

Nearby him great Ahasuerus stood,
   Esther his wife, and the just Mordecai
   whose word and deed were always one in good.   30

And as soap bubbles rise in air and seem
   full-bodied things, then rupture of themselves
   when the film about them breaks, just so that dream

vanished, and through my vision rose an image
   in which a maid cried: "O Queen! Queen no more!   35
   Your very being canceled by your rage!

All not to lose Lavinia? Ah, mother,
   now have you truly lost her. I am she,
   and mourn your death before I mourn another."

When strong light beats against a man's closed eyes   40
   his sleep is broken in him; yet, though broken,
   gives a last twitch before it wholly dies:

my vision fell from me exactly so
   the instant a new light beat on my face,
   a light outshining any that men know.   45

I was looking all about, as if to find
   where I might be, when a new voice that cried,
   "Here is the ascent," drove all else from my mind;

and kindled in my spirit such a fire
   to see who spoke, as cannot ever rest   50
   till it stand face to face with its desire.

But, as in looking at the Sun, whose rays
   keep his form hidden from our stricken eyes—
   so I lacked power to look into that blaze.

"A spirit of Heaven guides us toward the height: 55
   he shows us the ascent before we ask,
   and hides himself in his own holy light.

He does for us what men in the world's uses
   do only for themselves; for who sees need
   and waits a plea, already half refuses.   60

To such sweet bidding let our feet reply
   by striving as they may before night fall;
   for then they may not, till day light the sky."

So spoke my Guide, and he and I as one
   moved toward the ascent; and soon as I had mounted   65
   the first step cut into that ramp of stone,

I felt what seemed to be a great wing fan
    my face and heard: "Blessèd are the peacemakers,
    who feel no evil wrath toward any man."

The last rays, after which night rules the air,   70
    were now so far above us that already
    the stars began to shine through, here and there.

"O strength, why do you melt away?" I said
    several times over to myself, for now
    it seemed my legs were turning into lead.   75

We had come to where the stair ascends no more
    and we were stuck fast on the topmost step
    like a vessel half drawn up upon the shore.

I waited with my head cocked to one side
    for any sound that might reveal the nature   80
    of the new ledge. Then, turning to my Guide,

I said: "Dear Father, what impurity
    is washed in pain here? Though our feet must stay,
    I beg you not to stay your speech." And he:

"That love of good which in the life before   85
    lay idle in the soul is paid for now.
    Here Sloth strains at the once-neglected oar.

But that you may more clearly know The Way,
    give your entire attention to my words;
    thus shall you gather good fruit from delay.   90

Neither Creator nor his creatures move,
    as you well know," he said, "but in the action
    of animal or of mind-directed love.

Natural love may never fall to error.
    The other may, by striving to bad ends,   95
    or by too little, or by too much fervor.

While it desires the Eternal Good and measures
   its wish for secondary goods in reason,
   this love cannot give rise to sinful pleasures.

But when it turns to evil, or shows more   100
   or less zeal than it ought for what is good,
   then the creature turns on its Creator.

Thus you may understand that love alone
   is the true seed of every merit in you,
   and of all acts for which you must atone.   105

Now inasmuch as love cannot abate
   its good wish for the self that loves, all things
   are guarded by their nature from self-hate.

And since no being may exist alone
   and apart from the First Being, by their nature,   110
   all beings lack the power to hate That One.

Therefore, if I have parsed the truth of things,
   the evil that man loves must be his neighbor's.
   In mortal clay such bad love has three springs:

some think they see their own hope to advance   115
   tied to their neighbor's fall, and thus they long
   to see him cast down from his eminence;

some fear their power, preferment, honor, fame
   will suffer by another's rise, and thus,
   irked by his good, desire his ruin and shame;   120

and some at the least injury catch fire
   and are consumed by thoughts of vengeance; thus,
   their neighbor's harm becomes their chief desire.

Such threefold love those just below us here
   purge from their souls. The other, which seeks good, 125
   but without measure, I shall now make clear.—

All men, though in a vague way, apprehend
  a good their souls may rest in, and desire it;
  each, therefore, strives to reach his chosen end.

If you are moved to see good or pursue it,   130
  but with a lax love, it is on this ledge—
  after a proper penance—you will rue it.

There is another good which bears bad fruit:
  it is not happiness, nor the true essence
  of the Eternal Good, its flower and root.   135

The love that yields too much to this false good
  is mourned on the three Cornices above us;
  but in what way it may be understood

as a tripartite thing, I shall not say.
  That, you may learn yourself upon our way."   140

NOTES

1–3. *as moles do, through the skin:* Dante follows a medieval be-
lief that the eyes of moles were completely sealed by a membranous
covering through which they could see a diffused foggy light only.
Here the fog does for Dante what the skin covering was supposed to
do for the eyes of moles.

9. *the Sun, which now was almost down:* It is near sunset of
Easter Monday, the second day on the mountain.

10. *matching steps . . . once more:* Through the smoke, Dante has
stumbled along holding on to Virgil's shoulder. Now, once more in
the light, he is able to match Virgil's pace.

12. *already dead on the low shore:* Dante, it must be remem-
bered, conceives Purgatory to be on a scale unmatched by any
earthly mountain. The Sun, as seen from the mountain's base, would
already have set. At the Poets' altitude, however, the Sun is still in
sight. Since sunset would be at six o'clock on the earth's surface, it
must be a bit later than six now.

13–18. THE POWER OF FANTASY. Dante is about to describe the Rein of Wrath, which consists of another set of visions. Typically, he introduces the visions with a question on the nature of the imagination, and in developing his discussion makes clear, first, that the visions are from Heaven, and second, that he is utterly enrapt by them.

19–39. THE REIN OF WRATH. The three visions of the ruinous results of wrath may be taken as exemplifying wrath against kin, against neighbor, and against God (and self).

The first vision (lines 19–21) shows Procne killing her own son in wrath. The bird that most delights in song is the nightingale. Dante probably intends Procne as "she . . . who was changed." See IX, 15, note, which will also explain her act of great wrath.

The second vision (lines 25–30) is of the crucifixion of Haman, the powerful minister of Ahasuerus, King of Persia. Enraged against Mordecai, Haman persuaded Ahasuerus to decree the death of all the Jews in Persia. A cross (as Dante envisions it, though more likely it was a stake or a gibbet) was especially prepared for Mordecai. Queen Esther, however, persuaded Ahasuerus of Haman's iniquity and the decree was canceled. Not to waste a perfectly good cross, or perhaps because he was confused by the number of people who were making up his mind for him, Ahasuerus had Haman crucified in Mordecai's place. The basic story is told in *The Book of Esther.*

The third vision (lines 34–39) is of Amata killing herself for wrath. The incident is from the *Aeneid,* XII, 595 ff. Lavinia, daughter of the Latian king, was betrothed to Turnus, a neighboring king. War broke out between Turnus and Aeneas, and Queen Amata, mother of Lavinia, hoped Turnus would kill the invader and marry Lavinia. When a false rumor of Turnus' death reached Amata, she hanged herself for rage at the thought that she had lost Lavinia beyond all hope. Aeneas did later kill Turnus in a duel. Lavinia's words in line 39—"and mourn your death before I mourn another"—are prophetic of the death of Turnus. Lavinia later married Aeneas.

The incident itself will not, however, explain Dante's full intent in citing it unless one remembers Dante's partisan identification with the Trojans. (See especially *Inferno,* II, 13–30, and XXVI, 56–63, and notes.) Aeneas was God's chosen and was sent to Italy by Divine Will to found the Roman Empire as the seat of the True

Church. It was God's will, therefore, that Aeneas marry Lavinia, daughter of Italy, and thus bring together God's two chosen races. Amata's wrath, therefore, was not only against herself but against God's decree.

47. *a new voice:* The Angel of Meekness.

49–51. Dante's phrasing should be understood in two senses (and both at once). The first: "I was filled with that yearning that allows a man no rest till he have his wish." The second: "I was filled with such yearning that I shall never rest until, this life ended, I rise to stand once more before that Angel."

64–66. *as one:* Virgil leading and Dante a step behind, as they have been going. Thus when Dante switches from the "he and I" of line 64, to the "I" of line 65, he is not being careless but, rather, precise. He mounts the steps a pace behind Virgil. (Reason goes first.)

69. *evil wrath:* One might think wrath inherently evil, and the adjective, therefore, redundant. Dante distinguishes here between Wrath as an evil thing, and Righteous Indignation as a just thing. (See *Inferno,* VIII, 43, note.)

70–72. To read Dante is to educate the eye. The observation here is both subtle and exact. At high altitudes the setting Sun's rays shoot up so steeply that the first stars begin to appear before the last light of the Sun is gone. I do not know whether the phenomenon is observable from any earthly mountain, but it is easily observable in an airplane at high altitude.

77. *and we were stuck fast:* The Poets cannot ascend after darkness, but they have already finished the ascent to the Fourth Cornice. They are, therefore, free to continue on the level of the ledge. It is not darkness that stops them, but the contagion of Sloth that takes away their wills, though briefly. (See also XVIII, 87–90, and note to 87. And compare the pause they make in *Inferno,* XI, where the stench of Lower Hell is so great the Poets must wait till their nostrils adjust to it.)

85–87. SLOTH. The central sin (there are three deadly sins below it and three above it) is Acedia (from L. *accidia,* from Gr. roots meaning "not caring") or Sloth. Sloth, however, must not be understood as physical laziness or slovenliness but as torpor of the soul which, loving the good, does not pursue it actively enough. Dante's condition in the Dark Wood of Error, from which he embarked on his long journey, is best conceived as a recognition of the slothful worldliness of his soul up to that time. The entire journey, in fact, is Dante's active pursuit of the true good, his own purgation from Acedia.

Acedia, however, is not simply the failure to perform good works for others, though it readily involves that failure. It is, more specifically, the failure to pay enough attention to the good, to make enough demands upon oneself. Were one to give all of one's energy and attention to the pursuit of God's truth, good works would follow automatically. Acedia may consist in being too torpid to arrive at a vision of the good, or in achieving that vision but neglecting to pursue it.

90. *from delay:* Since Dante finds himself temporarily deprived of strength to continue, he seeks to win advantage from delay, thus showing a zeal of which the Slothful failed in their lives. (Here, also, compare *Inferno,* XI.)

93. *animal love:* Blind instinct. *mind-directed love:* Those desires shaped by the God-given light of reason.

95–96. Free will may err in three ways. First, by seeking bad goals (the self-love of Pride, which seeks to rise above others; of Envy, which resents the rise of others; and of Wrath, which seeks revenge at the cost of others). Second, by too little zeal for the known good (Sloth). And third, by too much love for the good things of this world (Avarice, Gluttony, and Lust).

97–98. *the Eternal Good:* God. *secondary goods:* The pleasures of the earth given to man for his delight. To deny these is to reject God's bounty; to seek them immoderately is to abandon God for His gifts.

106–108. *love cannot abate:* The doctrine here is Aquinian. Nothing in creation seeks anything but what it takes to be the good of love. Even suicide is an act motivated by self-love, the suicide believing he does himself more good in escaping life than in enduring it.

124. *those just below . . . purge:* Those on the first three Cornices.

125. *The other:* The other kind of love.

132. *after a proper penance:* After a penitent turning to God, and after the delay in Purgatory for the period of time they made God wait. After due penance, due punishment.

Canto XVIII

THE FOURTH CORNICE   *The Slothful*
        The Whip of Sloth
        The Rein of Sloth

*Virgil continues his DISCOURSE ON LOVE, explaining
THE RELATION OF LOVE AND FREE WILL, but warns
Dante that Reason is limited. Dante must seek the final an-
swer from Beatrice, for the question involves one of the mys-
teries of faith.*

*It is near midnight when Virgil concludes, and Dante is
starting to drowse, when he is suddenly brought awake by a
long train of souls who come running and shouting from
around the mountain. They are THE SLOTHFUL, the souls
of those who recognized The Good but were not diligent in
pursuit of it. As once they delayed, so now they are all hurry
and zeal, and will not even pause to speak to the Poets.*

*Two souls run before the rest shouting aloud THE WHIP
OF SLOTH, one citing Mary as an example of holy zeal, the
other citing Caesar as an example of temporal zeal.*

*Virgil hails the racing souls to ask the nearer way to the as-
cent, but not even the news that Dante is still alive slows them.
One soul, a former ABBOT OF SAN ZENO, shouts back an
answer while still running.*

*Behind the train come two more souls shouting THE REIN
OF SLOTH, citing as examples of the downfall of the laggard,
the Israelites in the desert, and those followers of Aeneas who
remained in Sicily.*

*The souls pass from sight and hearing. Dante, his head full
of confused thoughts, sinks into sleep. Instantly, his thoughts
are transformed into A DREAM.*

His explanation at an end, my Guide,
    that lofty scholar, scrutinized my face
    as if to see if I seemed satisfied.

And I, my thirst already sprung anew,
    said nothing, thinking, "He may well be tired   5
    of all this questioning I put him through."

But that true Father, sensing both my thirst
    and that I was too timid to reveal it,
    encouraged me to speak by speaking first.

I, therefore: "Master, in the light you shed   10
    my sight grows so acute that I see clearly
    all that your argument implied or said.

But, dear and gentle Father, please discourse
    more fully on that love in which you say
    all good and evil actions have their source."   15

And he: "Focus the keen eyes of your mind
    on what I say, and you will see made clear
    the error of the blind who lead the blind.

The soul, being created prone to Love,
    is drawn at once to all that pleases it,   20
    as soon as pleasure summons it to move.

From that which really is, your apprehension
    extracts a form which it unfolds within you;
    that form thereby attracts the mind's attention,

then if the mind, so drawn, is drawn to it,   25
    that summoning force is Love; and thus within you,
    through pleasure, a new natural bond is knit.

Then, just as fire yearns upward through the air,
    being so formed that it aspires by nature
    to be in its own element up there,   30

so love, which is a spiritual motion,
   fills the trapped soul, and it can never rest
   short of the thing that fills it with devotion.

By now you will, of course, have understood
   how little of the truth they see who claim   35
   that every love is, in itself, a good;

for though love's substance always will appear
   to be a good, not every impress made,
   even in finest wax, is good and clear."

"Your words and my own eager mind reveal   40
   exactly what Love is," I said, "but now
   there is an even greater doubt I feel:

if love springs from outside the soul's own will,
   it being made to love, what merit is there
   in loving good, or blame in loving ill?"   45

And he to me: "As far as reason sees,
   I can reply. The rest you must ask Beatrice.
   The answer lies within faith's mysteries.

Every substantial form distinct from matter
   and yet united with it in some way,   50
   has a specific power in it. This latter

is not perceivable save as it gives
   evidence of its workings and effects—
   as the green foliage tells us a plant lives.

Therefore, no man can know whence springs the light   55
   of his first cognizance, nor of the bent
   of such innate primordial appetite

as springs within you, as within the bee
   the instinct to make honey; and such instincts
   are, in themselves, not blamable nor worthy.   60

Now, that all later wills and this first bent
   may thrive, the innate counsel of your Reason
   must surely guard the threshold of consent.

This is the principle from which accrue
   your just desserts, according as it reaps   65
   and winnows good or evil love in you.

Those masters who best reasoned nature's plan
   discerned this innate liberty, and therefore
   they left their moral science to guide Man.

Or put it this way: all love, let us say,   70
   that burns in you, springs from necessity;
   but you still have the power to check its sway.

These noble powers Beatrice will comprehend
   as 'The Free Will.' Keep that term well in mind
   if she should speak of it when you ascend."   75

It was near midnight. The late-risen Moon,
   like a brass bucket polished bright as fire,
   thinned out the lesser stars, which seemed to drown.

It traveled retrograde across that sign
   the Sun burns when the Romans look between   80
   the Sards and Corsicans to its decline.

And he who made Piètola shine above
   all other Mantuan towns, had discharged fully
   the burden I had laid on him for love;

because of which I, being pleased to find   85
   such clear and open answers to my questions,
   was rambling drowsily within my mind.

I wakened in an instant to a pack
   of people running toward us, a great mob
   that broke around the mountain at my back: 90

as once, of old, wild hordes ran through the night
   along Ismenus' and Asopus' banks
   when Thebes invoked no more than Bacchus' might;

in such a frenzy, far as I could see,
   those who were spurred by good will and high love   95
   ran bent like scythes along that Cornice toward me.

They were upon us soon, for all that rout
   was running furiously, and out in front
   two spirits streaming tears were calling out:

"Mary *ran* to the hills"—so one refrain;   100
   and the other: "Caesar, to subdue Ilerda
   struck at Marseilles, and then *swooped* down on
     Spain."

"Faster! Faster! To be slow in love
   is to lose time," cried those who came behind;
   "Strive on that grace may bloom again above."   105

"O souls in whom the great zeal you now show
   no doubt redeems the negligence and delay
   that marred your will to do good, there below;

this man lives—truly—and the instant day
   appears again, he means to climb. Please show him   110
   how he may reach the pass the nearer way."

So spoke my Master, and one running soul
   without so much as breaking step replied:
   "Come after us, and you will find the hole.

The will to move on with all speed so fills us   115
   we cannot stop; we humbly beg your pardon
   if duty makes us seem discourteous.

I was abbot of San Zeno in the reign
   of the good emperor Frederick Barbarossa,
   of whom the Milanese still speak with pain.   120

And another with one foot now in the grave
   will shed tears for that monastery soon,
   and rue the evil orders he once gave.

For he has set his son up as the head—
   a man deformed in body, worse in mind,   125
   and bastard born—in its true Pastor's stead."

He had by then left us so far behind
   that if he said more, it was lost to me:
   but I was pleased to keep this much in mind.

My aid on all occasion, the prompt Master,   130
   said: "Look, for here come two who cry aloud
   the Scourge of Sloth, that souls may flee it faster."

At the tail end one runner cried: "They died
   before the Jordan saw its heirs, those people
   for whom the Red Sea's waters stood aside."   135

The other: "Those who found it too laborious
   to go the whole way with Anchises' son
   cut from their own lives all that was most glorious."

Then when those shades had drawn so far ahead
   that I could not make out a trace of them,   140
   a new thought seized upon me, and it bred

so many more, so various, and so scrambled,
   that turning round and round inside itself
   so many ways at once, my reason rambled;

I closed my eyes and all that tangled theme   145
was instantly transformed into a dream.

NOTES

18. *the blind who lead the blind:* Virgil means here the teachers of
Epicurean philosophy and their students, both spiritually blind in

Dante's view in that they teach that all desire (*i.e.*, all love, as Virgil calls it) is a good thing and should be gratified.

19 ff. VIRGIL'S DISCOURSE ON LOVE. The doctrine Dante puts into Virgil's mouth is typically medieval both in content and in the manner of its statement. The soul, Virgil posits, is made with a potential for love, *i.e.*, it is naturally drawn to that which pleases it. Such love passes to action in three stages.

Lines 22–24 describe the first stage. The apprehensive faculty (the senses plus the intellect) observes *that which really is* (any object that has real existence) and extracts from it a *form* (not the thing, but what the mind conceives the thing to be). This *form* is registered upon the soul.

Lines 25–27 describe the second stage. If the soul is drawn to that form, it yields to it with a natural tie of love. It is in this way that the soul has contact with creation.

Lines 28–33 describe the third stage. Just as fire is so conceived and made by Nature that it naturally yearns to rise "up there" (*i.e.*, to the Sphere of Fire) so the soul, by its very nature (its natural disposition to love) yearns for that which attracts it.

37–39. *love's substance:* Dante uses the philosophical term *matera, i.e.*, matter, which may be taken to mean either "the thing loved" (which will always appear as a good to one who loves it), or "the natural substance of love," *i.e.*, the soul's naturally created aptitude to love.

The Epicureans, according to Dante, err in not seeing that appearances may beguile the soul into loving a bad object (the Epicureans, of course, would reply that nothing that gives pleasure can be bad) and thus, that a force that is good in its potential may be exercised in such a way as to be evil in its action.

43–45. I have taken liberties here for the sake of clarity. The passage literally rendered would read: "If love is offered to us from outside, and the soul does not go with another foot (*i.e.*, has no other way of choosing its course), then whether it goes rightly or wrongly is not a matter of its own merit."

49. *substantial form:* A scholastic term for "the essence of a thing." The substantial form of man is his soul, which is distinct from matter, yet united with it. Each substantial form has its specific tendencies, characteristics, and capacities which are visible only in

its working and effects. Before what the Catholic Church declares to be the age of reason (approximately age seven) these powers are simply innate and neutral. Thereafter, there develops within the soul a capacity to reason, and in order to gather the soul into a harmonious unit, innate reason must decide what may and what may not pass the threshold of the soul and be gathered into its love. With reason as the principle of conduct, the soul is then responsible for its actions.

67. *those masters:* Aristotle and Plato. Both based their moral philosophy upon free will.

75. *if she should speak of it:* Beatrice discusses Free Will in the Sphere of the Moon, *Paradiso,* V, 19 ff.

76–81. Note that Dante does not say that the Moon rose at midnight, but only that it was near midnight and that the Moon was late-risen.

He then appends an astronomical figure too complicated to explain here in detail. In brief, the Moon in its monthly retrograde motion is in the sign of the zodiac (commentators dispute whether Dante means Scorpio or Sagittarius) in which the Sun is when a Roman sees it set in a position between Sardinia and Corsica.

82. *Piètola:* A village near Mantua. One legend—and Dante obviously follows it—has it that Virgil was born in Piètola rather than in Mantua proper. Thus Piètola outshines all other Mantuan towns because it was Virgil's birthplace.

83–84. *had discharged fully:* The burden of all the doubts Dante has laid upon him.

87. *was rambling drowsily:* Mental laxness seems to be contagious on this Cornice. Dante, satisfied with what he has learned, does not answer with his usual eagerness, but lets his mind wander off. The appearance of the band of the Slothful, however, awakens him instantly, their presence and the nature of their sin reproaching Dante for his self-indulgence.

91–93. *Ismenus and Asopus:* Boetian rivers. The ancient Thebans ran on their banks at night invoking the aid of Bacchus when they needed rain for their vines. Dante makes a careful point in his phrasing: the Thebans exerted themselves for no more than such a pagan and earthly deity as Bacchus could give, but here the sinners strain for the Supreme Good.

96. *bent like scythes:* Bent so in the speed of their race.

97–102. THE WHIP OF SLOTH. The examples here are shouted by two of the sinners who run before the others. The first example of zeal (spiritual) is Mary's haste, after the Annunciation, to go visit Elizabeth in the hill country of Juda (*Luke,* i. 39). The second (temporal) is Caesar's diligence in the conquest of Ilerda (the modern Spanish town of Lérida). He laid siege to Marseilles, left an army there under Brutus, and pushed by forced marches to take Ilerda.

Since all zeal must be either spiritual or temporal, two examples are enough to cover all possible categories.

109. *this man lives—truly:* Virgil is announcing the news that has amazed all other souls in Purgatory, but these souls are so intent on pursuing their purification that they pay no attention. Their attention is focused on the Supreme Good, and they shun the distraction of lesser things.

111. *the nearer way:* There is one ascent from each Cornice. Virgil's object on each ledge is to learn the short rather than the long way round the circle to it. As it has been on every other ledge, the nearer way is to the right.

118. *San Zeno:* There are three churches of San Zeno in Verona, one of which has a monastery attached. The speaker has not been positively identified, but the Abbot of San Zeno through most of Barbarossa's reign was Gherardo II, who died in 1187.

119. *Frederick Barbarossa:* Frederick Redbeard. Frederick I, Emperor from 1152 to 1190. Dante calls him "good" because he pursued the good of the Empire. Frederick quarreled with Pope Alexander III and was excommunicated by him. Frederick then warred on the Pope's adherents in Lombardy. He took Milan in 1163, pulled down its walls, burned the city, ploughed the ruins, and sowed the ground with salt that nothing might grow there. After other bloody successes, his fortunes turned, and he had to kneel to Alexander for pardon. He drowned while crusading in the Holy Land.

121–126. *another with one foot now in the grave:* Alberto della Scala, Lord of Verona, who died in September of 1301. Thus, in 1300 he already had one foot in the grave. He had three natural sons, among them the famous Can Grande della Scala, who was Dante's host and protector in exile. Another was Giuseppe, and it was this son Alberto forced upon the monks as Abbot of San Zeno, a post he held from 1292 to 1313. The speaker, as former abbot, is especially indignant that an unworthy man should hold so high an office. Giuseppe was triply disqualified, being mentally incapable, physically deformed, and a bastard. Except by special dispensation, the Catholic Church does not grant ordination to the illegitimate; the candidate for ordination must of course be mentally qualified, and he must be free of physical deformities that would interfere with the performance of his duties. (A priest with a mutilated hand, for example, might not be able to celebrate the mass properly. Nor could a deaf priest hear confessions.)

127. *left us so far behind:* The sinner never slackened pace as he spoke.

129. *but I was pleased to keep this much in mind:* Dante seems to relish his chance to fire a shot at Alberto della Scala, certainly not as a personal attack on the father of his great protector, but generally against all the temporal lords of Italy who used their power to corrupt the Church by imposing their will and politics upon its offices.

131–138. THE REIN OF SLOTH. As two of the sinners ran ahead to shout the examples of the Whip, so two more run behind the train shouting the examples that constitute the Rein.

As usual, the first example of the destruction of the laggard is from sacred history. It reminds the sinners that though the Lord delivered Israel from Egyptian bondage, opening the Red Sea for their passage, the people still muttered and would not follow Moses (*i.e.,* would not diligently pursue good); and that, therefore, the Lord doomed them to die in the wilderness. Of all Israel that crossed the Red Sea, only Joshua and Caleb reached the Promised Land of Jordan's waters. (*Numbers,* xiv, 26–34; *Exodus,* xiv, 10–20; *Deuteronomy,* i, 26–36.)

The second example, from secular history, reminds the sinners of those followers of Aeneas who chose to live at ease in Sicily rather than follow him to the great end that had been promised. Thus they did not share in the glory of founding Rome.

Note that both incidents provide a parable of a promised joy (Heaven) lost by lack of zeal in following the clearly indicated road.

Canto XIX

———— ◦◦◦◦◦ ————

Just before morning (when the truth is dreamed) Dante dreams of THE SIREN that lures the souls of men to incontinent worldliness. Hideous in her true form, the Siren grows irresistible in men's eyes as they look upon her. A HEAVENLY LADY races in upon the dream and calls to Virgil who, thus summoned, strips the Siren, exposing her filthy body. Such a stench rises from her, so exposed, that Dante wakens shuddering, to find Virgil calling him to resume the journey.

THE ANGEL OF ZEAL shows them the passage, and when his wings have fanned the Poets, Dante casts off his depression and lethargy, and rushes up the remaining length of the passage.

Arrived at THE FIFTH CORNICE, Virgil inquires the way of one of the souls of THE HOARDERS AND WASTERS, who lie motionless and outstretched, bound hand and foot, with their faces in the dust.

The soul of POPE ADRIAN V replies that, if they have incurred no guilt by Hoarding or Wasting, they may pass on to the right. Dante kneels in reverence to Adrian and is scolded for doing so. Adrian then dismisses Dante in order to resume his purification. Adrian's last request is that his niece, ALAGIA, be asked to pray for his soul.

184

At the hour when the heat of the day is overcome
　　by Earth, or at times by Saturn, and can no longer
　　temper the cold of the Moon; when on the dome

of the eastern sky the geomancers sight
　　Fortuna Major rising on a course　　　　　　　5
　　on which, and soon, it will be drowned in light;

there came to me in a dream a stuttering crone,
　　squint-eyed, clubfooted, both her hands deformed,
　　and her complexion like a whitewashed stone.

I stared at her; and just as the new Sun　　　　　10
　　breathes life to night-chilled limbs, just so my look
　　began to free her tongue, and one by one

drew straight all her deformities, and warmed
　　her dead face, till it bloomed as love would wish it
　　for its delight. When she was thus transformed,　　15

her tongue thus loosened, she began to sing
　　in such a voice that only with great pain
　　could I have turned from her soliciting.

"I am," she sang, "Sirena. I am she
　　whose voice is honeyed with such sweet enticements　20
　　it trances sailing men far out to sea.

I turned Ulysses from his wanderer's way
　　with my charmed song, and few indeed who taste
　　how well I satisfy would think to stray."

Her mouth had not yet shut when at my side　　　25
　　appeared a saintly lady, poised and eager
　　to heap confusion on the Siren's pride.

"O Virgil, Virgil! Who," she cried, "is this?"
　　Roused by her indignation, Virgil came:
　　his eyes did not once leave that soul of bliss.　　30

He seized the witch, and with one rip laid bare
   all of her front, her loins and her foul belly:
   I woke sick with the stench that rose from there.

I turned then, and my Virgil said to me:
   "I have called at least three times now. Rise and come   35
   and let us find your entrance." Willingly

I rose to my feet. Already the high day
   lit all the circles of the holy mountain.
   The Sun was at our backs as we took our way.

I followed in his steps, my brow as drawn   40
   as is a man's so bowed with thought he bends
   like half an arch of a bridge. And moving on,

I heard the words: "Come. This is where you climb,"
   pronounced in such a soft and loving voice
   as is not heard here in our mortal time.   45

With swan-like wings outspread, he who had spoken
   summoned us up between the walls of rock.
   He fanned us with his shining pinions then,

affirming over us as we went by
   "blessed are they that mourn"—for they shall have   50
   their consolation given them on high.

"What ails you?" said my Guide. "What heavy mood
   makes you stare at the ground?" (We were by then
   above the point at which the Angel stood.)

And I: "An apparition clouds my spirit,   55
   a vision from a dream so strange and dreadful
   I cannot seem to leave off thinking of it."

"Did you see that ageless witch," he said, "for whom
   —and for no other—those above us weep?
   And did you see how men escape her doom?   60

Let it teach your heels to scorn the earth, your eyes
   to turn to the high lure the Eternal King
   spins with his mighty spheres across the skies."

As falcons stare at their feet until they hear
   the wished-for call, then leap with wings outspread   65
   in eagerness for the meat that waits them there,

so did I move: filled with desire, I ran
   up the remaining length of the rock passage
   to the point at which the next great Round began.

When I stood on the fifth ledge and looked around,   70
   I saw a weeping people everywhere
   lying outstretched and face-down on the ground.

"My soul cleaves to the dust," I heard them cry
   over and over as we stood among them;
   and every word was swallowed by a sigh.   75

"O Chosen of God, spirits whose mournful rites
   both Hope and Justice make less hard to bear,
   show us the passage to the further heights."

"If you have not been sentenced to lie prone
   in the bitter dust, and seek the nearest way,   80
   keep the rim to your right as you go on."

So spoke the Poet, and so a voice replied
   from the ground in front of us. I took good note
   of what its way of speaking did not hide.

I turned my eyes to Virgil then, and he   85
   gave me a happy sign of his permission
   to do what my eyes asked. Being thus free

to act according to my own intention,
   I moved ahead and stood above that soul
   whose speaking had attracted my attention,   90

saying: "O Soul in whom these tears prepare
    that without which no soul can turn to God,
    put off a while, I beg, your greater care,

to tell me who you were, why you lie prone,   95
    and if there is some way that I may serve you
    in the world I left while still in flesh and bone."

"Why Heaven makes us turn our backs shall be
    made known to you," the spirit said, "but first
    scias quod ego fui successor Petri.

Between Sestri and Chiaveri, flowing on   100
    through a fair land, there is a pleasant river
    from which the title of my line is drawn.

A single month, a month and some few days
    I came to know on my own weary body
    how heavily the Papal Mantle weighs   105

upon the wearer who would take good care
    to keep it from the mire; compared to that
    all other burdens are as light as air.

My conversion, alas, came late; for only when
    I had been chosen Pastor of Holy Rome   110
    did I see the falseness in the lives of men.

I saw no heart's rest there, nor ease from strife,
    nor any height the flesh-bound soul might climb,
    and so I came to love this other life.

My soul was lost to God until that moment,   115
    and wholly given over to avarice;
    such was my sin, such is my punishment.

The nature of avarice is here made plain
    in the nature of its penalty; there is not
    a harsher forfeit paid on the whole mountain.   120

We would not raise our eyes to the shining spheres
   but kept them turned to mundane things: so Justice
   bends them to earth here in this place of tears.

As Avarice, there, quenched all our souls' delight   125
   in the good without which all our works are lost,
   so, here, the hand of Justice clamps us tight.

Taken and bound here hand and foot, we lie
   outstretched and motionless; and here we stay
   at the just pleasure of the Father on High."

I had knelt to him. Now I spoke once more.   130
   That spirit sensed at once my voice was nearer
   and guessed my reverence. "Why do you lower

your knees into the dust?" he said to me.
   And I: "My conscience troubled me for standing
   in the presence of your rank and dignity."   135

"Straighten your legs, my brother! Rise from error!"
   he said. "I am, like you and all the others,
   a fellow servant of one Emperor.

It is written in holy scripture *Neque nubent*;
   if ever you understood that sacred text,   140
   my reason for speaking will be evident.

Now go your way. I wish to be alone.
   Your presence here distracts me from the tears
   that make me ready. And to your last question:

I have a niece, Alagia, still on earth.   145
   If she can but avoid the bad example
   those of our line have set, her native worth

will lead her yet the way the blessed go.
And she alone remains to me below."

NOTES

1–3. An intricate passage based on the medieval belief that sunlight reflected from earth to the Moon produced warmth on the Moon, whereas sunlight reflected from the Moon to the earth produced cold on the earth. *At the hour:* Before dawn. The accumulated heat of the day would have been dissipated through the long night and could no longer temper the cold of the Moon. *overcome by Earth:* The last heat of the day is overcome by the night-chilled earth. *or at times by Saturn:* The times would be those in which Saturn draws close to the horizon. Saturn was believed to be a cold planet, as opposed to Mars, a hot planet.

5. *Fortuna Major:* A conjunction of the last stars of Aquarius and the first of Pisces, supposed to signify great good fortune. In this season these stars would be rising just before dawn; hence the sun is coming up behind them and their course will soon be drowned in light.

7 ff. DANTE'S DREAM. The Sirens were mythological creatures, usually of great beauty, and with the power of singing so entrancingly that they charmed the souls of men. They were usually presented as luring sailors at sea to their destruction.

Dante's Sirena is a Christian adaptation. She symbolizes the three remaining sins (Greed, Gluttony, and Lust), which is to say, the abandonment to physical appetites. So in lines 58–60 Dante calls her "the ageless witch, for whom—and for no other—those above us [on the three remaining ledges] weep." Dante's description of her tells all the rest: she is deformed and hideous in herself but grows beautiful in the eyes of men, and few of those she lures to her pleasures ever stray from the kind of satisfaction she gives them. Only when a Heavenly Voice (the unidentified Saintly Lady of lines 26–30) summons Reason to strip Sensual Abandon of its false trappings, does man waken from his dream to realize what abomination has entranced him.

Note that she cannot be taken to symbolize the Pleasures of the Appetite (for those were given by God for man's joy in His creation), but the Abandonment of the Soul to Excessive Physical Appetite.

22. *I turned Ulysses:* In the Homeric version Ulysses escapes the Siren's blandishments by stuffing his ears with wax and having him-

self lashed to the mast of his ship. Dante may, perhaps, be following another version of the myth, but more probably he means to portray the Siren as a liar, an allegorically significant point.

26. *a saintly lady:* She may be Beatrice, or she may be Provenient Grace, but any identification is speculative.

43. *I heard the words:* They are spoken by the Angel of Zeal. Note that Dante is moving along bowed in thought and rather slowly, his spirit still weighed by the vision of the Siren, until they pass the Angel. Once the Angel of Zeal has fanned them with his wings, however (and by now the reader knows, without being told, that the fourth *P* has disappeared from Dante's brow), Virgil, as Dante's own Reason, tells him what he should do, and Dante immediately loses his heaviness, and hurries eagerly up the remaining passage to the next Cornice.

50. *blessed are they that mourn:* The Fourth Beatitude. "Blessed are they that mourn: for they shall be comforted." (*Matthew,* iv, 5.)

73. *My soul cleaves to the dust:* Psalm CXIX.

76 ff. THE HOARDERS AND WASTERS. The sinfulness of Avarice is in the fact that it turns the soul away from God to an inordinate concern for material things. Since such immoderation can express itself in either getting or spending, the Hoarders and Wasters are here punished together and in the same way for the two extremes of the same excess, as in Hell.

84. *what its way of speaking did not hide:* The soul has said, "If you have not been sentenced to lie prone in the bitter dust." The implication is—and it is the first time the point has emerged clearly— that souls may pass through some of the Cornices without delay, if they are free of the taint of sin there punished. The speaker, his face in the dust, cannot know that Dante is a living man. He must have assumed, therefore, that Virgil's request for directions is that of a soul that has completed its purification on one of the lower Cornices, and that has no penance to do for Avarice. Dante, ever eager to grasp the nature of things, seizes upon the implication. In XIII, 133 ff., Dante makes it clear that he has penance to do for Pride, and some, though very little, for Envy. It is clear, therefore, that souls may be required to undergo penance on successive Cornices, and in

XXI and XXII Statius confirms that fact. Now we know that souls may pass through some of the Cornices without delay.

99. *scias quod ego fui successor Petri:* "Know that I was Peter's successor." The speaker is Pope Adrian V. He died in 1276 after having been Pope for thirty-eight days.

101. *a pleasant river:* The river is the Lavagna. It flows between Sestri and Chiaveri, small coastal towns near Genoa. Adrian, born Ottobuono de' Fieschi, was of the line of the Counts of Lavagna.

139. *Neque nubent:* ". . . they neither marry [nor are given in marriage but are as the angels of God in heaven]" (*Matthew,* xxii, 30). These were Christ's words when asked to which husband a re-married widow would belong in Heaven. Adrian obviously extends the meaning to include the cancellation of all earthly contracts, fealties, and honors. *Cf.* Cato's attitude toward Marcia in Canto I. It is well to remember, too, that the phrasing of the Christian marriage vow is "till death do us part."

145. *Alagia* (Ah-LAH-djah): Daughter of Niccolò di Tedisio di Ugone de' Fieschi (Oo-GO-ne day Fee-YEH-ski) and wife of Moroello (Moh-roh-ELL-oh) Malaspina, Marquis of Giovagallo (Djoe-vah-GAH-lo). Dante had been well received by Malaspina and knew and admired his wife for her good works.

Canto XX

THE FIFTH CORNICE   *The Hoarders and Wasters*
                             (The Avaricious)
            The Whip of Avarice
            The Rein of Avarice

Dante walks on after Adrian has dismissed him, wishing he might have continued the conversation, but bowing to Adrian's wish to resume his purification.

The Poets find the ledge so crowded with the souls of the Avaricious that only one narrow passage is left open to them. Dante hears a soul cry out THE WHIP OF AVARICE, a litany in praise of MARY, FABRICIUS, and ST. NICHOLAS. The sinner identifies himself as HUGH CAPET and proceeds to a DENUNCIATION OF THE CAPETIAN KINGS, the dynasty he himself founded, but which has degenerated into a succession of kings distinguished only for their bloodthirsty avarice.

Hugh Capet then explains THE REIN OF AVARICE, citing seven examples of the downfall of the Avaricious.

Dante has hardly left Capet when he feels the mountain shake as if stricken by AN EARTHQUAKE, and he hears A SHOUT OF TRIUMPH. Dante is frightened but Virgil reassures him. The Poets move on at top speed, but Dante remains deep in thought, his mind pondering these new phenomena.

What's willed must bow to what is stronger willed:
   against my pleasure, to please him, I drew
   my sponge back from the water still unfilled.

I turned: my Guide set off along the space
    left clear next to the rock; for they who drain,   5
    slow tear by tear, the sin that eats the race

left little room along the outer edge.
    Thus, as one hugs the battlements in walking
    atop a wall, we moved along the ledge.

Hell take you, She-Wolf, who in the sick feast   10
    of your ungluttable appetite have taken
    more prey on earth than any other beast!

You Heavens, in whose turnings, as some say,
    things here below are changed—when will he come
    whose power shall drive her from the light of day?   15

We moved along with measured step and slow,
    and all my thoughts were centered on those shades,
    their tears and lamentations moved me so.

And walking thus, I heard rise from the earth
    before us: "Blessed Mary!"—with a wail   20
    such as is wrung from women giving birth.

"How poor you were," the stricken voice went on,
    "is testified to all men by the stable
    in which you laid your sacred burden down."

And then: "O good Fabricius, you twice   25
    refused great wealth that would have stained your
        honor,
    and chose to live in poverty, free of vice."

These words had pleased me so that I drew near
    the place from which they seemed to have been
        spoken,
    eager to know what soul was lying there.   30

The voice was speaking now of the largesse
    St. Nicholas bestowed on the three virgins
    to guide their youth to virtuous steadiness.

"O soul," I said, "whose words recite such good,
   let me know who you were, and why no other   35
   joins in your praises of such rectitude.

If I return to finish the short race
   remaining of that life that ends so soon,
   your words will not lack some reward of grace."

"Not for such comfort as the world may give   40
   do I reply," he said, "but that such light
   of grace should shine on you while yet you live.

I was the root of that malignant tree
   which casts its shadow on all Christendom
   so that the soil bears good fruit only rarely.   45

But if Douay and Lille and Bruges and Ghent
   were strong again, their vengeance would be swift;
   and that it may, I pray the King of Judgment.

I was Hugh Capet in my mortal state.
   From me stem all the Philips and the Louis'   50
   who have occupied the throne of France of late.

I was born in Paris as a butcher's son.
   When the old line of kings had petered out
   to one last heir, who wore a monk's gray gown,

I found that I held tight in my own hand   55
   the reins of state, and that my new wealth gave me
   such power, and such allies at my command,

that my son's head, with pomp and sacrament
   rose to the widowed crown of France. From him
   those consecrated bones took their descent.   60

Till the great dowry of Provence increased
   my race so that it lost its sense of shame,
   it came to little, but did no harm at least.

That was the birth of its rapacity,
    its power, its lies. Later—to make amends—   65
    it took Normandy, Ponthieu, and Gascony.

Charles came to Italy, and—to make amends—
    he victimized Conrádin. Then he sent
    Saint Thomas back to Heaven—to make amends.

I see a time, not far off, that brings forth   70
    another Charles from France. It shall make clear
    to many what both he and his are worth.

He comes alone, unarmed but for the lance
    of Judas, which he drives so hard he bursts
    the guts of Florence with the blow he plants.   75

He wins no land there; only sin and shame.
    And what is worse for him is that he holds
    such crimes too lightly to repent his blame.

The third, once hauled from his own ship, I see
    selling his daughter, haggling like a pirate   80
    over a girl sold into slavery.

O Avarice, what more harm can you do?
    You have taken such a hold on my descendants
    they sell off their own flesh and blood for you!

But dwarfing all crimes, past or yet to be,   85
    I see Alagna entered, and, in His Vicar,
    Christ Himself dragged in captivity.

I see Him mocked again and crucified,
    the gall and vinegar once more sent up.
    He dies again—with *live* thieves at His side.   90

I see another Pilate, so full of spite
    not even that suffices: his swollen sails
    enter the very Temple without right.

O God, my Lord, when shall my soul rejoice
   to see Thy retribution, which, lying hidden,   95
   sweetens Thine anger in Thy secret choice?

What you first heard me cry in adoration
   of that one only Bride of the Holy Ghost,
   which made you turn and ask an explanation,

is the litany we add to every prayer   100
   as long as it is day. When the Sun sets
   we raise the counter-cry on the night air.

We cry then how Pygmalion of old
   was made a traitor, thief, and parricide
   by his insatiable sick lust for gold;   105

how Midas suffered when his miser's prayer
   was answered, and became forever after
   the legend of a ludicrous despair;

and then we tell how Achan, covetous,
   stole from the booty, for which Joshua's rage   110
   still falls upon him—so it seems to us.

We cry Sapphira's and her husband's blame;
   we praise the hooves that battered Heliodorus;
   then round the ledge runs Polymnestor's name,

foul to all time with Polydorus' blood.   115
   Then we conclude the litany crying: 'Crassus,
   you supped on gold—tell us, did it taste good?'

We wail or mutter in our long remorse
   according to the inner spur that drives us,
   at times with more, at others with less force: 120

thus I was not the only one who praised
   the good we tell by day; but, as it happened,
   the only one nearby whose voice was raised."

We had already left him to his prayers
   and were expending every ounce of strength   125
   on the remaining distance to the stairs,

when suddenly I felt the mountain shake
   as if it tottered. Such a numb dread seized me
   as a man feels when marching to the stake.

Not even Delos, in that long ago   130
   before Latona went there to give birth
   to Heaven's eyes, was ever shaken so.

Then there went up a cry on every side,
   so loud that the sweet Master, bending close
   said: "Do not fear, for I am still your Guide."   135

"Glory to God in the Highest!" rang a shout
   from every throat—as I could understand
   from those nearby, whose words I could make out.

We stood there motionless, our souls suspended—
   as had the shepherds who first heard that hymn—   140
   until the ground grew still and the hymn ended.

Then we pushed on our holy way once more,
   studying those prostrate souls who had already
   resumed their lamentation, as before.

I never felt my soul assaulted so—   145
   unless my memory err—as in that war
   between my ignorance and desire to know

the explanation of that shock and shout;
   nor dared I ask, considering our haste;
   nor could I of myself, looking about,   150

find anywhere the key to what I sought.
So I moved on, timid and sunk in thought.

NOTES

2. *him:* Adrian. Dante's wish to know more had to bow to Adrian's greater wish to resume his purification. Thus, Dante had to withdraw the sponge of his desire to know, from the water of Adrian's presence, before he had absorbed all he wished for.

4–9. THE CROWDING OF THE LEDGE. The point, of course, is that Avarice is so common a sin that the ledge is jammed full of sinners, so many in fact that the space between their shades and the open side of the ledge is too narrow for safe passage. Virgil leads Dante, therefore, along the narrow space between the bodies and the inner cliff-face.

10–15. *She-Wolf:* See the three beasts encountered by Dante in *Inferno*, I, 33 ff. *have taken more prey:* As in lines 4–9, above, Avarice has infected more souls than has any other sin. *when will he come:* Another reference to the mysterious Greyhound who will come to make the world pure again and who will drive the She-Wolf from the light of day, back into Hell. (See *Inferno*, I, 95–104, and note.)

20–33. THE WHIP OF AVARICE. Once more the examples that make up the Whip are cried aloud by the sinners themselves. On this Cornice, however, all the sinners cry out the examples as impulse moves them, adding them as a litany to each prayer they recite as part of their penance. The prayer of this Cornice is, of course, from Psalm CXIX, "My soul cleaves to the dust." (See Canto XIX, 73.)

A further peculiarity of the Whip and the Rein on this ledge is that the sinners recite the Whip by day and the Rein by night.

The first example of the Whip (lines 20–24) praises the blessed poverty of Mary. So great was it that she gave birth to Jesus in a manger. Yet in such poverty she achieved blessedness in comparison with which all the possessions of the world are as baubles.

The second example (lines 25–27) praises the honorable poverty of Fabricius Caius Luscinus, Roman Consul in 282 B.C. and Censor in 275. He refused to deal in the bribes and gifts which were normally assumed to be perquisites of such high offices, and he died so poor that the state had to bury him, and had also to provide dowries for his daughters.

The third example (lines 31–33) cites Saint Nicholas, Bishop of

Myra in Lycia, who was born rich and gave all his riches to the poor. A local minor nobleman found himself so poor that he could not provide dowries for his daughters. He was about to turn them over to a life of sin in order that they might make a living, when Nicholas heard of their plight and threw three bags of gold through the nobleman's window, one on each of three successive nights. Thus the father was able to buy husbands for the girls, and thus Nicholas guided their youth to "virtuous steadiness."

34–96. *Hugh Capet:* Dante seems to confuse Hugh, Duke of the Franks (died 956), and his son, Hugh Capet (King of France 987–996), into one person. Hugh Capet founded the Capetian dynasty of French kings, succeeding Louis V, the last of the Carlovingian line founded by Charlemagne.

Hugh Capet begins by replying to Dante's customary promise of earthly recollection that he has little interest in any good the world can do him. Since he has been in Purgatory 344 years (by 1300), it seems reasonable enough to assume that he is well advanced in otherworldliness.

He then laments the degeneracy of the line he himself founded and prays God's vengeance upon it soon, as it would already have fallen had Flanders the power to avenge itself. Douay, Lille, Bruges, and Ghent are the four principal cities of Flanders. Philip the Fair, King of France, and his brother, Charles of Valois, warred on Flanders. In 1299 Charles negotiated the surrender of Ghent by making liberal promises, which he later ignored, dealing harshly with the conquered. The vengeance Hugh Capet prayed for as of 1300 had already taken place by the time Dante wrote these lines, the Flemish having inflicted a major defeat upon the French at the Battle of Courtrai in 1302.

50. *all the Philips and the Louis':* From 1060 to 1300 all the Kings of France bore one or another of these names.

52. *a butcher's son:* Dante follows here a popular but erroneous legend: the meat business was not that good in tenth-century France. King Hugh Capet, as noted, was the son of Hugh Capet, Duke of France, of Burgundy, and of Aquitaine, and Count of Paris and of Orleans. The history that follows is full of similar confusions, some of which may best be left to scholars, but some of which must be explained for a basic understanding of the text.

53. *the old line of kings:* The Carlovingian dynasty.

54. *one last heir, who wore a monk's gray gown:* There is no evidence that Charles of Lorraine, the last of the Carlovingians, took holy orders. He died in prison, put there by Hugh Capet. Two sons born to him while he was in prison were hustled away to Germany, where they disappeared.

58. *my son's head:* The son of King Hugh Capet was Robert I, but Dante is clearly having King Hugh speak now as if he were Duke Hugh.

60. *those consecrated bones:* The Capetian kings. By the sacramental anointment which was part of the coronation, the King's person became sacred.

61–63. *the great dowry of Provence:* Raymond Berengar was Count of Provence. After the Count's death, Louis IX (St. Louis) married the eldest of the Count's four daughters, and Louis' brother, Charles of Anjou, married one of the younger daughters. The brothers then seized all of Provence, claiming it as their wives' dowry. *lost its sense of shame:* Dante may have meant that in seizing Provence they acquired a title so ancient that it wiped out the taint of low origin Dante ascribes to the Capets. The more obvious meaning is that in waxing great on so much wealth, they lost all sense of just reckoning.

65. *to make amends:* The triple repetition is meant as bitter irony: after each bad action the French kings "make amends" by doing something worse.

66. *Normandy, Ponthieu, and Gascony:* Philip II took Normandy from England in 1202. Philip the Fair took Ponthieu and Gascony from England in 1295.

67. *Charles:* Charles of Anjou, brother of Louis IX. When Clement IV excommunicated Manfred (see III, 103 ff., note), he summoned Charles to Italy and crowned him King of Sicily. In 1266 Charles defeated Manfred at Benevento. In 1268 he defeated Conradin, Manfred's nephew, at Tagliacozzo, and had him beheaded.

68–69. *sent Saint Thomas back to Heaven:* Dante is following an unfounded popular legend that Charles had Thomas Aquinas poisoned.

71. *another Charles:* Charles of Valois, brother of Philip the Fair. He was called Charles Sans Terre. Boniface VIII called him to Florence in 1301, presumably as peacemaker, but actually to destroy all who opposed Papal policy.

76. *He wins no land there:* A taunt at the fact that Charles had inherited no land. He will not improve his temporal state, says Hugh, and will only blacken his honor and his soul.

79. *The third:* The third Charles is Charles II of Anjou (Charles the Lame), King of Naples and of Apulia. He was born in 1243 and died in 1309. *once hauled from his own ship:* In June of 1284 the admiral of Peter III of Aragon sailed into the Bay of Naples. Charles, against express orders left by his father, allowed himself to be lured out to meet the Aragonese and was easily taken prisoner. Two hundred of his court were taken with him and were executed by the Aragonese to avenge the death of Conradin. Charles escaped with his life but remained a prisoner in Sicily until 1288.

80. *selling his daughter:* In 1305 Charles concluded a marriage contract between his very young daughter and Azzo (or Ezzo) VIII of Este, then forty-two. For the honor of marrying the king's daughter, Azzo settled for practically no dowry, and made very valuable gifts to his father-in-law.

85–93. *But dwarfing all crimes, past or yet to be:* The crime was the capture and humiliation of Pope Boniface VIII at the instigation of Philip the Fair. Philip had charged Boniface with heresy, and Boniface had prepared a bull excommunicating Philip. On September 7, 1303, before the bull could be published, Philip sent a large force to Alagna (now Anagni) under Guillaume de Nogaret and Sciarra (SHAH-rah) Colonna. They ransacked the palace and the cathedral treasury, and subjected Boniface to great indignities, threatening to haul him off in chains to execution. Boniface, then eighty-six, was released in a few days but his mind seems to have cracked, and he died of "hysterical seizures" in Rome within a few weeks, on October 12, 1303.

Dante's attitude in this matter is characteristic. Much as he loathed Boniface for his corruption of the Papacy, Dante saw the office itself as sacred, for Boniface was officially Christ's Vicar on Earth. Thus to offend his person was to offend the person of Christ

Himself. King Philip's all-dwarfing crime, therefore, was against the very body of Christ.

90. *He dies again—with* live *thieves at His side:* Christ died between dead thieves who had been crucified with Him. In the person of Boniface, He "died" again, but with live thieves (de Nogaret and Colonna) at His side.

91. *another Pilate:* Philip. As Pilate turned Christ over to His tormentors, so Philip turned Him over—in the person of His Vicar—to de Nogaret and Colonna.

93. *enter the very Temple:* Philip out-Pilated Pilate by breaking into the Temple. The reference here is to Philip's suppression of the Knights Templars and the seizure of their lands and treasuries in 1314. He tortured those he captured and forced Pope Clement V to legalize the action. (See VII, 109, note.)

95–96. *which, lying hidden:* God's retribution. It lies hidden from men, but is known to God in His omniscient prevision, and will take place at His pleasure. His anger, therefore, is sweetened by the fact that His vengeance is already calculated and certain.

97–120. THE REIN OF AVARICE. The Rein of Avarice consists of seven examples of the downfall caused by Avarice. Note that although Dante divides Avarice into its two extremes of Hoarding and Wasting, the examples of the downfall of the Avaricious are all of what might be called Acquisitive Avarice.

(103–105) *Pygmalion:* Brother of Queen Dido. He killed King Sichaeus in the temple, stole his gold, and drove Dido into exile. Dante calls him a parricide because Sichaeus was not only his brother-in-law but his uncle. (He is not to be confused with the Pygmalion of Greek legend who fell in love with a statue.) Thus Avarice led him to damnation. If Pygmalion's crime is taken to be Treachery to his Host or Master, there is a strong probability (see *Inferno,* XXXIII, 128–147) that his soul instantly descended to Ptolomea or Judaïca, while his body still lived.

(106–108) *Midas:* The famous King of Phrygia who did a favor for Bacchus and was promised the fulfillment of a wish. Midas wished for the power to change all things to gold at his touch. Bacchus granted the wish, but Midas began to starve since even his food turned to gold, and he had to beg Bacchus to take the power from him. The best-known version of the story is in Ovid's *Metamorphoses*, XI, 85–145.

(109–111) *Achan:* After the fall of Jericho, Joshua commanded that all the booty should go into the Temple as the Lord's. Achan pilfered some treasures for himself and Joshua had him and his family stoned to death. (*Joshua,* vii, 1–26.)

(112) *Sapphira and her husband:* They were entrusted to sell some property held in common by the apostles, but they returned only part of the sale price, representing it as the whole sum. When St. Peter reproved them for their fraud, they fell dead at his feet. (*Acts,* v, 1–11.)

(113) *Heliodorus:* He was sent to Jerusalem by the King of Syria with orders to steal the Treasury but was driven from the Temple by the apparition of a great horse that battered him with its forefeet. "And it seemed that he that sat upon the horse had complete harness of gold." (*II Maccabees,* iii, 25.)

(114) *Polymnestor:* King of Thrace and a friend of King Priam. During the siege of Troy, Priam sent his youngest son, Polydorus, into Thrace for Polymnestor's protection. A considerable treasure accompanied the boy, and Polymnestor killed him for it as soon as Troy fell. Hecuba, mother of Polydorus, later avenged her son by blinding Polymnestor and killing him. *Aeneid,* III, 19–68; *Metamorphoses,* XIII, 429–575; and Euripides' *Hecuba* all recount part of the story. (See also *Inferno,* XXX, 16, note.)

(116) *Crassus:* Marcus Licinius Crassus (114–53 B.C.), Triumvir of Rome with Julius Caesar and Pompey, and infamous for his avarice, bribe taking, and plundering. He was taken in battle by the Parthians and his head was brought to King Hyrodes, who had molten gold poured into its mouth, thus mocking the memory of Crassus' bloody avarice by serving his severed head a last feast of gold.

130–132. *Not even Delos . . . Latona . . . Heaven's eyes:* Latona was pregnant by Jupiter and was chased from place to place by the jealous Juno. According to one legend, Jupiter caused an earthquake to raise the island of Delos from the bottom of the sea as a place of refuge for Latona. According to another, Delos was a floating island left over from the original division of the sea and the land and tossed about by waves until Jupiter fixed it in place for Latona. On Delos, Latona gave birth to Apollo (the Sun) and Diana (the Moon), hence, the twin eyes of Heaven. Dante regularly draws parallel-and-contrasting examples from both the Classical and the Judeo-Christian worlds. Note that in this example and the next he cites divine birth in both of those worlds.

140. *who first heard that hymn:* The shepherds of Bethlehem. It was first sung, according to *Luke,* ii, 14, to announce the birth of Christ.

145–152. I have taken substantial liberties with these lines in trying to make Dante's intent clear. A literal rendering might read: "No ignorance ever with so much war [within me] made me so desirous to know—if my memory does not err in this—as I seemed to be at this time, pondering [the explanation of the earthquake and the shout]; nor, since we were hurrying so, did I dare ask; nor could I by myself see anything [that would explain them] there: thus I moved on, timid and deep in thought."

Canto XXI

THE FIFTH CORNICE   *The Hoarders and Wasters*
                                      (The Avaricious)
                          Statius

Burning with desire to know the cause of the "shock and shout," Dante hurries after Virgil along the narrow way. Suddenly they are overtaken by a figure that salutes them. Virgil answers, and the new soul, taking the Poets to be souls who may not enter Heaven, expresses astonishment at finding them in this place.

Virgil explains his and Dante's state and asks the explanation of the earthquake and of the great cry. The new soul explains that these phenomena occur only when a soul arises from its final purification and begins its final ascent to Heaven. The newcomer then reveals that he is STATIUS and recites his earthly history, ending with a glowing statement of his love for the works of Virgil. To have lived in Virgil's time, says Statius, he would have endured another year of the pains he has just ended.

Virgil warns Dante, with a glance, to be silent, but Dante cannot suppress a half smile, which Statius notices, and asks Dante to explain. He thus learns that he is, in fact, standing in the presence of Virgil. Immediately he kneels to embrace Virgil's knees, but Virgil tells him to arise at once, for such earthly vanities are out of place between shades.

The natural thirst that nothing satisfies
    except that water the Samaritan woman
    begged of Our Lord, as St. John testifies,

burned me; haste drove me on the encumbered way
   behind my Guide, and I was full of grief   5
   at the just price of pain those spirits pay;

when suddenly—just as Luke lets us know
   that Christ, new risen from the tomb, appeared
   to the two travelers on the road—just so

as we moved there with bowed heads lest we tread   10
   upon some soul, a shade appeared behind us;
   nor did we guess its presence till it said:

"Brothers, God give you peace." My Guide and I
   turned quickly toward his voice, and with a sign
   my Master gave the words their due reply.   15

Then he began: "May the True Court's behest,
   which relegates me to eternal exile,
   establish you in peace among the blest."

"But how, if you are souls denied God's bliss,"
   he said—and we forged onward as he spoke—   20
   "have you climbed up the stairs as far as this?"

My Teacher then: "You cannot fail to see,
   if you observe the Angel's mark upon him,
   that he will reign among the just. But she

whose wheel turns day and night has not yet spun   25
   the full length of the thread that Clotho winds
   into a hank for him and everyone.

Therefore, his soul, sister to yours and mine,
   since it cannot see as we do, could not
   climb by itself. And, therefore, Will Divine   30

has drawn me out of the great Throat of Woe
   to guide him on his way, and I shall lead him
   far as my knowledge gives me power to go.

But tell me, if you can, what was the shock
   we felt just now? And why did all the mountain   35
   cry with one voice down to its last moist rock?"

He struck the needle's eye of my desire
   so surely with his question, that my thirst,
   by hope alone, lost something of its fire.

The shade began: "The holy rules that ring   40
   the mountain round do not permit upon it
   any disordered or unusual thing,

nor any change. Only what Heaven draws
   out of itself into itself again—
   that and nothing else—can be a cause.   45

Therefore, there never can be rain nor snow,
   nor hail, nor dew, nor hoarfrost higher up
   than the little three-step stairway there below.

Neither dense clouds nor films of mist appear,
   nor lightning's flash, nor Thaumas' glowing daughter,   50
   who shifts about from place to place back there;

nor can dry vapors raise their shattering heat
   above the top of these three steps I mentioned
   upon which Peter's vicar plants his feet.

Shocks may occur below, severe or slight,   55
   but tremors caused by winds locked in the earth
   —I know not how—do not reach to this height.

It trembles here whenever a soul feels
   so healed and purified that it gets up
   or moves to climb; and then the great hymn peals.   60

The soul, surprised, becomes entirely free
   to change its cloister, moved by its own will,
   which is its only proof of purity.

Before purgation it does wish to climb,
    but the will High Justice sets against that wish   65
    moves it to will pain as it once willed crime.

And I, who in my torments have lain here
    five hundred years and more, have only now
    felt my will free to seek a better sphere.

It was for that you felt the mountain move   70
    and heard the pious spirits praise the Lord—
    ah may He call them soon to go above!"

These were the spirit's words to us, and mine
    cannot express how they refreshed my soul,
    but as the thirst is greater, the sweeter the wine.   75

And my wise Leader: "Now I see what snare
    holds you, how you slip free, why the mount trembles,
    and why your joint rejoicing fills the air.

Now it would please me greatly, if you please,
    to know your name and hear in your own words   80
    why you have lain so many centuries."

"In the days when the good Titus, with the aid
    of the Almighty King, avenged the wounds
    that poured the blood Iscariot betrayed,

I lived renowned back there," replied that soul,   85
    "in the most honored and enduring name,
    but still without the faith that makes us whole.

My verses swelled with such melodious breath
    that, from Toulouse, Rome called me to herself,
    and there I merited a laurel wreath.   90

Statius my name, and it still lives back there.
    I sang of Thebes, then of the great Achilles,
    but found the second weight too great to bear.

The sparks that were my seeds of passion came
   from that celestial fire which has enkindled   95
   more than a thousand poets; I mean the flame

of the *Aeneid,* the mother that brought forth,
   the nurse that gave suck to my song. Without it
   I could not have weighed half a penny's worth.

And to have lived back there in Virgil's time   100
   I would agree to pass another year
   in the same banishment from which I climb."

Virgil, at these last words, shot me a glance
   that said in silence, "Silence!" But man's will
   is not supreme in every circumstance: 105

for tears and laughter come so close behind
   the passions they arise from, that they least
   obey the will of the most honest mind.

I did no more than half smile, but that shade
   fell still and looked me in the eye—for there   110
   the secrets of the soul are most betrayed.

"So may the road you travel lead to grace,"
   he said, "what was the meaning of the smile
   that I saw flash, just now, across your face?"

Now am I really trapped on either side: 115
   one tells me to be still, one begs me speak.
   So torn I heave a sigh, and my sweet Guide

understands all its meaning. "Never fear,"
   he says to me, "speak up, and let him know
   what he has asked so movingly to hear."   120

At which I said: "Perhaps my smiling thus
   has made you marvel, Ancient Soul; but now
   listen to something truly marvelous:

this one who guides my eyes aloft is he,
    Virgil, from whom you drew the strength to sing   125
    the deeds of men and gods in poetry.

The only motive for my smiling lay
    in your own words. If you conceived another,
    as you love truth, pray put the thought away."

He was bending to embrace my Teacher's knee,   130
    but Virgil said: "No, brother. Shade you are,
    and shade am I. You must not kneel to me."

And Statius, rising, said: "So may you find
    the measure of the love that warms me to you
    when for it I lose all else from my mind,   135

forgetting we are empty semblances
and taking shadows to be substances."

NOTES

1. *The natural thirst:* "All men naturally desire knowledge." (Aristotle, *Metaphysics*, I, 1.) *that nothing satisfies:* "In acquiring knowledge, there always grows the thirst for more." (*Il Convivio*, IV, 12.)

2–3. *that water the Samaritan woman begged:* At Jacob's Well, Jesus asked the Samaritan woman for a drink, and she showed surprise that a Jew should make such a request of her, but Jesus replied that had she known who he was, she would have asked him for a drink and he would have given her the living water of the truth. "The woman saith unto him, Sir, give me this water that I thirst not. . . ." (*John,* iv, 6–15.)

7. *as Luke lets us know:* "And behold two of them [James and John] went that same day to a village called Emmaus. . . . And it came to pass that, while they communed together and reasoned, Jesus himself drew near, and went with them." (*Luke,* xxiv, 13–15.)

11. a shade appeared: The shade is Statius, for whom see note to
lines 82 ff.

14–15. with a sign . . . due reply: There were regular formulas for
greeting and reply among monks of the Middle Ages. Most com-
monly, "God give you peace" or "God's peace be with you," would
be answered, "And with thy spirit." Virgil's answer is not verbal. He
replies with what must have been a gesture of benediction.

23. the Angel's mark: The three remaining *P*'s on Dante's brow,
which identify him as a saved soul, *i.e.,* as one who will enter
Heaven when he has completed his purification.

24–27. she: Lachesis. She is the Fate (or Parca) who spins the
Thread of Life. Her sister Clotho winds each man's thread about her
distaff, forming it into a hank begun at each man's birth. The third
sister, Atropos, cuts the thread at the end of the man's life. Virgil
means simply that Dante is not yet dead, *i.e.,* his thread has not been
cut. (The Poets are on the western side of the mountain with the sun
in the east, and Dante casts no identifying shadow.)

36. cry with one voice down to its last moist rock: I.e., "Down to
the shore where the reeds grow." "Rock" is rhyme-forced. Dante
says, literally, "down to its moist feet," and the shore is described
not as rocky but as muddy.

40 ff. STATIUS' REPLY. Virgil has asked the reason for the
earthquake and the shout. Statius begins his elaborate reply in good
scholastic form by explaining the principles on which the answer
must be based, and having stated them in brief, he goes on to de-
velop each in detail.

The first principle is that nothing on the mountain is subject to
change except within itself, for nothing there is subject to external
forces. Every soul in Purgatory is effectively in Heaven, and beyond
the Gate evil does not exist.

The second principle follows from the first. The soul issues from
the hand of God. When the soul goes from Purgatory to Heaven,
therefore, it is not entering from outside. Heaven is simply receiving
its own again. Only that motion of Heaven's receiving its own from
itself to itself can, therefore, be a *cause* on the mountain, "cause"
being "that which gives rise to an effect."

48. *the little three-step stairway:* The three steps that lead to the Gate of Purgatory mark the highest point to which the weathers of the world (literally and in every extended sense) can reach. Above them, all that is, is from God.

50. *Thaumas' glowing daughter:* Iris, the rainbow. Daughter of the Centaur Thaumas and of Electra. Her sisters were the Harpies. Like her sisters, she was a messenger of the Gods and came and went by way of the rainbow, with which she became identified.

The rainbow is an especially apt symbol of mutability. Note, too, that it always appears *away* from the Sun, never between the Sun and the observer. Taking Iris to represent changeableness and the Sun to represent God, one may pursue a number of interesting allegories.

52. *dry vapors:* For Dante's theory of wet and dry vapors as the origin of storms, see *Inferno,* XXIV, last note. The theory is from Aristotle. Wet vapors cause rain, hail, dew, and hoarfrost, as specified in lines 46–47. Dry vapors, if they are free, produce lightning and thunder. If, however, they enter the earth as winds and are locked inside, they cause earthquakes. But such terrestrial earthquakes (lines 55–60) cannot be felt above the three steps at the Gate.

58. *whenever a soul feels:* Once again the point is made that the Purgatorial souls are free of external restraints. Each decides within itself when it is free to move up.

59. *that it gets up:* If the soul has been crawling with the Proud, seated with the Envious, or lying with the Avaricious, its moment of purity is achieved when it feels the will to get up.

60. *or moves to climb:* If the soul has been circling with the Wrathful, the Slothful, the Gluttonous, or the Lustful, it would not need to get up: its moment of purity would be achieved when it feels moved to stop circling and to move toward the ascent. *to climb:* Statius must mean "to climb to Paradise" rather than merely to a higher ledge. As Dante has already hinted, and as Statius soon demonstrates, a soul may pass unchecked through those ledges that punish sins of which it is not guilty. Thus on completing a given penance, a soul may move on to another, or directly to Paradise. There is no conclusive evidence that the mountain shakes and the hymn peals only when souls achieve their final purification, but the very scale of the celebration suggests that it is reserved for graduation exercises

only. If the shock and shout occurred every time a soul moved from one ledge to another, there is every likelihood that Dante would have touched things off every time he passed up one of the stairways, or every time an Angel removed one of his *P*'s.

62. *cloister:* An especially apt choice in that "cloister" implies (a) confinement, (b) confinement of one's own free will, and (c) a life ordered by strict rules of worship and discipline. Dante, because "soul" is feminine in Italian, uses "convent."

64–66. *wish . . . will:* I am not happy about these terms, but they are the only ones I could make work within prosodic necessity. The intended distinction is between "impulse" (the *relative will* of scholastic philosophy) and what might be called "innate desire" (the *absolute will* of scholastic philosophy). Thus the passage in extended paraphrase: "Before purification it does have a relative will to climb, but the absolute will that High Justice sets against that relative will, gives the soul the same sort of will to suffer penitential pain that it once had [in life] toward the crime it now expiates." (Compare the state of the Infernal souls who cross Acheron driven by their own absolute will to yearn for what they fear.)

82 ff. STATIUS. Publius Papinius Statius (*c.* A.D. 45–96) is a central figure of the *Purgatorio* and an especially complex one. He remains with Dante till the very end of the ascent. Thus Dante completes his climb to the presence of Beatrice (Divine Love) in the company of Virgil as Human Reason, and of Statius, who must be taken as a symbol of the soul's triumphant redemption.

Thus Statius has a major role, though his known history hardly serves to explain it. In life he was a Latin poet much admired by Dante, though it is difficult to see why Dante, himself so stylistically sparse, should admire a writer as prolix as was Statius. Statius' main work was the *Thebaid,* an epic of the Seven against Thebes (so line 92: "I sang of Thebes"). He was engaged in an epic of the Trojan War, the *Achilleid,* at his death (so line 93, "but found the second weight too great to bear," *i.e.,* he died bearing it). An earlier collection of poems, the *Silvae,* came to light after Dante's time.

Statius was born in Naples and lived in Rome. Dante confused him in part with Lucius Statius Ursulus, a rhetorician of Toulouse, and has Statius give his birthplace accordingly in line 89.

Why Dante should have chosen Statius to represent the triumph

of the purified soul is a matter open to any careful reader's specula-
tion. The very fact that so little is known of Statius' life may be a
point in favor, for it leaves Dante free to attribute qualities to Statius
without embarrassment from history. (There is, for example, no
slightest historical evidence that Statius turned Christian.)

If, as seems likely, Dante himself invented this legend, its own el-
ements best explain it, for so interpreted, Statius becomes a sym-
bolic figure joining the Roman and the Christian past, a theme
always dear to Dante. Thus Statius may be seen as a lesser Virgil and
a greater: a less perfect writer, but a greater soul in the gift of
Christ's redemption. Thus he may be taken as springing from that
cardinal point in Church history at which the greatness of the Ro-
man past and the glory of the Christian present are joined. So Dante
may now climb guided not only by Virgil (as Human Reason, Phi-
losophy, and the Classic Virtues of Ancient Rome) but by Statius
(those same qualities transformed by Faith and thus nearer to God).
Between Virgil and Statius, that is, Dante now climbs in the com-
pany of the total Roman tradition.

Dramatically, of course, the possibilities inherent in presenting
Statius to Virgil must have been especially inviting.

82. *the good Titus:* Roman Emperor, A.D. 79–81. In A.D. 70 in the
reign of his father, Vespasian, Titus besieged and took Jerusalem.
Thus, with God's help, Rome avenged the death (the wounds) of
Christ. So Dante, within his inevitable parochialism, chose to take
that passage of history. The Jews, one may be sure, found less cause
for rejoicing in the goodness of Titus.

86. *in the most honored and enduring name:* Of poet.

Canto XXII

———◆◆◆———

THE ASCENT TO THE SIXTH CORNICE
THE SIXTH CORNICE   *The Gluttons*
                 The Tree
          The Whip of Gluttony

*The Poets have passed the Angel who guards the ascent, and
Dante has had one more P removed from his forehead. So
lightened, he walks easily behind Virgil and Statius despite
their rapid ascent, listening eagerly to their conversation.*

*Virgil declares his great regard for Statius, and Statius ex-
plains that he was on the Fifth Cornice for Wasting rather
than for Hoarding. He adds that he would certainly have
been damned, had Virgil's poetry not led him to see his error.
For Virgil, he acknowledges, not only inspired his song, but
showed him the road to faith, whereby he was baptized, though
secretly, for fear of the persecutions—a lukewarmness for
which he spent four hundred years on the Fourth Cornice.*

*Statius then names his favorite poets of antiquity and asks
where they are. Virgil replies that they are with him in Limbo.
He then cites many who have not been mentioned before as
being among his eternal companions.*

*At this point the Poets arrive at THE SIXTH CORNICE
and, moving to the right, come upon AN ENORMOUS TREE
laden with fruits. From its foliage a voice cries out the exam-
ples of abstinence that constitute THE WHIP OF GLUTTONY.*

We had, by now, already left behind
    the Angel who directs to the Sixth Round.
    He had erased a stigma from my brow,

and said that they who thirst for rectitude
   are blessèd, but he did not say "who hunger"   5
   when he recited that Beatitude.

I, lighter than on any earlier stairs,
   followed those rapid spirits, and I found it
   no strain at all to match my pace to theirs.

Virgil began: "When virtue lights in us   10
   a fire of love, that love ignites another
   within the soul that sees its burning. Thus,

ever since Juvenal came down to be
   one of our court in the Infernal Limbo,
   and told me of your great regard for me,   15

my good will toward you has been of a sort
   I had not felt for any unseen person;
   such as will make the climb ahead seem short.

But tell me—and if I presume too much
   in slackening the rein this way, forgive me   20
   as a friend would and answer me as such:

how, amid all the wisdom you possessed—
   and which you won to by such diligence—
   could Avarice find a place within your breast?"

At these words Statius let a brief smile play   25
   across his lips, and fade. Then he replied:
   "I hear love's voice in every word you say.

Often, indeed, appearances give rise
   to groundless doubts in us, and false conclusions,
   the true cause being hidden from our eyes.   30

Seeing me on the ledge from which I rose,
   you have inferred my sin was Avarice;
   an inference your question clearly shows.

Know then that my particular offense
   was all too far from Avarice: I wept   35
   thousands of months for riotous expense.

Had I not turned from prodigality
   in pondering those lines in which you cry,
   as if you raged against humanity:

'To what do you not drive man's appetite   40
   O cursèd gold-lust!'—I should now be straining
   in the grim jousts of the Infernal night.

I understood then that our hands could spread
   their wings too wide in spending, and repented
   of that, and all my sins, in grief and dread.   45

How many shall rise bald to Judgment Day
   because they did not know this sin to grieve it
   in life, or as their last breaths slipped away!

For when the opposite of a sin, as here,
   is as blameworthy as the sin itself,   50
   both lose their growth together and turn sere.

If, then, I lay so long in my distress
   among the Avaricious where they weep,
   it was to purge the opposite excess."

"But when you sang of the fierce warfare bred   55
   between the twin afflictions of Jocasta,"
   the singer of the sweet *Bucolics* said,

"from what you said when Clio tuned your strain,
   it would not seem that you had found the faith
   without the grace of which good works are vain.   60

If that be so, what Sun or beacon shone
   into your mist that you set sail to follow
   the Fisherman?" And that long-waiting one:

"You were the lamp that led me from that night.
    You led me forth to drink Parnassian waters;   65
    then on the road to God you shed your light.

When you declared, 'A new birth has been given.
    Justice returns, and the first age of man.
    And a new progeny descends from Heaven'—

you were as one who leads through a dark track   70
    holding the light behind—useless to you,
    precious to those who followed at your back.

Through you I flowered to song and to belief.
    That you may know all, let me stretch my hand
    to paint in full what I have sketched in brief.   75

The world, by then, was swollen with the birth
    of True Belief sown by those messengers
    the Everlasting Kingdom had sent forth.

Those words of yours I quoted, so agreed
    with the new preachers', that I took to going   80
    to where they gathered to expound the Creed.

In time, they grew so holy in my eyes
    that in the persecutions of Domitian
    the tears burst from me when I heard their cries.

And long as I remained upon the vexed   85
    shores of that life, I helped them, and they taught me,
    by their strict ways, to scorn all other sects.

Before my poem sang how the Greeks drew near
    the Theban rivers, I had been baptized,
    but kept my faith a secret, out of fear,   90

pretending to be pagan as before;
    for which lukewarmness I was made to circle
    the Ledge of Sloth four hundred years and more.

Now may you please to tell me—you who rent
    the veil that hid me from this good I praise—   95
    while we have time to spare in the ascent,

where is our ancient Terence now? and where
    Caecilius, Varro, Plautus?—are they damned?
    and if they are, what torments must they bear?"

—"All these are there with Persius and the rest,   100
    myself among them, who surround that Greek
    who outsucked all men at the Muses' breast.

All walk the first ledge of the dark of Hell;
    and we speak often of the glorious mountain
    on which the Nine who suckled us still dwell.   105

Euripides is with us, Antiphon,
    Athenian Agathon, Simonides,
    and many more who wore the laurel crown.

And there, of your own people, one may see
    Ismene, mournful as she was before,   110
    Deiphyle, Argia, Antigone,

Hypsipyle, who led to Langia's water,
    Thetis, Deidamia with her sisters,
    and there, too, one may see Tiresias' daughter."

We stepped from the walled stairs to level ground,   115
    and both the Poets now had fallen still,
    attentive once again to look around.

Of the day's handmaids, four had fallen back,
    and now the fifth stood at the chariot's pole,
    pointing the bright tip on its upward track,   120

when Virgil said: "I think we ought to go
    with our right shoulders to the outer edge,
    circling the slope as we have done below."

So custom served to guide us, and we went
    as Virgil said, with all the more assurance   125
    since Statius' silence gave us his consent.

They walked ahead and I came on behind
    treasuring their talk, which was of poetry,
    and every word of which enriched my mind.

But soon, in mid-road, there appeared a tree   130
    laden with fragrant and delicious fruit,
    and at that sight the talk stopped instantly.

As fir trees taper up from limb to limb,
    so this tree tapered down; so shaped, I think,
    that it should be impossible to climb.   135

From that side where the cliff closed-off our way
    a clear cascade fell from the towering rock
    and broke upon the upper leaves as spray.

The Poets drew nearer, reverent and mute,
    and from the center of the towering tree   140
    a voice cried: "You shall not eat of the fruit!"

Then said: "Mary thought more of what was due
    the joy and honor of the wedding feast
    than of her mouth, which still speaks prayers
        for you.

Of old, the mothers of Rome's noble blood   145
    found joy in water. And great wisdom came
    to holy Daniel in despising food.

Bright as pure gold was mankind's state at first:
    then, hunger seasoned acorns with delight,
    and every rill ran sweet to honest thirst.   150

No wine nor meat were in the wilderness.
    Honey and locusts—that and nothing more
    nourished the Baptist in his holiness;

and to that fact is his great glory due,
as the Gospel clearly testifies to you."   155

NOTES

1–6. We had, by now . . . : The Poets, now three, are climbing the
stairway to the Sixth Cornice, having passed the Angel posted at the
entrance to the Ascent. Since this Angel must represent the virtue
opposite both Avarice and Prodigality, he may best be called the An-
gel of Moderation.

The Angel has lightened Dante's soul by striking away one more *P,*
and has speeded the Poets on their way by reciting a Beatitude, but
with an interesting variation. The whole Beatitude would be *Beati qui
esuriunt et sitiunt justitiam*—"Blessed are they who hunger and thirst
after righteousness." But the Angel left out *esuriunt* ("they hunger")
and said only "Blessed are they who thirst after righteousness." The
"who hunger" will be spoken by the next Angel; appropriately, for the
Gluttons. Dante was forced into some such device if he was to make
six Beatitudes do for seven Cornices. Certainly, the aptness of his in-
vention under such pressures is the mark of his structural genius.

11. that love ignites another: Cf. *Inferno,* V, 100: "Love, which
permits no loved one not to love. . . ."

13. Juvenal: Decius Junius Juvenal, satiric poet born about A.D. 47,
died about A.D. 130. His long life almost entirely overlapped that of
Statius. Since both lived in Rome, and both were poets (Juvenal
mentions Statius in his *Seventh Satire*), he would be a natural choice
as the bearer of tidings of Statius.

17. for any unseen person: For any person one has not met.

18. such as will make the climb ahead seem short: Since it will be
passed in such happy company.

27 ff. STATIUS' REPLY. Statius smiles briefly at Virgil's error in
forgetting that Avarice and Prodigality are twin sins, both of which
absorb the soul into an immoderate concern for material matters.
(*Cf.* Wordsworth, "Getting and spending we lay waste our powers.")
Statius then explains that he was not a miser but a waster, and that
his sin was riotous expense.

He then pays tribute to Virgil, explaining that it was a passage from the *Aeneid* (as he quotes in lines 40–41) that led him to correct his ways, else he would at that moment be in Hell rolling the enormous weights that the Hoarders and Wasters send crashing against one another there. There is no historic evidence either that Statius was a wasteful spender or that he turned Christian. On the contrary, Juvenal's *Seventh Satire* mentions Statius as being so poor that he would have starved without a patron.

Dante's reasons for both these inventions will have to be inferred from the text itself. Obviously, in making Statius' sin wasteful spending, Dante makes an opportunity to discuss Wasting along with Hoarding as related extremes of Avarice. Even more obviously, Statius could not be in Purgatory at all unless Dante established him as a Christian.

40–41. *To what do you not drive . . . :* These lines are from the *Aeneid* (III, 56–57)—*quid non mortalia pectora cogis Auri sacra fames* ("to what do you not drive mortal appetites, O sacred [god-like] hunger for gold?"). In the Italian, Dante seems to have rendered these lines: "Why do you not control mortal appetites, O sacred hunger for gold?" rendering Virgil's *quid* as "why" instead of as "to what" and thereby not only praising gold-hunger, but making it responsible for the control of Avarice. The hunger could, of course, be called "sacred" in that it is God-given, whereby only its excesses would be evil.

No lines in the *Divine Comedy* have called forth more critical argument. Did Dante make a ludicrous mistake? Was he so familiar with the text that he rendered it carelessly in a sleepy moment? Has the text been corrupted? Was he indulging in a sermonizer's license to twist the text to some obscure purpose? Was he using "sacred" in a special reverse way meaning "cursed," a usage still current in some parts of Italy? All these are puzzles for scholars. Dante is probably reading into Virgil an idea of Aristotelian moderation.

42. *the grim jousts:* Of the Hoarders and Wasters in the Fourth Circle of Hell (*Inferno*, VII).

46. *rise bald to Judgment Day:* Cf. *Inferno*, VII, 56–57, where Dante says of the Hoarders and Wasters:

one crew will stand tight-fisted, the other stripped
of its very hair at the bar of Judgment Day.

49–51. *when the opposite of a sin . . . is as blameworthy:* On this Cornice, as noted, Hoarding and Wasting are the two opposite faces of Avarice and are equally blameworthy. The opposites of Pride, Envy, and Anger, on the other hand, are the virtues of Humility, Caritas, and Meekness. The force of "when" is exactly in the fact that not every opposite is blameworthy.

55–57. *the twin afflictions of Jocasta:* Eteocles and Polynices, the twin sons of Oedipus by his own mother, Jocasta. When they succeeded to the throne of Thebes they agreed to rule in alternating years, the nonruling brother to pass the year in exile. Eteocles occupied the throne the first year and then refused to surrender it when Polynices came to claim it. Thereupon there broke out the war of the Seven against Thebes which Statius celebrated in his *Thebaid. the singer of the sweet Bucolics:* Virgil. So identified in preparation for the reference to *Eclogue* IV in line 67. This is the first time Virgil has been cited as the author of any work but the *Aeneid.*

58. *when Clio tuned your strain:* I.e., in the *Thebaid,* which Statius began with an invocation to Clio, the Muse of History. Virgil is saying that there is no sign in Statius' work to indicate that he had turned Catholic (as, in fact, he almost certainly had not).

59–60. *the faith without the grace of which good works are vain:* Virgil is citing the doctrine that there can be no salvation except through the Catholic Church. The doctrine has only very recently been modified and was the object of some controversy in the United States in the late 1940's.

61. *what Sun:* Divine Illumination. *or beacon:* Power of Reason. (Probable interpretations only.)

63. *the Fisherman:* St. Peter.

64. *You were the lamp:* Allegorically, Statius was guided by Human Reason.

67. *A new birth . . . :* These are the words of the Sybil in Virgil's *Eclogue* IV, 5–7, from his *Bucolics.* Virgil, as a courtier, was celebrating the birth of a son to the well-placed Asinius Pollio. Medieval readers were quick to interpret the lines as a prophecy of the birth of Christ, thus giving rise to the legend of Virgil as a powerful soothsayer and magician.

77. *those messengers:* The Apostles.

88–90. *drew near the Theban rivers:* The ninth book of the *Thebaid* relates the arrival of the Greeks under Adrastus to the Theban rivers, the Ismenus and the Asopus. The *Thebaid* consists of twelve books in all. Thus Statius would have had to write something more than three books (plus his work on the *Achilleid*) without letting slip any slightest indication that he was a Christian. Such a lack is sufficiently explained historically by the fact that there is no slightest evidence that Statius was converted. Within Dante's legend, however, that lack is further evidence of the Sloth of Statius, for which he spent more than four hundred years on the Fourth Cornice.

Statius must also have spent a considerable time in Ante-Purgatory or at the Mouth of the Tiber, or both, for he had been dead for 1,204 years by 1300. If "over four hundred years" plus "over five hundred years" is taken to equal as much as "about a thousand" there are still two centuries unaccounted for. Statius died at fifty-four. If he had been made to wait in Ante-Purgatory for as long as his entire life, there would still remain a century and a half unaccounted for. Some of that time may have been spent in doing minor penances on the other ledges, but he probably spent most of it at the Mouth of the Tiber waiting for the Angel Ferryman's approval.

95. *this good I praise:* The True Faith.

97–99. *Terence ... Caecilius, Varro, Plautus:* All those here mentioned were Latin poets of the third and second centuries B.C. Since all of them died before Christ, none could have won to salvation.

100. *Persius:* Latin poet, A.D. 34–62.

101. *that Greek:* Homer.

104. *the glorious mountain:* Parnassus.

105. *the Nine:* The Muses. Here, as in line 102, they are conceived as the mothers at whose breasts poets sucked the milk of inspiration. Homer, who outsucked all others, is, therefore, the foremost poet.

106–108. *Euripides ... Antiphon ... Agathon, Simonides:* All those here mentioned were Greek poets of the Golden Age.

109 ff. *of your own people:* Virgil means "of the people you wrote about in the *Thebaid*." All those listed may be taken as characters of the poem, only two of whom here require further explanation: *Ismene, mournful as she was:* Daughter of Oedipus and Jocasta, sister of Antigone and of Eteocles and Polynices. She had good reason to mourn, having witnessed the death of all her family and of her betrothed, and having been sentenced to death by Creon. *who led to Langia's water:* When the Seven Heroes who fought against Thebes were dying of thirst on their march through Boetia, Hypsipyle showed them the way to a spring called Langia. For the rest of her story see XXVI, 94–96, note.

118–120. THE TIME. In Canto XII Dante has established the fact that he means the hours when he speaks of the "handmaids of the day." Here he presents them as directing the chariot of the Sun in turn, each handing over her position at the chariot's pole to her successor. Four have already fallen back. It is, therefore, at least four hours since dawn (which was at 6:00 A.M.). The fifth hour is now pointing the bright tip of the chariot's pole (bright because it is approaching noon) toward the zenith. It is, therefore, between 10:00 and 11:00 A.M.

133 ff. THE TREE. The description of this tree has led to many strange speculations. A number of the early commentators thought of it as growing upside down and it is so illustrated in some old manuscripts. I take Dante's central idea to be of an unclimbable tree with a great spreading top.

140 ff. THE WHIP OF GLUTTONY. It is prefaced (line 141) by a voice that cries from amid the luscious fruits, denying them to the sinners. Note how much the phrasing suggests God's first command prohibiting the Fruit of Knowledge.

The voice then cites great examples of abstinence and moderation. It cites first (lines 142–144) the example of Mary at the marriage feast at Cana in Galilee (*cf.* XIII, 28–30) and how she thought only of the good of others, not of her own appetite.

The voice then cites (lines 145–146) the matrons of ancient Rome. It was the custom during the Republic for noble matrons not to drink wine. Thus they "found joy in water."

The third example (lines 146–147) is based on *Daniel,* i, 8 and 17. Daniel determined not to defile himself with the king's wine and meat . . . "and Daniel had understanding in all visions and dreams."

The fourth example (lines 148–150) cites mankind's earliest and most natural state, when men lived in accord with nature and had not developed the cookery that leads men to gluttonous feasting, nor the wine (distilled spirits were not developed till the eighteenth century) that leads to drunkenness. Then, according to the voice, acorns and water were enough to delight men.

The final example (lines 151–155) cites John the Baptist, who ate only honey and locusts in the desert (*Matthew,* iii, 4) and won thereby to the glory the Gospel attests (*Matthew,* xi, 11, and *Luke,* vii, 28).

Canto XXIII

———————— >>>◦<<< ————————

*Dante stares up into the tree to see who has spoken but he is
called away by Virgil who leads on, talking to Statius, while
Dante walks behind, drinking in their conversation. Sud-
denly, from behind him, Dante hears a psalm, and turning, he
sees a band of GLUTTONS overtaking them, souls so emaci-
ated that one can read in their sunken eyes and in the lines of
the cheeks and nose the word "OMO."*

*After some difficulty Dante recognizes one of the hideously
wasted souls as his old friend FORESE who had died only
five years before, but who had been advanced into Purgatory
and directly to this Cornice by the prayers of his widow,
Nella.*

*In praising Nella for her devotion, Forese takes occa-
sion to deliver a rather salty INVECTIVE AGAINST THE
WOMEN OF FLORENCE for their immodest dress and
behavior.*

*In answer to Forese's plea (for the souls have all seen
Dante's shadow), Dante explains how he has mounted into
Purgatory and with whom he is traveling.*

In hope of seeing who had cried those words
    I drew near and peered up at the green boughs
    like one who wastes his lifetime stalking birds.

At that, my more-than-father said: "My son,
    come now, for we must portion out more wisely   5
    the time allotted us." And he moved on.

I looked down and turned round to join those sages
   in the same instant. And their talk was such
   that every step I took paid double wages.

Then suddenly at my back I heard the strain   10
   of *Labia mea, Domine,* so sung
   that it was both a hymn and cry of pain.

"Father," I said, "what is this sound?" And he:
   "Spirits who, circling so, loosen perhaps
   the knot of debt they owe Eternity."   15

As pilgrims wrapped in holy meditation,
   when they encounter strangers on the way,
   look, but do not pause for conversation,

so from behind us, turning half about
   to stare as they went by, a band of souls   20
   came up and passed us, silent and devout.

The sockets of their eyes were caves agape;
   their faces death-pale, and their skin so wasted
   that nothing but the gnarled bones gave it shape.

I doubt that even Erysichthon's skin,   25
   even when he most feared that he would starve,
   had drawn so tight to bone, or worn so thin.

"Behold," I thought, although I did not speak,
   "the face of those who lost Jerusalem
   when Miriam ripped her son with her own beak."   30

Their eye pits looked like gem-rims minus gem.
   Those who read OMO in the face of man
   would easily have recognized the *M.*

Who could imagine, without knowing how,
   craving could waste souls so at the mere smell   35
   of water and of fruit upon the bough?

I was still wondering how they could have grown
   so thin and scabby (since what famished them
   had not yet been made clear to me), when one,

turning his eyes from deep inside his skull,   40
   stared at me fixedly, then cried aloud:
   "How have I earned a grace so bountiful?"

I never would have recognized his face,
   but in his voice I found that which his features
   had eaten from themselves without a trace.   45

That spark relit my memory and, in awe,
   I understood beneath those altered features
   it was Forese's very self I saw.

"Ah, do not stare," he pleaded, "at my hide,
   bleached like a leper's by these flaming scabs,   50
   nor at the fleshless bones I bear inside;

but tell me all about yourself, and who
   these two souls are that bear you company;
   and tell me with all haste, I beg of you."

"I wept to see your face once when it lay   55
   in death," I said, "and I weep no less now
   to see what pain has wasted it away;

in God's name tell me how. Do not demand
   I speak while still bemused, for he speaks badly
   whose mind is too full to be at command."   60

And he: "From the Eternal Counsel flow
   the powers whereby the water and the tree
   we have just passed, emaciate us so.

All those who sing while weeping in their pain
   once loved their stomach-sacs beyond all measure.   65
   Here, thirst and hunger wring them clean again.

Hunger and thirst that nothing can assuage
   grow in us from the fragrance of the fruit
   and of the spray upon the foliage.

And not once only as we round this place   70
   do we endure renewal of our pain.
   —Did I say 'pain'? I should say 'gift of grace.'

For the same will that drives us to the Tree
   drove Christ on gladly to cry 'Eli! Eli!'
   when he paid with his blood to set us free."   75

And I to him: "Forese, from the day
   in which you changed worlds for the better life,
   less than five years, as yet, have passed away.

If your ability to sin had fled
   before the hour of that sublime sweet sorrow   80
   that weds us back to God, among his blessèd,

how have you reached so high in the great climb?
   I thought to find you still below, with those
   who sit and wait, repaying time for time."

"My Nella's flood of tears," he answered me,   85
   "have borne me up so soon to let me drink
   the blessed wormwood of my agony.

Her sighs and prayers were heard where Love abounds:
   they raised me from the slope where I lay waiting
   and set me free of all the other Rounds.   90

The dearer and more pleasing in God's sight
   is the poor widow of my love, as she
   is most alone in doing what is right.

For the Barbagia of Sardinia breeds
   chaste women as compared to that Barbagia   95
   in which I left her to her widow's weeds.

O my dear brother, what is there to say?
  In vision I already see a time—
  and it is not far distant from this day—

in which the pulpit shall denounce by writ   100
  the shameless jades that Florentines call ladies,
  who go about with breasts bare to the tit.

What Moslem woman ever has required
  a priestly discipline, or any other,
  before she would go decently attired?   105

But if the chippies only could foresee
  swift Heaven's punishment, they'd have their
    mouths
  already open to howl misery.

For if what we foresee here does not lie,
  they shall be sad before those sons grow beards   110
  who can be soothed now with a lullaby.

Now, brother, answer in your turn. You see
  your shadow there, and how these other souls
  are staring at the spot along with me."

I then: "If you call back to mind from here   115
  my past life in your company, yours in mine,
  memory will seem too great a load to bear.

I was recalled from such ways by that one
  who leads me here, and just the other day
  when that one's sister" (pointing to the Sun)   120

"was at the full. Through the profoundest night
  of final death he led me in this flesh
  which follows him to find the final Right.

From there with many a sweet encouragement
  he led me upward and around the mountain   125
  which straightens in you what the world has bent.

And he has pledged himself to go with me
   until I stand by Beatrice, above.
   Then I must do without his company.

The one who pledges this" (and as I spoke   130
   I pointed to him standing there) "is Virgil.
   The other is the shade of him who woke

to blessedness just now when every rim,
the mountain round, shook in releasing him."

NOTES

11. *Labia mea, Domine:* "O Lord, open Thou my Lips, and my mouth shall pour forth Thy praise." From the Fifty-first Psalm of the Vulgate. The psalm is part of the service of Lauds for Tuesdays, and the time is now Easter Tuesday. A second aptness is in the mention of lips being opened for praise, rather than for eating and drinking.

21. *silent and devout:* Virgil (lines 14–15) seems to have implied that the souls go circling the ledge endlessly uttering their mixed hymn and lament. Here they are presented as silent and devout. The only possible inference seems to be that they circle the ledge in devout and silent meditation until they reach the tree, and then cry aloud.

25. *Erysichthon:* Erysichthon mocked the goddess Ceres by felling an oak in her sacred grove, and Ceres visited an insatiable hunger upon him. He ate up all his own substance, sold his daughter in order to buy more food, consumed that, and finally devoured his own limbs. (*Metamorphoses,* VIII, 726–881.) He does admirably as the archetype of gluttony, for the glutton consumes his soul just as Erysichthon consumed his body.

29–30. *who lost Jerusalem . . . Miriam:* Josephus (*Jewish Wars,* VI, 3) relates that when Titus was besieging Jerusalem in A.D. 70 (see XXI, 82, note), the people were so reduced by hunger that a woman named Mary or Miriam, the daughter of Eleazar, killed her son, cooked him, and ate half his body. *with her own beak:* As if she were a bird of prey, a creature reduced from all humanity. So gluttony reduces the soul.

32. *Those who read OMO in the face of man:* A medieval notion held that the Creator had signed His creation (thoughtfully anticipating the Latin alphabet) *OMO DEI,* "Man [is] of God"; the eyes forming the two *O*'s, the brows, nose, and cheekbones forming the *M,* the ears the *D,* the nostrils the *E,* and the mouth the *I.* Dante mentions only the *OMO,* making the point that these souls were so emaciated that one could readily see the *M.*

34. *without knowing how:* Dante's wonderment here concerns the nature of souls. How can insubstantial spirits become so hideously wasted by the craving aroused by the mere smell of food and water? (One need only inhale the moist air near a fountain or waterfall to know what Dante means by the "smell" of water.) In XXV the question arises again and is answered in detail.

42. *How have I earned a grace so bountiful:* The grace of seeing Dante again.

46. *That spark:* The soul's voice.

48. *Forese:* Forese Donati (For-RAY-zeh) died July 28, 1296. Gemma Donati, Dante's wife, was Forese's kinswoman. Forese was the brother of Corso Donati, head of the Black Guelphs, and Dante was a passionate White, but before politics separated them they had been warm friends. Forese had been something of a poet, and he and Dante had exchanged rhymed lampoons in one of which Dante had accused him of Gluttony; and of Pride and Prodigality as well.

70. *And not once only:* Dante may mean that the pain is renewed over and over as the souls circle past the one tree, or that there are more trees on the Cornice, each of them sharpening the hunger and thirst of these souls. Dante's phrasing of line 73 seems, despite the disagreement of many commentators, to suggest that only one tree so functions. The idea of the renewal of pain upon the completion of each full circle was well established in ancient writings, and has already been made use of in the *Inferno* in the *bolgia* of the Sowers of Discord.

74. *drove Christ on gladly to cry 'Eli! Eli!':* At the ninth hour of his agony Christ cried, *Eli, Eli, lama sabachthani?*—"My God, my God, why hast thou forsaken me?" (*Matthew,* xxvii, 46.) Dante does not mean that Christ rejoiced in his final despair but, rather, that foreseeing it, he still went gladly toward it. The desire of these sin-

ners to endure their terrible suffering is thus compared to Christ's eagerness to endure the pain that would redeem the souls of men.

76–84. DANTE'S QUESTION. Dante's phrasing is difficult here. It must be understood to be Dante's personal knowledge that Forese did not give up gluttony until he was too weak to eat any more, *i.e.,* in his final hour. Then only did he achieve the sweet sublime sorrow of repentance. But since he died in 1295, only five years before the present meeting, Dante would have expected to find him outside The Gate, his purifying pains delayed for as long as he made God wait. So line 84, "repaying time for time."

85. *Nella:* Forese's wife, Giovanna, a name whose affectionate diminutive is Giovanella, whence Nella. Dante clearly offers her as the type of the good Christian wife. Her virtue puts all the more to shame the decadence of the other women of Florence.

90. *set me free of all the other Rounds:* Nella's prayers have not only moved Forese out of Ante-Purgatory, but have freed him of all the pains of the Rounds below, on which he might have suffered (if Dante's charge in his rhymed lampoons had any substance) for Pride and Prodigality.

94. *the Barbagia of Sardinia:* Barbagia, a wild region in the Sardinian mountains, was dominated by the Barbacini, a bandit clan said to have been landed by the Vandals. They were reputed to be savages and idolaters. St. Gregory speaks of them as living like animals. Other medieval sources report their women as going half-naked; and inevitably some later sources (Dante's son Pietro among them) drop the "half" and report the Barbagian women to be naked savages. Thus, Forese is saying that the naked savages of the Sardinian Barbagia are chaste as compared to the women of that other Barbagia, *i.e.,* Florence, Barbagia-on-the-Arno.

109. *For if what we foresee here does not lie:* As usual, it does not, the calamities here foreseen, as of 1300, having already befallen Florence by the time Dante wrote this prophecy. In November of 1301 (see XX, 70–78) Charles de Valois entered Florence and sowed disaster. In 1302 Fulcieri da Calboli introduced his reign of terror (XIV, 58 ff.), and a great famine occurred in the same year. In 1303 Florence was interdicted, and shortly thereafter a bridge collapsed, killing many people. (See also *Inferno,* XXVI, 7–12.) It

would take about fifteen years for male children to progress from lullabies to beards, and by 1315 Florence had more than enough to mourn.

120. *that one's sister (pointing to the Sun):* The Moon. As Diana, she was said to be the sister of Apollo, the Sun. (See note to XX, 130–132.) Dante is, of course, referring to the Moon of the night of Holy Thursday when he was in the Dark Wood of Error (*Inferno,* I).

121–122. *the profoundest night of final death:* Hell.

Canto XXIV

The Tree of Knowledge
The Rein of Gluttony

*The Poets move on as Dante continues his talk with Forese,
who identifies many of the souls of the Gluttons, among them
BONAGIUNTA OF LUCCA. Bonagiunta mutters a prophecy
concerning Dante's future meeting with GENTUCCA. He
then questions Dante about THE SWEET NEW STYLE and
ends by concluding that had he and the others of his school of
poetry grasped the principle of natural expression, they
would have written as well as do the poets of Dante's school.*

*All the other souls speed ahead, but Forese remains to
prophesy the death of his brother, CORSO DONATI, leader of
the Black Guelphs. Then he speeds away and soon disappears.*

*The Poets move on and come to THE TREE OF KNOWL-
EDGE from which a voice cries THE REIN OF GLUTTONY,
citing EVE, THE CENTAURS, and THE ARMY OF GIDEON.
Having skirted the tree carefully, warned away by the voice, the
Poets move ahead and meet THE ANGEL OF ABSTINENCE,
who shows them to the ascent.*

Talk did not slow our steps, nor they in turn
    our talk, but still conversing we moved on
    like ships at sea with a brisk wind astern.

And all those shades, looking like things twice dead,
    were drinking in through their sepulchral eyes   5
    the awe of seeing me as I had been bred.

And I, continuing as I had begun,
    said: "His ascent, I think, is somewhat slower
    than it would be but for that other one.

—But where now is Piccarda? Do you know?   10
    And is there anyone of special note
    among these people who stare at me so?"

"My sister, who was good as she was fair,
    and fair as good, sits crowned on High Olympus,
    rejoicing in eternal triumph there."   15

Thus he began. Then: "To identify
    anyone here is certainly permitted,
    for abstinence has milked our features dry.

This" (and he pointed to him) "dearest brother,   20
    was Bonagiunta of Lucca. That behind him,
    his face more sunken in than any other,

once fathered Holy Church. Of Tours his line;
    and here in the long fast he expiates
    Bolsena's eels and the Vernaccia wine."

Then he named many others, one by one,   25
    at which I saw not one black look among them,
    but all seemed pleased at being thus made known.

Ubaldino della Pila hungered there,
    and Boniface, shepherd to all those bellies—
    they were so starved they used their teeth on air.   30

I saw my Lord Marchese. Before he died
    he drank with somewhat less thirst at Forlì,
    yet no man ever saw him satisfied.

As one who notes one face especially
    among a crowd, I noted him of Lucca   35
    who seemed most to desire a word with me.

He muttered something, and I seemed to hear
   the word "Gentucca" issue from the wound
   where most he felt High Justice pluck him bare.

"Spirit," I said, "since you seem so intent 40
   on talking to me, do so audibly,
   and speaking so, make both of us content."

"Though men may mock my city," he replied,
   "she who will teach you how to treasure it
   is born there, though she is not yet a bride. 45

This presage you shall take with you from here,
   and if you misconstrued what I first muttered
   the facts themselves, in time, will make it clear.

But is this really the creator of
   those new *canzoni,* one of which begins 50
   'Ladies who have the intellect of Love'?"

And I: "When Love inspires me with delight,
   or pain, or longing, I take careful note,
   and as he dictates in my soul, I write."

And he: "Ah, brother, now I see the thong 55
   that held Guittone, and the Judge, and me
   short of that sweet new style of purest song.

I see well how your pens attained such powers
   by following exactly Love's dictation,
   which certainly could not be said of ours. 60

And if one scan the two styles side by side,
   that is the only difference he will find."
   With that he fell still, as if satisfied.

Just as the cranes that winter by the Nile
   form close-bunched flights at times, then, gathering speed, 65
   streak off across the air in single file,

so all the people there faced straight ahead,
    and being lightened by both will and wasting,
    quickened their paces, and away they sped.

And as a runner who must take a rest   70
    lets his companions pull ahead, and walks
    till he has eased the panting in his chest,

just so Forese let that blessed train
    outdistance him, and held his pace to mine,
    and said to me: "When shall we meet again?"   75

"I do not know how long my life will be,"
    I said, "but I cannot return so soon
    but what my wish will reach the shore before me;

for from that city where I came to life
    goodness is disappearing day by day;   80
    a place foredoomed to ruin by bloody strife."

"Take heart," he said, "for I see him whose crime
    exceeds all others' dragged at a beast's tail
    to where sin lasts beyond the end of time.

At every stride the beast goes faster, faster,   85
    until its flashing hooves lash out, and leave
    the foul ruin of what was once its master.

Those Spheres" (and he looked toward the Heavens here)
    "will not turn far before what I have said,
    and may not add to now, shall be made clear.   90

Now I must leave you far behind: your pace
    has cost me a considerable delay;
    and time is precious to us in this place."

At times during a horse charge, one brave knight
    will spur ahead, burning to claim the honor   95
    of having struck the first blow in the fight;

just so his lengthened stride left us behind,
  and I trailed on, accompanied by those two
  who were such mighty marshals of mankind.

And when, in such haste, he had pulled ahead   100
  so far that I could only make him out
  as I could understand what he had said,

we turned a corner and there came in sight,
  not far ahead, a second tree, its boughs
  laden with fruit, its foliage bursting bright.   105

Sometimes when greedy children beg and screech
  for what they may not have, the one they cry to
  holds it in plain sight but beyond their reach

to whet their appetites: so, round that tree,
  with arms raised to the boughs, a pack of souls   110
  begged and was given nothing. Finally

they gave up and moved on unsatisfied,
  and we drew close in our turn to that plant
  at which such tears and pleadings were denied.

"Pass on. Do not draw near. The tree whose fruit   115
  Eve took and ate grows further up the slope,
  and this plant sprouted from that evil root."

—Thus, from the boughs, an unknown voice called
    down.
  And thus warned, Virgil, Statius, and myself
  drew close, and hugged the cliff, and hurried on.   120

"Recall," the voice went on, "those cursed beasts
  born of a cloud. When they had swilled the wine,
  Theseus had to slash their double breasts.

Recall those Jews who once showed Gideon
  how to abandon all to thirst, whereat   125
  he would not lead them down the hills to Midian."

So we strode on along the inner way
    while the voice cried the sins of Gluttony
    which earn, as we had seen, such fearful pay.

Then the road cleared, and with more room for walking 130
    we spread out, and had gone a thousand paces
    in meditation, with no thought of talking;

when suddenly a voice cried, startling me
    as if I were a panic-stricken colt:
    "What are you thinking of alone, you three?" 135

I looked up to see who had spoken so:
    no man has ever seen in any furnace,
    metal or glass raised to so red a glow.

"If your wish is to ascend," I heard one say, 140
    "this is the place where you must turn aside.
    All you who search for Peace—this is the way."

His glory blinded me. I groped and found
    my Teacher's back and followed in his steps
    as blind men do who guide themselves by sound.

Soft on my brow I felt a zephyr pass, 145
    soft as those airs of May that herald dawn
    with breathing fragrances of flowers and grass;

and unmistakably I felt the brush
    of the soft wing releasing to my senses
    ambrosial fragrances in a soft rush. 150

And soft I heard the Angel voice recite:
    "Blessed are they whom Grace so lights within
    that love of food in them does not excite

excessive appetite, but who take pleasure
in keeping every hunger within measure." 155

NOTES

6. *as I had been bred:* In the flesh of the first life.

8. *His ascent, I think, is somewhat slower:* Dante is speaking of Statius, continuing his answer to Forese's question from the last Canto. Statius is now free to ascend to the top of the Mount, and thence to Heaven, but is slowing his ascent in order to be with Virgil that much longer. Were Statius to climb with the speed of the almost-weightless (for, barring last rites, his soul is now purified and free) he would have to leave Virgil, who is still slowed by his need to keep pace with Dante, who is still slowed by his flesh.

Clearly, however, Dante is making an exception to the rule of his own great concept, for Statius is delaying his ascent to God (making God wait) in favor of Virgil. Such a choice would certainly emerge as sinful were Dante to apply his own rule impartially, and in Canto XXX Dante himself receives a substantial tongue-lashing from Beatrice when he mourns the disappearance of Virgil.

10. *Piccarda:* Sister of Forese. She took vows as a nun but was later forced by her other brother, Corso, into a political marriage in violation of her vows. Dante will meet her in the lowest sphere of Paradise.

14. *High Olympus:* Heaven. Another of Dante's easy adaptations of pagan themes and concepts to Christian belief.

16. *Thus he began. Then:* As at many other points in the *Divine Comedy,* Dante has asked two questions. "Thus he began" signifies that the preceding speech was in answer to the first question (line 10). "Then" begins the answer to the second (lines 11–12).

17. *is certainly permitted:* Their emaciation being such that they could never be recognized by their appearances.

19. *(and he pointed to him):* Dante seems to have discovered this device at the end of the last Canto, and to have become so taken by it that he uses it three times in thirty-one lines.

20. *Bonagiunta of Lucca:* See below, note to line 35.

20–21. *That* [one] *behind him . . . :* Simon de Brie, of Tours, Pope from 1281–1285 as Martin IV. Italians, with their normal proprietary arrogance toward Vatican matters, frowned at the thought of a French Pope, but generally granted him to be a good one, though gluttonous. Since in Dante the punishment is always meant to fit the crime, the fact that his face is more sunken-in than any other would indicate that he was, in life, the most gluttonous of all. Or it may indicate that his exalted position as Pope made his gluttony that much more sinful.

24. *Bolsena's eels and the Vernaccia wine:* The eels of Lake Bolsena, near Viterbo, are still especially prized. Vernaccia is a rich, sweet white wine of the mountains near Genoa. Eels were prepared by dropping them alive into a vat of wine. The eels, thus pickled alive, died and were roasted. Martin IV gorged incessantly on such eels and died of an attack brought on by overindulgence.

28. *Ubaldino della Pila:* A knight of the Ubaldini. Brother of the Cardinal of the Ubaldini who is roasting in Hell with Farinata, among the Epicureans (*Inferno,* X). Another brother was Ugolino d'Azzo, who is mentioned with great honor in XIV. Ubaldino was the father of Archbishop Ruggieri who is serving as lunch for Ugolino in the cooler of Hell (*Inferno,* XXXII–XXXIII). He was a great feaster and entertainer, once playing host for several months—in necessarily lavish style—to the Pope and his whole court.

29. *Boniface:* Archbishop of Ravenna, 1274–1294. He was rather more drawn to political than to spiritual affairs. Dante's charge against him involves a word play I could not render without taking considerable liberties. Literally: "Who pastured so many people with his crozier [*i.e.,* shepherd's staff]." But there is the spiritual pasturage the archbishop should provide for his flock of souls, and there is the material pasturage that filled the bellies of all the retainers Boniface kept about him as political boss of his district and its patronage. Thus the essential sarcasm of Dante's charge is that Boniface was shepherd to the bellies rather than to the souls of his archdiocese. There is no evidence outside of Dante that Boniface was a glutton.

31. *my Lord Marchese:* Messer Marchese of Forlì, *podestà* of Faenza in 1296. He once asked what the people thought of him. When told they spoke of nothing but his incessant drinking, he replied that they should remember he was always thirsty.

35. *him of Lucca:* Bonagiunta (Bon-ah-DJOON-tah) degli Overardi. Poet and orator of some repute in Lucca, but one whose lan-

guage Dante condemns in *De Vulgari Eloquentia*, I, xiii. He was a famous glutton and tippler. Died 1297.

38. *Gentucca:* Is probably best taken as the name of a lady Dante met when he went to live with a friend at Lucca, probably about 1314–1316.

38–39. *the wound where most he felt High Justice pluck him bare:* Another of Dante's mixed metaphors. "Pluck him bare" can only be understood as "waste him away." "The wound" where he would most feel his wasting is his mouth, now reduced to a wound in his ruined face, but originally the part of him through which he sinned.

43. *Though men may mock my city:* Dante is certainly not more scornful of Lucca than of the other cities of Tuscany. Throughout the *Comedy* he enjoys taking pot shots at all of them.

44. *she:* Gentucca. In 1300 she had been born and was living in Lucca but as a girl not yet married.

49–51. Literally: "But tell me if I truly behold him who brought forth the new rhymes beginning . . ." The line quoted is the first line of a *canzone* of the *Vita Nuova* (XIX).

Bonagiunta already knows who Dante is. His phrasing is not, therefore, for identification. He has just prophesied a Platonic love into which Dante will enter with Gentucca. His thoughts turn naturally to the past Platonic love that Dante celebrated in his *Vita Nuova*. As a poet himself, Bonagiunta would be interested in discussing the "sweet new style" with its foremost practitioner.

49–62. BONAGIUNTA AND THE SWEET NEW STYLE. Bonagiunta, Guittone d'Arezzo (who first perfected the form of the Italian sonnet), and Jacopo da Lentino (known as "Il Notaro," *i.e.,* The Judge)—a Sicilian poet to whom Dante gives some qualified praise in *De Vulgari Eloquentia* (I, xii)—were all practitioners of a kind of conventionalized verse modeled after the most decadent phase of Provençal poetry. They flourished in the first half of the thirteenth century. Dante was a prime mover in the later "sweet new style" of more natural expression. In lines 55–57 Bonagiunta regrets that his school failed to discover the principle of the sweet new style, for only the adherence to that principle of natural expression, he adds (lines 61–62), distinguishes the one style from the other. His implication is that, had his school observed that principle, he and his fellows would have written as well as the new poets, being their equals in all else. And with this final wishful assertion, Bonagiunta seems satisfied, and says no more.

It is possible to interpret Bonagiunta's remarks as a lament over his failure to discover the new style and thereby to write better, but the first interpretation seems firmer.

64–66. Compare Dante's description of the Carnal, *Inferno*, V, 46–47.

68. *being lightened by both will and wasting:* Sin is equated to heaviness and purity to lightness throughout the *Comedy*. These souls are made lighter both by their own will to endure the purifying penance and by the wasting that resulted from it. Dante seems to imply that an emaciated incorporeal essence weighs less than a normal one. If so, the explanation must lie in one of the mysteries of faith.

76–81. DANTE'S ANSWER TO FORESE. Forese, moved by love, has expressed his longing to see Dante again, but obviously he cannot until Dante is dead. To a soul in Purgatory, to be sure, death is not a tragedy but an arrival. Yet Forese phrases his question delicately, aware that he is speaking to a living man. Dante, on the other hand, understands Forese's intent, and answers without circumlocution: however soon his return to the second life, his wish will be there before him.

78. *the shore:* Of Purgatory. Dante will have some time to spend on the Cornice of Pride (and perhaps of Wrath), but he may yet overtake Forese in the final ascent.

79. *that city:* Florence.

82. *him:* Corso Donati. Forese's brother and head of the Black Guelphs. It was Corso who persuaded Boniface VIII to send Charles of Valois to Florence in 1300. Thus the crimes of Charles are indirectly his. In 1309 Corso tried a coalition that would make him the supreme authority in Florence, but the Blacks, whom he had done so much so bloodily to put into power, discovered his plot and condemned him to death. He fled but was pursued and killed. Dante follows an account (line 83) that has him dragged to death by his horse.

84. *where sin lasts beyond the end of time:* Hell.

88. *Those Spheres:* Of Heaven, as indicated by the parenthetical stage direction.

90. *and may not add to now:* Forese has already overstayed and must rejoin his band.

92. *a considerable delay:* In matching his pace to Dante's when he should be speeding toward his expiation with the other spirits.

100–105. These two tercets present fairly typical problems of Dantean interpretation. In 100–102 Dante says he can follow Forese with his eyes only as he could follow in his mind (*i.e.,* understand) what Forese had said. Hence if Forese was still remotely in sight, it would follow that Dante had some glimmer of the meaning of his prophecy. If, on the other hand, Dante meant he could not grasp the prophecy at all, Forese must have disappeared.

At that very instant, however (103–105), the Poets round a bend in the cliff. If they are that close to a turning (and the circles at this altitude would turn on a shortened radius), Forese must have long since disappeared around the bend. It must follow, therefore, that Dante means he had no idea whatever of the meaning of Forese's prophecy—as, in fact, he could not have known in 1300 how Corso would die in 1309.

104. *a second tree:* Various attempts have been made to relate this tree to the first, as they must, indeed, be related since from one the Whip of Gluttony is spoken, and from the other, the Rein. This one, we are told by the voice, is sprung from the same root as the Tree of Knowledge from which Eve ate. Among other things, therefore, it is the Tree of Death. By simple opposites the other may be argued to be the Tree of Life. Or the two may be seen as the Tree of Mortal Woe (death included) and the Tree of Eternal Life, the former containing the voice of the ruin brought on by sin, the latter the voice of the eternal joy that arises from obedience.

115–126. THE REIN OF GLUTTONY. (115–117) The first admonition cites the downfall of Eve (aptly cited from an offshoot of the original tree). Gluttony, in Dante's view, is sinful because it rejects God in favor of appetite: the Glutton thinks of his belly rather than of his soul. Eve's act is, therefore, the supreme Gluttony in that it lost God to all mankind until the coming of Christ. In Dante's geography, the Garden of Eden stands at the top of the Mount of

Purgatory. Thus the tree from which Eve ate, and from whose roots this tree springs, must stand above it.

(121–123) The second admonition cites the drunkenness of the Centaurs and the grief to which it brought them. Invited to a wedding feast by the neighboring Lapithae, the Centaurs became so drunk they tried to make off with the bride, whereupon Theseus and the Lapithae seized arms and killed great numbers of the Centaurs. The Centaurs are spoken of as "born of a cloud" (line 122) because they were supposed to have been sired by Ixion upon the cloud Nephele whom Jupiter had formed into the likeness of Juno, beloved of Ixion. They are said to have double breasts (line 123) because of their two natures, half-horse and half-human.

(124–126) The third admonition is based on *Judges,* vii, 5–6. When Gideon was leading the army of the Jews against Midian, he was instructed by the Lord to lead his men to the river and to watch how they drank. Those who threw aside all caution at the sight of water and plunged their faces into the river were to be set aside. Those who stayed alert despite their thirst, drinking cautiously by scooping the water up in their hands and remaining watchful, were to be chosen. Three hundred were so chosen, and with them alone Gideon moved down to victory.

127. *the inner way:* Along the cliff-face.

130–131. *the road cleared, and with more room . . . :* One must remember that the tree grows in the middle of the ledge. The voice had warned the Poets not to draw near. Since the ledge is narrow and the tree spreads wide, the Poets had to draw far to one side along the inner cliff-face, naturally drawing close together. Now, with the road cleared, they once more draw apart for better walking.

135. *alone:* As Dante has made clear, the souls in Purgatory go normally in great bands. Three alone is an exception the Angel could not fail to note.

135–155. THE ANGEL OF ABSTINENCE. The combined fieriness and softness of the Angel of Abstinence makes him an especially memorable figure, and an especially appropriate one, his office considered. The fieriness of his aura may be taken to symbolize raging appetite, perhaps prefiguring the Fire of *Luxuria* (lust) of

the next Canto; his softness to symbolize the sweetness of absti-
nence in its conquest of such fire.

His blessing to the Poets is based on the second half of the Fifth
Beatitude, the first half of which was recited by the Angel of Moder-
ation on the ledge just below. (See opening lines of XXII.) That An-
gel had left out "who hunger" in his version of the Beatitude. This
Angel leaves out "who thirst" but puts in "who hunger."

Canto XXV

DEPARTURE FROM THE SIXTH CORNICE   *The Ascent*
       The Discourse of Statius
THE SEVENTH CORNICE   *The Lustful*
       The Whip of Lust

*It is 2:00 P.M. as the three Poets leave the Cornice of the Glut-
tonous and begin their hurried ASCENT TO THE SEVENTH
CORNICE.*

*Dante, burning with eagerness to ask how the Gluttons could
give the appearance of advanced starvation despite the fact
that they are airy bodies and do not need food, fears to speak
but is finally encouraged to do so by Virgil. Dante immediately
offers his question, and Virgil, as an act of courtesy, invites Sta-
tius to answer it. The rest of the rapid ascent is then occupied by
THE DISCOURSE OF STATIUS ON THE NATURE OF THE
GENERATIVE PRINCIPLE, THE BIRTH OF THE HUMAN
SOUL, and THE NATURE OF AERIAL BODIES.*

*By the time Statius is finished, the Poets have reached the
Seventh Cornice. There, enwrapped in sheets of flame, the
souls of THE LUSTFUL sing over and over the hymn Sum-
mae Deus Clementiae. At each conclusion of the hymn, they
cry out in praise of an example of High Chastity. These exam-
ples form THE WHIP OF LUST. It is in this way, singing and
praising as they move through the flames, that the Lustful
perform their purification.*

It was an hour to climb without delay.
    Taurus succeeded to the Sun's meridian,
    and Scorpio to Night's—a world away;

thus, as a man spurred on by urgent cause
    will push ahead, no matter what appears   5
    along the way inviting him to pause—

just so we filed, one of us at a time,
    into the gap, and started up those stairs
    whose narrowness divides all those who climb.

And as a little stork, eager to fly   10
    but afraid to leave the nest, will raise a wing
    then let it fall again—just such was I,

the will within me now strong and now weak,
    eager to ask, but going only so far
    as to make me clear my throat, and then not speak.   15

The pace was swift; nor did my Sweet Lord slow
    his stride, but said: "I see the bow of speech
    drawn back to the very iron. Let it go."

My doubts resolved, I did not hesitate
    to use my mouth. "How can they grow so thin,"   20
    I said, "who need no food in their new state?"

"Recall Meleager wasting as the brand
    wasted in fire," he said, "and you will find
    the matter not so hard to understand.

Or think how your least move before a glass   25
    is answered by your image, and what seemed hard
    is bound to grow much clearer than it was.

But this wish burns you, I know, and to put out
    all of its flames, I shall beg Statius now
    to be the one to heal the wounds of doubt."   30

"If, in your presence," Statius first replied,
    "I explain eternal things, let my excuse
    be only that your wish be not denied."

And then to me: "Son, let it be your task
    to hear and heed my words, and they will be   35
    a light upon the 'how' of what you ask.

Perfect blood—that pure blood that remains
    as one might say, like food upon the table,
    and never goes to slake the thirsty veins—

acquires, within the heart, formative power   40
    over all human organs; as that which flows
    into the veins forms *them*. It is once more

changed in the heart, then flows down to that place
    the better left unmentioned. Thence, it drips
    over another blood in its natural vase.   45

There, the two commingle; and one blood shows
    a passive bent, while the other blood is active,
    due to the perfect place from which it flows.

So joined, the active force within the latter
    first clots, then quickens what it has made firm   50
    of the former blood to serve as working matter.

The active force has now become a soul
    like that of a plant, but with the difference
    that this begins where that achieves its goal.

Soon, like some sea-thing, half-beast and half-weed,   55
    it moves and feels. It then begins to form
    those powers of sense of which it is the seed.

Now, my son, the formative power expands
    and elongates within, till every member
    takes form and place as nature's plan commands.   60

But how this animal-thing grows human powers
    you do not yet see; and this very point
    has led astray a wiser head than yours.

By him, the *possible intellect* was thought   65
   (since it occupied no organ) to be disjoined
   from the *vegetative soul*—and so he taught.

Open your heart to the truth I shall explain,
   and know that at the instant articulation
   has been perfected in the foetal brain,

that instant the First Mover turns to it.   70
   And there, rejoicing at such art in nature,
   breathes into it a new and powerful spirit.

All that is active there, this spirit draws
   into itself, forming a single soul
   that lives, and feels, and measures its own cause.   75

(Consider, if you find these words of mine
   too strange to understand, how the Sun's heat
   joined to the sap of the vine turns into wine.)

Then when Lachesis' flax is drawn, it frees
   itself from flesh, but takes with it the essence   80
   of its divine and human faculties—

its lower powers grown passive now and mute;
   but memory, intelligence, and will
   more active than they were, and more acute.

Miraculously then, by its own will,   85
   it falls at once to one or the other shore.
   There it first learns its way, for good or ill.

And once inclosed in that new atmosphere,
   the *formative power* rays out, as it did first
   in shaping the bodily parts it left back there.   90

Then, as the air after a rain will glow
   inside itself, reflecting an outer ray,
   and clothe itself in many colors—so

wherever the soul may stop in its new hour,
   the air about it takes on that soul's image.   95
   Such is the virtue of the *formative power.*

Thereafter, in the same way one may see
   flame follow fire wherever it may shift,
   the new form follows the soul eternally.

From air it draws its visibility. Hence,   100
   it is called a *shade.* And out of air it forms
   the organs of sight, speech, and every sense.

Thus are we able to speak and laugh. And thus
   are we able to weep such tears and breathe such sighs
   as you have seen and heard, passing among us.   105

As desire, or other feelings move us, so
   our shades change their appearances. And that
   is that cause of what amazed you just below."

—We had come, by then, to the last turn of the stairs
   from which we bore to the right along the Cornice,   110
   and our minds were drawn already to other cares.

Here, from the inner wall, flames blast the ledge,
   while from the floor an air-blast bends them back,
   leaving one narrow path along the edge.

This path we were forced to take as best we might,   115
   in single file. And there I was—the flames
   to the left of me, and the abyss to the right.

My Leader said: "In this place, it is clear,
   we all must keep a tight rein on our eyes.
   To take a false step would be easy here."   120

"Summae Deus clementiae," sang a choir
   inside that furnace, and despite my road
   I could not help but look into the fire.

Then I saw spirits moving through the flames,
   and my eyes turned now to them, now to my feet,   125
   as if divided between equal claims.

When they had sung the hymn, those souls in pain
   cried out in full voice: *"Virum non cognosco."*
   Then, softly, they began the hymn again.

That done, they cried: "Diana kept to the wood,   130
   and drove Helicé from her when that nymph
   had felt Venus' poison in her blood."

Then, once again, the hymn swelled from their choir;
   and after it they praised husbands and wives
   who were chaste as virtue and marriage vows require. 135

And in this way, I think, they sing their prayer
   and cry their praise for as long as they must stay
   within the holy fire that burns them there.

Such physic and such diet has been thought fit
before the last wound of them all may knit.   140

Notes

1. *It was an hour to climb without delay:* Afternoon. Hence there was no time to waste, for darkness will come soon.

2–3. *Taurus succeeded to the Sun's meridian:* The Sun is in the sign of Aries, which is succeeded by the sign of Taurus. If Taurus has replaced the Sun at the meridian, the Sun must have moved lower toward the west. And since the signs of the Zodiac each represent two hours (twelve of them for twenty-four hours), it must be two hours past noon. *and Scorpio to Night's—a world away:* Night is personified here. A world away (above Jerusalem), Night would have reached its meridian point (midnight) in the sign of Libra, but has now passed on and Scorpio is the ruling sign. It is, therefore, 2:00 A.M. in Jerusalem.

7. *one of us at a time:* The probable order is: Virgil, Statius, Dante. (*Cf.* XXVI, 1.)

9. *whose narrowness divides all those who climb:* A clear allegorical meaning not to be overlooked here is that each soul must ultimately climb to salvation alone, inside itself, no matter how much assistance it may receive from others. Another would be the soul's loneliness in meeting sexual temptation.

10–15. *eager . . . afraid:* Dante is burning to ask how such insubstantial entities as shades, who need no physical nourishment, could have every appearance of advanced starvation, as is the case with the souls of the Gluttonous. This eagerness to ask, along with the need to hurry on, is implicit in all of Dante's phrasing in lines 1–6.

17–18. *the bow of speech . . . :* Dante's speech is conceived to be a bow that he has bent back to the very iron (the head) of the arrow, in his eagerness to let fly, but which he has been afraid to release.

22. *Meleager:* Son of Oeneus, King of Calydon, and of Althaea. When he was born, the Fates threw a branch into the fire and decreed that he should live until fire had consumed it. Althaea pulled it out of the fire and hid it.

When he had grown, Meleager fell in love with Atalanta, famous for the story of the golden apples. He slew a great bear for her and gave her the skin. His own brothers stole the skin from Atalanta and Meleager, in his rage, killed them. Althaea thereupon brought the fatal branch out of hiding and threw it into the fire. As the flames consumed it, Meleager's life was consumed.

29. *I shall beg Statius now:* Some commentators see Virgil's action in calling upon Statius as signifying that Human Reason has begun to surrender its function to the redeemed soul. Certainly, however, there is nothing in what Statius goes on to say that lies beyond the province of Virgil as Human Reason. Statius' long reply, in fact, would have been taken as a scientific disquisition in Dante's time.

Virgil's action is better taken, I believe, as a courtesy to Statius. Rather than have Statius stand by while Virgil lectures on matters that Statius knows perfectly well, Virgil invites Statius to take over the lecture—a courtesy to a visiting professor. Statius returns the courtesy by pointing out that he can say nothing not known to Virgil, but undertakes the lecture because Virgil has been so gracious in requesting that he do so.

36. *the "how":* Dante had asked (line 20): "How can they grow so thin?"

34–108. THE DISCOURSE OF STATIUS. The long discourse into which Statius launches cannot fail to present unusual difficulties to modern readers, yet it is worth special attention as an illustration of what Dante meant by "Science," as a series of outdated but interesting theories, and especially as an example of how carefully Dante led up to and then introduced his inquiries into the nature of things as an important part of the total scheme of the *Commedia*.

The discourse may be divided into three parts: I. The Nature of the Generative Principle; II. The Birth of the Human Soul; and III. The Nature of Aerial Bodies. An extended paraphrase is perhaps the best way to deal with the complexities of the discourse.

I. *The Nature of the Generative Principle:*

31–39. Dante's concept of blood includes not only blood as we understand it, but a pre-substance (perfect blood), some of which flows into the veins (*i.e.,* the arteries), but some of which remains apart (like food left untouched and in its original state).

40–42. This perfect blood enters the heart (without entering into the general circulation of the bloodstream) and acquires the power (which we now associate with the genes) to determine the development of the bodily organs and members. Similarly, the blood that flows into the "veins" has the power to determine *their* form and function. *formative power:* a technical term from Scholastic philosophy. It may be thought of as "the generative principle." It is derived entirely from the male parent.

43–45. Within the heart of the father, this "perfect blood" undergoes a change into sperm. It then flows down to the male organs ("better left unmentioned") and, in the act of conception, drips over the blood of the female in the womb ("another blood in its natural vase").

46–48. These two bloods commingle. One of them (the female blood) is passive, *i.e.,* it is menstrual, tending to flow away rather than to take form. The other (the male blood), because of the perfect place from which it flows (the heart), is active, *i.e.,* it seeks to generate form.

49–51. The active blood then causes the passive blood to clot. It thus forms it into solid and workable matter, which it then quickens into life. Conception has taken place.

II. *The Birth of the Human Soul:*

52–54. With conception the soul is born, not as a coinheritance from the mother and father, but from the active force (the formative power) of the father-blood alone, the maternal blood providing only the matter for the formative power to work on. (Dante's views here are pure Aquinian doctrine.)

This newly formed soul is like that of a plant (vegetative only), but with the difference that the plant soul is fully formed at this stage, whereas the human soul is only beginning.

55–57. From this plant-like state (possessing only "vegetative faculties") the soul grows capable of elementary motion and sensation (the "sensitive faculties"). It has achieved the state of some "sea-thing." Dante says not "sea-thing" but "sea-fungus." He probably meant some coelenterate, such as the hydra, sea anemone, or jellyfish. In Dante's time such life-forms were believed to be single living masses without differentiated organs of any sort.

58–60. From this "sea-thing" stage, the *formative power* of the soul (from the father) moves within the maternal material shaping each organ and member into its form and place in human anatomy, according to nature's plan.

61–63. One must still ask how this animal foetus acquires the power of human reason (in Scholastic phrasing, "the possible intellect"). And here, before propounding the true doctrine as he sees it, Statius pauses to refute the teaching of Averroës ("a wiser head than yours"), who erred on this point.

64–66. To grasp the importance to Dante's doctrine of the error of Averroës, one must understand that in Scholastic teaching the soul possesses (1) the *vegetative faculty,* which is to say it lives, (2) the *sensitive or perceiving faculty,* which is to say it feels and receives impressions, and (3) the *reflective faculty,* called the *possible intellect,* which is to say it has the power of reasoning from the known to the unknown, and of extracting forms and concepts from nature.

The vegetative and sensitive faculties receive particular impressions only. The organ of those faculties, common to both man and beast, is the brain. Where then was the organ of the higher intellectual faculty, the possible intellect?

Since he could find no such organ, Averroës postulated a generalized universal rationality from which all men could draw rational faculties during their lives, but which was lost to them at death. It must follow, therefore, that no individual and rational soul could be summoned to eternal judgment, since the soul would have lost its possible intellect (rationality) at death. Church scholars would necessarily be required to reject such a doctrine since it denied the very basis of free will and of just reward and punishment.

67–75. Having refuted error, Statius then explains the truth: the instant the brain is fully formed in the human foetus, God turns to it in his joy at the art of nature in forming so perfect a thing, and breathes into it a powerful spirit peculiar to man. This God-infused spirit draws all the life forces (vegetative, sensitive, and rational) into a single soul. Note especially, in reply to Averroës, that the soul so formed is individualized, self-measuring, and, therefore, self-responsible.

76–78. Statius then compares the change wrought by the new spirit with the way the heat of the Sun is transformed into the quickened wine when joined to the relatively inert sap of the vine.

III. *The Nature of Aerial Bodies:*

79–81. Then when Lachesis (the Fate who draws out the flaxen thread of life—see XXI, 24–27, note) measures the end of the mortal life, the soul goes free of the flesh but takes with it, by virtue of that essence God breathed into it, all of its faculties both human (vegetative and sensitive) and divine (rational).

82–84. These lower (vegetative and sensitive) faculties grow passive and mute after death, since they have left behind the organs whereby they functioned. The higher faculties, however, since they are God-inspired and now free of their mortal involvement in materiality, become more active and acute.

85–87. At the instant of death the soul miraculously falls, by an act of its own will, either to the shore of Hell for damnation, or to the mouth of the Tiber to await transport to Purgatory.

88–90. As soon as the soul feels itself inclosed in the new atmosphere of the afterlife, the *formative power* from the heart of the father (line 40) sends out its rays, as it first did through the matter of the maternal blood to shape the living organs of the body.

91–93. The process is compared to the way the Sun's rays (a force from without) work upon moist air to form a rainbow (within the air). Note that the power of the Sun's rays is, allegorically, from God the Father, just as the formative power of the soul is from the mortal father, and that both work upon passive matter to give it form.

94–96. Wherever (*i.e.*, on whichever shore, as in line 86) the soul lights, the inclosing air takes on the image of that soul by virtue of the soul's indwelling formative power.

97–99. Then, ever after, and just as flame follows fire, the new form follows the soul, wherever it may move.

100–102. This new form is called a *shade* because it is made of insubstantial air, and because out of air it forms all the organs of sense.

103–105. Not only is the shade able to receive sensory impressions, but to produce sounds and appearances that can be registered by mortal senses. (As well as by other shades, as the narrative has made clear at many points.)

106–108. The appearance of the shade, moreover, conforms in detail to the inner feelings of the soul. Thus, if God fills the souls of the gluttonous with a craving for food which is then denied them, their shades appear to wither and starve, their outward appearance conforming to their inner state. It is this phenomenon that amazed Dante on the ledge below. (Note, too, the difference made clear here between men and shades. Men may appear virtuous by hiding their inner evil desires, and thus practice fraud. But shades cannot hide their inner workings: as they are within themselves, so must they appear. This doctrine applied retrospectively, especially to the souls in Hell, will immediately suggest another dimension to be considered when reading Dante's descriptions of the souls he meets.)

119. *we all must keep a tight rein on our eyes:* On the narrative level, Virgil means simply, we must watch our dangerous path with great care. On the allegorical level, however, he can certainly be read to mean that lust (the excess of love) is the most readily inviting

sin, but that it is as dangerous as a fall off the cliff, and that all men must guard their souls against it and refuse, like the souls of the Carnal now in Hell, to "abandon reason to their appetites." It was a convention of the "sweet new style," moreover, that love always enters through the eyes.

121. *"Summae Deus clementiae":* God of clemency supreme. These words are the beginning of the old hymn (now revised) which was sung at Matins on Saturday. The hymn is a prayer for chastity, begging God, of his supreme clemency, to burn lust from the soul and to leave the suppliant chaste.

128 ff. THE WHIP OF LUST. The Whip of Lust consists of examples of chastity which are called forth in praises by the sinners themselves, one example being cried forth at each completion of the Hymn they sing endlessly. The first example (Holy chastity) is, as always, from the life of Mary. The second (Natural chastity) cites Diana. In subsequent intervals between the hymn-singing, the sinners cry out the praise of various husbands and wives (not specified by Dante) who were chaste as required by natural virtue and the sacramental vows of matrimony. They might be called examples of Catholic chastity.

128. *"Virum non cognosco":* "I know not a man." These words were spoken by Mary at the Annunciation. Gabriel had said, "Behold, thou shalt conceive in thy womb, and bring forth a son." Mary replied, "How shall this be, seeing I know not a man?" (*Luke*, i, 26–38.)

130 ff. *"Diana kept to the wood . . .":* In order to preserve her virginity, Diana lived in the woods and became a huntress. One of her attendant nymphs, Helicé, felt the urging of lust (the *poison* of Venus, as opposed to love itself, which would also be from Venus, but not as poison) and gave herself to Jove. After she had been driven away by Diana, Helicé was changed into a bear by Juno. Jove, who seemed systematically incapable of keeping his wife under control where his philandering was concerned, made his new she-bear a questionable sort of recompense by placing her in the sky as Ursa Major, the Big Dipper. (Ovid, *Metamorphoses,* II, 401–530.)

Canto XXVI

*Dante's shadow falls on the wall of flame and it is noticed by
the souls of the Lustful who approach (without leaving the
flames) to question him. Dante's answer, however, is inter-
rupted by the approach of a second band of souls from the
opposite direction. These are THE SODOMITES. The two
bands of souls exchange brief embraces and then cry out
THE REIN OF LUST as they move on, drawing rapidly
apart.*

*The first group again approaches Dante and the soul of
GUIDO GUINIZELLI speaks to him. Dante pays high homage
to Guinizelli and discusses with him the growth of the Sweet
New Style.*

*With a final request for a prayer for his soul, Guido with-
draws and Dante then addresses ARNAUT DANIEL, who an-
swers in the* langue d'oc, *and also begs that Dante say a
prayer for him. His petition made, Daniel disappears into the
purifying flame.*

So, one before the other, we moved there
    along the edge, and my Sweet Guide kept saying:
    "Walk only where you see me walk. Take care."

The Sun, already changing from blue to white
    the face of the western sky, struck at my shoulder,   5
    its rays now almost level on my right;

and my shadow made the flames a darker red.
   Even so slight an evidence, I noticed,
   made many shades that walked there turn their head.

And when they saw my shadow, these began   10
   to speak of me, saying to one another:
   "He seems to be no shade, but a living man!"

And some of them drew near me then—as near
   as they could come, for they were ever careful
   to stay within the fire that burned them there.   15

"O you who trail the others—with no desire
   to lag, I think, but out of deference—
   speak to me who am burned by thirst and fire.

Not I alone need what your lips can tell:
   all these thirst for it more than Ethiopes   20
   or Indians for a drink from a cold well:

how is it that you cast a shadow yet,
   making yourself a barrier to the Sun,
   as if death had not caught you in its net?"

—So one addressed me. And I should have been   25
   explaining myself already, but for a new
   surprising sight that caught my eye just then;

for down the center of that fiery way
   came new souls from the opposite direction,
   and I forgot what I had meant to say.   30

I saw them hurrying from either side,
   and each shade kissed another, without pausing,
   each by the briefest greeting satisfied.

(Ants, in their dark ranks, meet exactly so,
   rubbing each other's noses, to ask perhaps   35
   what luck they've had, or which way they should go.)

As soon as they break off their friendly greeting,
   before they take the first step to pass on,
   each shade outshouts the other at that meeting.

"Sodom and Gomorrah," the new souls cry.   40
   And the others: "Pasiphaë enters the cow
   to call the young bull to her lechery."

As if cranes split into two flocks, and one
   flew to the Rhipheans, one to the sands,
   these to escape the ice, and those the Sun—   45

so, then, those shades went their opposing ways;
   and all returned in tears to their first song,
   and each to crying an appropriate praise.

Then those who came my way drew close once more—
   the same shades that had first entreated me.   50
   They seemed as eager to hear me as before.

I, having had their wish presented twice,
   replied without delay: "O souls assured—
   whenever it may be—of Paradise,

I did not leave my limbs beyond the flood,   55
   not green nor ripe, but bear them with me here
   in their own jointure and in their own blood.

I go to be no longer blind. Above
   there is a lady wins us grace, and I,
   still mortal, cross your world led by her love.   60

But now I pray—so may it soon befall
   you have your greater wish to be called home
   into that heaven of love that circles all—

tell me, that I may write down what you say
   for all to read, who are you? and those others   65
   who move away behind you—who are they?"

Just as our mountaineers, their first time down,
   half-wild and shaggy, gape about the streets
   and stare in dumb amazement at the town—

just such a look I saw upon those shades;   70
   but when they had recovered from their stupor
   (which from a lofty heart the sooner fades),

the first shade spoke again: "Blessèd are you
   who for a better life, store in your soul
   experience of these realms you travel through!   75

Those souls you saw going the other way
   grew stained in that for which triumphant Caesar
   heard his own legions call him 'Queen' one day.

Therefore their band, at parting from us, cries
   'Sodom!'—as you have heard—that by their shame   80
   they aid the fire that makes them fit to rise.

We were hermaphroditic in our offenses,
   but since we did not honor human laws,
   yielding like animals to our lusting senses,

we, when we leave the other band, repent   85
   by crying to our shame the name of her
   who crouched in the mock-beast with beast's intent.

And now you know our actions and our crime.
   But if you wish our names, we are so many
   I do not know them all, nor is there time.   90

Your wish to know mine shall be satisfied:
   I am Guido Guinizelli, here so soon
   because I repented fully before I died."

In King Lycurgus' darkest hour, two sons
   discovered their lost mother: I was moved   95
   as they had been (but could not match their actions)

when I heard his name, for he had fathered me
   and all the rest, my betters, who have sung
   sweet lilting rhymes of love and courtesy.

Enraptured, I can neither speak nor hear   100
   but only stare at him as we move on,
   although the flames prevent my drawing near.

When at last my eyes had fed, I spoke anew;
   and in such terms as win belief, I offered
   to serve him in whatever I could do.   105

And he to me then: "What you say has made
   such a profound impression on my mind
   as Lethe cannot wash away, nor fade.

But if the words you swore just now are true,
   let me know why you show by word and look   110
   such love as I believe I see in you?"

And I to him: "Your songs so sweet and clear
   which, for as long as modern usage lives,
   shall make the very ink that writes them dear."

"Brother," he said, "that one who moves along   115
   ahead there," (and he pointed) "was in life
   a greater craftsman of the mother tongue.

He, in his love songs and his tales in prose,
   was without peer—and if fools claim Limoges
   produced a better, there are always those   120

who measure worth by popular acclaim,
   ignoring principles of art and reason
   to base their judgments on the author's name.

So, once, our fathers sent Guittone's praise,
   and his alone, bounding from cry to cry,   125
   though truth prevails with most men nowadays.

And now, if you enjoy such privilege
    that you are free to go up to that cloister
    within which Christ is abbot of the college,

say an Our Father for me in that host,   130
    as far as it may serve us in this world
    in which the very power to sin is lost."

With that, perhaps to yield his place with me
    to someone else, he vanished through the fire
    as a fish does to the dark depths of the sea.   135

I drew ahead till I was by that shade
    he had pointed to, and said that in my heart
    a grateful place to feast his name was laid.

And he replied at once and willingly:
    "Such pleasaunce have I of thy gentilesse,   140
    that I ne can, ne will I hide from thee.

Arnaut am I, and weepe and sing my faring.
    In grievousnesse I see my follies past;
    in joie, the blistful daie of my preparing.

And by that eke virtue, I thee implour,   145
    that redeth thee, that thou amount the staire,
    be mindful in thy time of my dolour."

Then he, too, hid himself within the fire
that makes those spirits ready to go higher.

NOTES

4–8. *changing from blue to white . . . the western sky:* It is now
4:00 P.M., or a bit later, of the third day on the mountain. At that hour
of a clear day Dante sees the Sun as washing the blue out of the
western sky and turning it whiter and brighter than the east. *struck at
my shoulder . . . now almost level on my right:* If the circumference
of the mountain is taken as a compass rose, the Poets have moved

beyond WNW and are moving toward W. The Sun is in about the same position in the sky and getting low (perhaps a bit less than 30°), and Dante says its rays are almost level. In point of fact, the mean distance of the Sun from the earth is approximately 93,000,000 miles and to be level with it at one-third of its altitude, Dante would have to be about 30,000,000 miles up: an altitude that makes it a considerable mountain even as hyperbole goes. In any case, the shadow of Dante's body falls on the wall of flame to his left, where it is noticed by many of the shades within the fire. This fact, too, is certainly impossible: Dante is treating the wall of flame as if it were a fog bank.

20–21. *all these:* All these others who walk with me here. *Ethiopes or Indians:* Dante thought of Ethiopia and India as nothing but parched and burning wastes.

29 ff. THE SODOMITES. The first shades Dante met on this Cornice walked along bearing to the right (from east to west, the direction of the Sun, and the natural way of going on the mountain). These new souls, to Dante's surprise, walk in the opposite direction, *i.e.,* against the natural way. They are The Sodomites. (See further note to 37–42, below.)

31. *them:* Both bands of sinners.

32. *and each shade kissed another:* In accordance with the Apostolic admonition: "Salute one another with a holy kiss." (*Romans,* xvi, 16.) These holy kisses not only remind them of the libidinous kisses of their sin, but help expiate it. *without pausing:* Throughout, Dante is moving behind Virgil and Statius as rapidly as possible along that dangerous path. Thus, all his exchanges with these sinners are carried on at a fast walk, the Sodomites walking the opposite way and soon passing from view, the other shades retaining their same relative positions to Dante in their course along the ledge.

37–42. THE REIN OF LUST. The Rein consists here of a single admonition against *unnatural lust,* and of another against *natural lust.*

(40) *Sodom and Gomorrah:* Ancient cities destroyed in a rain of fire from Heaven as punishment for the fact that homosexuality was a general practice in them.

(41–42) *Pasiphaë:* Daughter of Apollo by the nymph Perseis. Wife of King Minos of Crete. Poseidon sent Minos a black bull to be offered as a sacrifice, but Minos put it in his herd. For revenge, Poseidon made Pasiphaë fall in love with the bull. She had Daedalus make a cunning effigy of a cow with wicker or wooden ribs, over which a cowhide was spread. She then crouched inside in order to be possessed by the bull. The Minotaur (see *Inferno*, XII, 12–18, note) was born of the union. Thus, lust gave birth to a monster.

Note that Dante reserves "sodomy" specifically for "homosexuality." In modern usage "sodomy" includes "sexual relations with animals." Pasiphaë's example, though it may seem unnatural enough to us, does not violate natural law, but only human law. See 82–84, note, below.

43–45. *the Rhipheans:* The Rhiphean Mountains, a mythical range that occurs "somewhere in the north" on some old maps. Dante's phrasing is best understood to mean north in a generic sense. *the sands:* Of the African desert. Note that Dante does not say cranes actually behave in this way (he could not fail to know that cranes do not migrate both north and south in the same season), but only that it is *as if* cranes did so behave. Clearly the figure relates to the cranes of *Inferno*, V, 46–47, thereby suggesting both a parallelism and a contrast.

46–48. *their opposing ways:* The Sodomites go away from Dante. The others continue along in his direction. *their first song: Summae Deus clementiae. each . . . an appropriate praise:* The appropriate praises are the miscellaneous exhortations from The Whip of Lust. The sinners sing their hymn, then shout a praise, then sing again. After the first hymn they praise Mary. After the second, Diana. After the third, and before starting the cycle over, each cites his own example of chastity, probably an example that stands directly opposite his particular sin.

55. *beyond the flood:* Across the sea. Hence, in the world.

59. *a lady:* Dante could mean either Beatrice or the Virgin Mary.

63. *that heaven . . . that circles all:* The Empyrean. *of love:* Note the special aptness of "holy love" to the state of these sinners whose crime was unholy love.

77–78. *Caesar ... "Queen":* Suetonius (*Caesar,* 49) reports Caesar's homosexual relation with Nicomedes, the conquered King of Bithynia, and that he was called "The Queen of Bithynia" for it, his soldiers singing a lampoon that ran:

> *Gallias Caesar subegit, Nicomedes Caesarem;*
> *Ecce Caesar nunc triumphat, qui subegit Gallias;*
> *Nicomedes non triumphat, qui subegit Caesarem.*

The point of the lampoon lies in a pun on the word *subegit*—"put under" or "conquered." Thus:

> Caesar put Gaul under; Nicomedes, Caesar.
> Now behold Caesar triumphant who put Gaul under,
> But not Nicomedes who put Caesar under.

80–81. *by their shame they aid the fire:* To do its purifying work. The pains of Purgatory are willed joyously by those who endure them. Both the flame and the shame therefore are a gladly offered penance. In Dante's view, the fire itself would be meaningless (and Infernal rather than Purgatorial) without the shame (a true act of contrition).

82–84. *hermaphroditic:* Heterosexual. These sinners were guilty of abandoning themselves to lust, but not of mating with their own sex. *human laws:* Those restraints that govern human but not animal behavior, and which are the functions of intelligence and of a moral sense. To lose those restraints is to be bestial, and therefore the example of Pasiphaë in the Rein of Lust.

87. *the mock-beast:* The "cow" in which Pasiphaë crouched, and which consisted of a hide stretched over a framework.

92. *Guido Guinizelli:* Guido di Guinizelli de' Principi (GWEE-doh dee Gwee-nee-TZEH-lee day PREEN-chee-pee). Vernacular poet of the mid-thirteenth century, esteemed as a forerunner of the sweet new style. Died 1276. *here so soon:* Since Guido had been dead only twenty-four years by 1300, his full repentance spared him a long delay.

94–96. *Lycurgus' darkest hour:* Hypsipyle, wife of Jason, to whom she had borne twin sons, Thoas and Euneus, was captured by pirates and sold to Lycurgus, King of Nemea. She was appointed nurse of the king's infant son.

When she met the parched heroes who fought against Thebes (XXII, 112, note) she put the baby down on the grass long enough to point out the spring called Langia. While she was gone, the infant was bitten by a poisonous snake. Lycurgus condemned her to death for negligence, and she was on the point of being executed when her sons (they had been sent to Nemea by Dionysus) discovered her, rushed to embrace her, and won her release.

Dante's point is that he felt upon discovering the identity of Guinizelli as the twins had felt on discovering their lost mother. He adds, however, that he could not match their actions in racing to embrace her, for he was prevented by the fire. (Note, also, that in basing his figure on an incident narrated in the *Thebaid,* Dante is once more registering the presence of Statius.) Statius' earlier feeling for Virgil forms another parallel.

98. *my betters:* There is some disagreement as to whether or not Dante meant to rate himself among the six greatest poets of all time in narrating his reception in Limbo. Considering his confessed pride, and his willingness to point out how well he can accomplish certain poetic feats that no other has equaled (see *Inferno,* XXV, 91–99, and XXXII, 7–9), I believe Dante knew very well how good he was, and that he had few betters. This phrasing, therefore, is best taken as a compliment to the generation of poets that preceded him, its tone set by his wish to honor Guido Guinizelli. One must also recognize, however, that Dante distinguished between *poeti* (poets) and *rimatori* (versifiers). Here, "betters" could mean "as versifiers."

113. *modern usage:* Of writing about love in the spoken tongue rather than in Latin or in elaborate euphuisms. The Sweet New Style.

119–120. *Limoges produced a better:* Girault de Bornelh, of Limoges, a rival poet.

121–123. I have all but abandoned Dante's phrasing here in attempting to convey his meaning. Literally rendered, the passage reads: "They turn their faces to rumor (*i.e.,* to what is being said, *i.e.,* to reputation) more than to the truth (of merit in the writing) and so they fix their opinions before they have heeded art or reason."

124. *Guittone:* See XXIV, 56, and note. *our fathers:* Dante says *antichi,* the primary meaning of which is "the ancients" but which

can also mean simply "gone by." Guittone died in 1294, and Guinizelli, though only thirty-two years old, in 1276.

131. *as far as it may serve:* The souls in Purgatory cannot yield to temptation, for their power to sin has been taken from them. Thus the supplication "and lead us not into temptation but deliver us from evil" could not apply to them. One could argue, too, that Purgatorial souls do not need their "daily bread," but "bread" can, of course, be taken to mean "spiritual sustenance." In any case, the point is that not all of the Lord's Prayer is apt to the state of the Purgatorial souls.

136–139. *that shade he had pointed to:* Arnaut Daniel, Provençal poet of the second half of the twelfth century. He was especially given to intricate rhyme structures and elaborate phrasing and is generally credited with having invented the sestina. Many commentators have wondered why Dante held him up for such high praise, for his work seems rather more elaborate than compelling to most readers. Perhaps it was Dante's particular passion for elaborate structural relations and for such devices as the *UOM* of Canto XII that drew him to Daniel.

140–147. DANIEL'S REPLY. Daniel replies, in the original, not in Italian, but in the *langue d'oc,* the Provençal tongue in which he wrote. Since some obvious shift of language is necessary here, and since Daniel's would seem an antique and a courtly tongue to Dante, I have rendered his lines into what can best be called a desperate attempt at bastard Spenserian. *faring:* going. *blistful:* blissful. *redeth:* leads. *amount:* mount.

Canto XXVII

---◆◆◆◆◆---

THE SEVENTH CORNICE   *The Angel of Chastity*
The Wall of Fire
THE EARTHLY PARADISE   *The Angel Guardian*

A little before sunset of the third day on the Mountain the Poets come to the further limit of the Seventh Cornice and are greeted by THE ANGEL OF CHASTITY, who tells them they must pass through the wall of fire. Dante recoils in terror, but Virgil persuades him to enter in Beatrice's name.

They are guided through the fire by a chant they hear coming from the other side. Emerging, they find it is sung by THE ANGEL GUARDIAN of the Earthly Paradise, who stands in a light so brilliant that Dante cannot see him. (It is probably here that THE LAST P is stricken from Dante's brow. Or perhaps it was consumed by the fire.)

The Angel hurries them toward the ascent, but night overtakes them, and the Poets lie down to sleep, each on the step on which he finds himself. (For Statius it will be the last sleep, since there is no night in Heaven.) There, just before dawn, Dante has a prophetic DREAM OF LEAH AND RACHEL, which foreshadows the appearance, above, of Matilda and Beatrice.

Day arrives; the Poets rise and race up the rest of the ascent until they come in sight of THE EARTHLY PARADISE. Here VIRGIL SPEAKS HIS LAST WORDS, for the Poets have now come to the limit of Reason, and Dante is now free to follow his every impulse, since all motion of sin in him has been purged away.

273

As the day stands when the Sun begins to glow
   over the land where his Maker's blood was shed,
   and the scales of Libra ride above the Ebro,

while Ganges' waters steam in the noonday glare—
   so it stood, the light being nearly faded,   5
   when we met God's glad Angel standing there

on the rocky ledge beyond the reach of the fire,
   and caroling *"Beati mundo corde"*
   in a voice to which no mortal could aspire.

Then: "Blessèd ones, till by flame purified   10
   no soul may pass this point. Enter the fire
   and heed the singing from the other side."

These were his words to us when we had come
   near as we could, and hearing them, I froze
   as motionless as one laid in his tomb.   15

I lean forward over my clasped hands and stare
   into the fire, thinking of human bodies
   I once saw burned, and once more see them there.

My kindly escorts heard me catch my breath
   and turned, and Virgil said: "Within that flame   20
   there may be torment, but there is no death.

Think well, my son, what dark ways we have trod . . .
   I guided you unharmed on Geryon:
   shall I do less now we are nearer God?

Believe this past all doubt: were you to stay   25
   within that womb of flame a thousand years,
   it would not burn a single hair away.

And if you still doubt my sincerity,
   but reach the hem of your robe into the flame:
   your hands and eyes will be your guarantee.   30

My son, my son, turn here with whole assurance.
   Put by your fears and enter to your peace."
   And I stood fixed, at war with my own conscience.

And seeing me still stubborn, rooted fast,
   he said, a little troubled: "Think, my son,   35
   you shall see Beatrice when this wall is past."

As Pyramus, but one breath from the dead,
   opened his eyes when he heard Thisbe's name,
   and looked at her, when the mulberry turned red—

just so my hard paralysis melted from me,   40
   and I turned to my Leader at that name
   which wells forever in my memory;

at which he wagged his head, as at a child
   won over by an apple. Then he said:
   "Well, then, what are we waiting for?" and smiled.   45

He turned then and went first into the fire,
   requesting Statius, who for some time now
   had walked between us, to bring up the rear.

Once in the flame, I gladly would have cast
   my body into boiling glass to cool it   50
   against the measureless fury of the blast.

My gentle father, ever kind and wise,
   strengthened me in my dread with talk of Beatrice,
   saying: "I seem already to see her eyes."

From the other side, to guide us, rose a paean,   55
   and moving toward it, mindless of all else,
   we emerged at last where the ascent began.

There I beheld a light that burned so brightly
   I had to look away; and from it rang:
   "Venite benedicti patris mei."   60

"Night falls," it added, "the Sun sinks to rest;
   do not delay but hurry toward the height
   while the last brightness lingers in the west."

Straight up through the great rock-wall lay the way
   on such a line that, as I followed it,   65
   my body blocked the Sun's last level ray.

We had only climbed the first few stairs as yet
   when I and my two sages saw my shadow
   fade from me; and we knew the Sun had set.

Before the vast sweep of the limned horizon   70
   could fade into one hue and night win all
   the immeasurable air to its dominion,

each made the step on which he stood his bed,
   for the nature of the Mount not only stopped us
   but killed our wish to climb, once day had fled.   75

As goats on a rocky hill will dance and leap,
   nimble and gay, till they find grass, and then,
   while they are grazing, grow as tame as sheep

at ease in the green shade when the Sun is high
   and the shepherd stands by, leaning on his staff,   80
   and at his ease covers them with his eye—

and as the herdsman beds down on the ground,
   keeping his quiet night watch by his flock
   lest it be scattered by a wolf or hound,

just so we lay there, each on his stone block,   85
   I as the goat, they as my guardians,
   shut in on either side by walls of rock.

I could see little ahead—rock blocked the way—
   but through that little I saw the stars grow larger,
   brighter than mankind sees them. And as I lay,   90

staring and lost in thought, a sleep came on me—
 the sleep that oftentimes presents the fact
 before the event, a sleep of prophecy.

At the hour, I think, when Venus, first returning
 out of the east, shone down upon the mountain—   95
 she who with fires of love comes ever-burning—

I dreamed I saw a maiden innocent
 and beautiful, who walked a sunny field
 gathering flowers, and caroling as she went:

"Say I am Leah if any ask my name,   100
 and my white hands weave garlands wreath on
  wreath
 to please me when I stand before the frame

of my bright glass. For this my fingers play
 among these blooms. But my sweet sister Rachel
 sits at her mirror motionless all day.   105

To stare into her own eyes endlessly
 is all her joy, as mine is in my weaving.
 She looks, I do. Thus live we joyously."

Now eastward the new day rayed Heaven's dome
 (the sweeter to the returning wanderer   110
 who wakes from each night's lodging nearer home),

and the shadows fled on every side as I
 stirred from my sleep and leaped upon my feet,
 seeing my Lords already standing by.

"This is the day your hungry soul shall be   115
 fed on the golden apples men have sought
 on many different boughs so ardently."

These were the very words which, at the start,
 my Virgil spoke to me, and there have never
 been gifts as dear as these were to my heart.   120

Such waves of yearning to achieve the height
   swept through my soul, that at each step I took
   I felt my feathers growing for the flight.

When we had climbed the stairway to the rise
   of the topmost step, there with a father's love   125
   Virgil turned and fixed me with his eyes.

"My son," he said, "you now have seen the torment
   of the temporal and the eternal fires;
   here, now, is the limit of my discernment.

I have led you here by grace of mind and art;   130
   now let your own good pleasure be your guide;
   you are past the steep ways, past the narrow part.

See there the Sun that shines upon your brow,
   the sweet new grass, the flowers, the fruited vines
   which spring up without need of seed or plow.   135

Until those eyes come gladdened which in pain
   moved me to come to you and lead your way,
   sit there at ease or wander through the plain.

Expect no more of me in word or deed:
   here your will is upright, free, and whole,   140
   and you would be in error not to heed

whatever your own impulse prompts you to:
   lord of yourself I crown and mitre you."

NOTES

1–4. *As the day stands:* Meaning of this passage: It is shortly before sunset of the third day on the Mountain. Dante's details here are the reverse of those given at the opening of II, which see. *the land where his Maker's blood was shed:* Jerusalem. *the Ebro:* For Spain.

6. *God's glad Angel:* The Angel of Chastity. He is standing on the narrow rocky path outside the wall of fire.

8. *Beati mundo corde:* "Blessed are the pure in heart [for they shall see God]." (*Matthew,* v, 8.)

10–12. THE WALL OF FLAMES. It is, of course, the fire in which the Lustful are purified. It is also the legendary wall of fire that surrounded the Earthly Paradise. Note that all souls must pass through that fire. The readiest interpretation of that fact is that every soul must endure some purification before it can approach God (theoretically, a soul could climb Purgatory and endure no pain but this). Since no man's soul is perfect in its love, moreover, it must endure the fire that purifies impure love. Additionally, the allegorical intent may be that no man is entirely free of Lust. Having reached the Earthly Paradise, the soul has reached the Perfection of the Active Life. Below, its motion has been *toward* perfection. Now, after a few final rituals, the soul *becomes* perfect, and therefore changeless.

16. *I lean forward over my clasped hands:* Dante's hands must be clasped a bit below the waist. It is an odd posture, but it is also oddly Dantean.

17–18. *bodies I once saw burned:* Dante must mean as a witness at an execution. Burnings at the stake generally took place in public squares. They were a rather common spectacle. Dante's sentence of exile, it is relevant to note, decreed that he was to be burned if taken on Florentine territory.

23. *Geryon:* The Monster of Fraud. See *Inferno,* XVII, 1 ff., note.

37–39. *Pyramus . . . Thisbe:* Famous tragic lovers of Babylon. Ovid (*Metamorphoses,* IV, 55–166) tells their story. At a tryst by a mulberry (which in those days bore white fruit) Thisbe was frightened by a lion and ran off, dropping her veil. The lion, his jaws bloody from a recent kill, tore at the veil, staining it with blood. Pyramus, arriving later, saw the stained veil, concluded that Thisbe was dead, and stabbed himself. Thisbe, returning, found him and cried to him to open his eyes for his Thisbe. At that name Pyramus opened his eyes, looked at her, and died. Thisbe, invoking the tree to darken in their memory, thereupon stabbed herself. (*Cf.* Shakespeare's *Romeo and Juliet.*) The mulberry roots drank their blood and the fruit turned red ever after.

40. *my hard paralysis melted:* Note how Dante describes his emotions throughout this passage. He is afraid, to be sure. But the fear is of his human body and habit. His soul yearns forward, but his body will not obey until Reason has overcome mortal habit.

58. *a light:* This is the Angel Guardian of the Earthly Paradise. He corresponds to the Angel guarding the Gate. At every other ascent in Purgatory, Dante has met one angel. Here, he meets two, one on either side of the fire. It is the song of this Angel that has guided the Poets through the flames. In all probability, too, it is this Angel that strikes away the final *P* from Dante's brow (or perhaps it was consumed in the fire). It is unlikely that the final *P* was removed by the Angel of Chastity, since the Poets had not yet been through the fire, *i.e.,* had not really crossed all of the Cornice.

60. *Venite benedicti patris mei:* "Come ye blessèd of my Father." (*Matthew,* xxv, 34.)

68. *my shadow:* Virgil and Statius, of course, cast none.

94. *At the hour . . . when Venus, first returning:* Venus is in the sign of Pisces, which immediately precedes Aries, in which sign the Sun now is. It is, therefore, Venus Morningstar. Thus it is the hour before dawn, in which the truth is dreamed.

97–108. DANTE'S DREAM. Leah and Rachel were, respectively, the first- and second-born daughters of Laban and the first and second wives of Jacob. Many authors before Dante had interpreted them as representing the Active and the Contemplative Life of the Soul. Leah's white hands (*le belle mani*) symbolize the Active Life, as Rachel's eyes (lines 104–108) symbolize the Contemplative Life.

Since it is the truth Dante is dreaming, these figures must foreshadow others, as the eagle of his earlier dream (IX, 19 ff.) represented Lucia. Thus Leah prefigures Matilda, who will appear soon, and Rachel prefigures Beatrice, who will appear soon thereafter. But just as the eagle is not to be confused with Lucia, so Leah and Rachel are not to be narrowly identified with Matilda and Beatrice except as allegorical dream equivalents, for Matilda and Beatrice may very well be taken, as part of their total allegory, to represent the Active and the Contemplative Life of the Soul.

127 ff. *"My son,"* he said: These are Virgil's last words, for the Poets have now reached the extreme limit of Reason's (and Art's)

competence. Virgil continues awhile with Dante into the Earthly
Paradise (walking, one should note, behind rather than ahead of
Dante) but he has no more to say. A little later in fact (XXIX, 55–57)
when Dante turns to Virgil out of old habit as if for an explanation of
the strange and marvelous sights he comes on, he receives in answer
only a look as full of awe as his own. And later yet (XXX, 43 ff.),
when Dante turns from Beatrice to look for him, Virgil has vanished.

For Virgil has now performed all that he had promised at their
first meeting (*Inferno,* I, 88 ff.), and Dante's soul is now free to obey
its every impulse, for it now contains nothing but Good.

143. *I crown and mitre you:* Crown as king of your physical self
and mitre (as a bishop) as lord of your soul. Dante has not, by much,
achieved the full lordship of his soul, but he has achieved as much as
Virgil (Reason) can confer upon him. A bishop's mitre, though it
confers great authority, does not confer final authority. And a king,
for that matter, may still be subject to an emperor, as he certainly
would be, in Dante's view, to God.

Canto XXVIII

THE EARTHLY PARADISE   *Lethe*

*It is the morning of the Wednesday after Easter, Dante's fourth
day on the Mountain, and having been crowned Lord of Him-
self by Virgil, Dante now takes the lead for the first time, wan-
dering at his leisure into THE SACRED WOOD of the Earthly
Paradise until his way is blocked by the waters of LETHE.*

*His feet stopped, Dante sends his eyes on to wander that
Wood and there suddenly appears to him a solitary lady
singing and gathering flowers. She is MATILDA, who sym-
bolizes THE ACTIVE LIFE OF THE SOUL.*

*In reply to Dante's entreaty, Matilda approaches to the other
bank of the river. So standing, three paces across from him, she
offers to answer all that Dante wishes to ask. Dante replies that
he is in some confusion about the sources of the wind and the
water of the Earthly Paradise. Matilda promises to dispel the
mists from his understanding and proceeds to explain in great
detail THE NATURAL PHENOMENA OF THE EARTHLY
PARADISE, which is to say, the source of the wind, the vege-
tation, and the water. She further explains the special powers
of the waters of LETHE and of EUNOË and concludes with
some remarks on the errors of the ancient poets in the loca-
tion of the Earthly Paradise. At her last words, Dante turns to
his two ancient poets to see how they are taking her remarks.
Finding them smiling, he turns back once more to Matilda.*

Eager now to explore in and about
    the luxuriant holy forest evergreen
    that softened the new light, I started out,

without delaying longer, from the stair
   and took my lingering way into the plain
   on ground that breathed a fragrance to the air.   5

With no least variation in itself
   and with no greater force than a mild wind,
   the sweet air stroked my face on that sweet shelf,

and at its touch the trembling branches swayed,   10
   all bending toward that quarter into which
   the holy mountain cast its morning shade;

yet not so far back that in any part
   of that sweet wood the small birds in the tops
   had reason to stop practicing their art;   15

but bursting with delight those singing throngs
   within their green tents welcomed the new breeze
   that murmured a sweet burden to their songs

like that one hears gathering from bough to bough
   of the pine wood there on Chiassi's shore   20
   when Aeolus lets the Sirocco blow.

I had already come, slow bit by bit,
   so far into that ancient holy wood
   I could not see where I had entered it,

when I came upon a stream that blocked my way.   25
   To my left it flowed, its wavelets bending back
   the grasses on its banks as if in play.

The purest waters known to man would seem
   to have some taint of sediment within them
   compared to those, for though that holy stream   30

flows darkly there, its surface never lit
   in its perpetual shade by any shaft
   of sun or moon, nothing could hide in it.

My feet stopped, but my eyes pursued their way   35
    across that stream, to wander in delight
    the variousness of everblooming May.

And suddenly—as rare sights sometimes do,
    the wonder of them driving from the mind
    all other thoughts—I saw come into view

a lady, all alone, who wandered there   40
    singing, and picking flowers from the profusion
    with which her path was painted everywhere.

"Fair lady who—if outward looks and ways
    bear, as they ought, true witness to the heart—
    have surely sunned yourself in Love's own rays,   45

be pleased," I said to her, "to draw as near
    the bank of this sweet river as need be
    for me to understand the song I hear.

You make me see in my imagining
    Persephone as she appeared that day   50
    her mother lost a daughter; she, the Spring."

As a dancer, keeping both feet on the ground
    and close together, hardly putting one
    before the other, spins herself around—

so did she turn to me upon the red   55
    and yellow flowerlets, virgin modesty
    making her lower her eyes and bow her head.

And she did all I asked, for she came forward
    till I not only heard the melody
    of what she sang, but made out every word.   60

And when she stood where the bright grasses are
    bathed and bent by the waves of the clear river,
    she raised her eyes—and gave my soul a star.

I cannot think so glorious a ray
  shot out of Venus' eyes that time her son   65
  wounded her inadvertently in play.

There, on the other bank, smiling she stood
  and gathered to her arms more of the flowers
  that sprang up without seeds in that high wood.

The stream between us was three paces wide,   70
  but the Hellespont where Persian Xerxes crossed
  to leave a dire example to all pride,

in its raging between Sestos and Abydos,
  caused less hate in Leander than this in me,
  for not dividing so that I might cross.   75

"You are newcomers, and perhaps you find
  because I smile," she said, "here in this place
  chosen to be the nest of humankind,

some doubt that makes you wonder at the sight.
  To pierce such mists as gather on your thoughts   80
  the psalm, *Delectasti me,* will give you light.

And you in front who first entreated me,
  speak if you would know more. I came prepared
  to answer you as fully as need be."

"The way the wood hums and the waters flow,"   85
  I said then, "are at odds with the conclusions
  I drew from what I heard a while ago."

"I shall explain from what cause," she replied,
  "these things that have confused your mind proceed,
  and thus brush its obscuring mist aside.   90

That Highest Good which only Itself can please
  made man good, and for goodness, and It gave him
  this place as earnest of eternal peace.

But man defaulted. All too brief his stay.
   Defaulted, and exchanged for tears and toil   95
   his innocent first laughter and sweet play.

When vapors of the earth and water meet
   a storm is born, below there. Now these vapors
   reach up, as far as possible, toward heat.

To guard man from such warring elements   100
   this mountain soared so high that no earth vapor
   could rise above the gate of penitence.

Now since the air revolves in one conjoint
   and perfect circuit with The Primal Motion,
   unless its wheel is broken at some point,   105

here at this altitude, where it goes round
   in its pure state, it strikes the foliage
   which, being dense, is made to give off sound.

The stricken plant impregnates the pure air
   with its particular powers, which are then borne   110
   on the great wheel and scattered everywhere;

and the other earth, according to the powers
   of soil and climate in its various zones,
   conceives and bears its various fruits and flowers.

When this is understood there, no man need   115
   believe it strange when plants take root and spring
   out of the earth without apparent seed.

Know, too, the sacred soil on which you stand
   is bursting-full of species of all sorts,
   and bears fruits never picked by human hand.   120

The water you see here is from no source
   that needs replenishment from cloudy vapors,
   like streams that rise and fall: with constant force

it leaves a fountain that receives again,
   from God's Will, every drop that it pours forth   125
   to the two streams it sends across this plain.

On this side, it removes as it flows down
   all memory of sin; on that, it strengthens
   the memory of every good deed done.

It is called Lethe here: Eunoë there.   130
   And one must drink first this and then the other
   to feel its powers. No sweetness can compare

with the savor of these waters. And although
   you may at once, and with no more instruction,
   drink your soul's fill from the eternal flow,   135

let me bestow one thing more for good measure.
   Though I exceed my promise, I cannot think
   what I add now will meet with your displeasure.

Those ancients who made songs to celebrate
   man's Age of Gold, placed probably on Parnassus   140
   this perfect garden of his first pure state.

Here mankind lived its innocent first days.
   Here is the Eternal Spring and every fruit.
   This is the nectar that the poets praise."

She paused. I turned around to face my lords,   145
   the poets whose strains had honored ancient song,
   and saw they had received her final words

with smiles that lingered yet upon their faces;
then turned back to that lady of glad graces.

Notes

3. *softened the new light:* In its green shade. It is the morning of
the Wednesday after Easter, the beginning of Dante's fourth day on

the Mountain, and the last of his Divine Journey, for he will complete his tour of Heaven in less than a day. *I started out:* Note that for the first time it is Dante who leads the way in his new state as "king of himself."

11. *that quarter:* The West.

20. *the pine wood there on Chiassi's shore:* Chiassi (now Classe) was the seaport of Ravenna in 1300. It is now a desolate place left behind by the recession of the Adriatic.

21. *Aeolus:* In ancient mythology the god who kept the winds in his cave and controlled their blowing. *the Sirocco:* The South Wind, which in Italy is the wind from Africa.

36. *everblooming May:* See line 143. It is eternally springtime in the Earthly Paradise.

40. *a lady, all alone:* Matilda. She may be taken, as foreshadowed in Dante's dream of Leah and Rachel, to symbolize the Active Life of the Soul. She is the innocence that guides Dante through the Earthly Paradise to Beatrice. Thus, she is the intermediary between Human Reason and the various manifestations of Beatrice as Divine Love, Faith, the Contemplative Life of the Soul, and the Church Triumphant, among others.

There has been a great deal of speculation among commentators concerning her possible historical identity. Dante clearly treats her as someone he recognizes at once, for he does not ask her name. And later (XXXIII, 119) when her name is mentioned, he asks none of his usual questions about her identity.

Nevertheless there seems to be no point in trying to identify her with any historic person. The allegorical point may very well be that, having achieved the Earthly Paradise by his own active pursuit of the Good, Dante instantly recognizes the Active Life of the Soul. He has, moreover, just had a prophetic dream of her coming.

45. *sunned yourself in Love's own rays:* In the light of God.

50. *Persephone:* Daughter of Demeter (whose name signifies "Mother Earth"), the goddess of vegetation. One day, as Persephone was gathering flowers in a field, she was carried off to the lower world by Hades (with the consent of Zeus, her father). At the insistence of Demeter, Zeus sent Hermes to fetch her back. Persephone,

however, had eaten a quarter of a fateful pomegranate and, in consequence, could only return for three quarters of each year, being forced to return to the lower world for the fourth quarter.

Thus Persephone represents the vegetative cycle, spending spring, summer, and fall with Demeter (as Mother Earth) but descending to the lower world (into the ground) for the winter. When she is in the lower world she rules beside her husband as the goddess of the dead, but she forever returns to her mother as the virgin daughter (spring). Matilda not only reminds Dante of Persephone, but of Persephone as she was in that original springtime before she was carried off to the lower world.

51. *she, the Spring:* The flowers fell from Persephone's arms when Hades abducted her. Dante certainly means "the Spring" as both those lost flowers, and as the unchanging springtime of the world's first innocence. The myth, of course, is obviously concerned with the idea of virgin innocence, and as obviously related to the Christian myth of the Fall.

65–66. *Venus' . . . her son:* Cupid was playing with his mother one day when one of the arrows in his quiver scratched her breast by accident and she was smitten with love of Adonis, the son of Myrrha by her own father (see *Inferno,* XXX, 38, and note). Ovid tells the story in *Metamorphoses,* X, 525 ff.

69. *that sprang up without seeds:* Here and below in 109–111, 114–117, and 118–119, Dante refers to seeds and to plants springing up without seed. At this point he seems quite clearly to intend, as suggested by *Genesis,* that the newly created earth brought forth of itself. At other times he seems to intend something like the distribution of plants by wind-borne seeds. I have not been able to satisfy myself on the exact nature of his theory on this point. Note that he does not deny that most earthly plants grow from seed, but declares that *some* plants spring up without apparent seed. He could mean that *new species* arise in consequence of wind-borne influences from the Earthly Paradise, thereafter reproducing themselves from their seed.

70. *three paces:* May symbolize the three steps to true repentance (contrition, confession, and the rendering of satisfaction), thereby repeating the motif of the three steps that lead to the Gate.

71. *Hellespont:* Now called the Dardanelles, the strait between Europe and Asia Minor. It is famous for its raging currents. *Xerxes:* Son of Darius, the Persian king. In 485 B.C. Xerxes crossed the Hellespont on a bridge of ships to invade Greece. Decisively defeated in a sea battle off Salamis, Xerxes fled back across the Hellespont undone, thus leaving to all posterity a dire example of the downfall of pride.

73–74. *Sestos and Abydos:* Cities on the Hellespont in, respectively, Greece and Asia Minor. The Hellespont is about a mile wide between them. *Leander:* A young man of Abydos who fell in love with Hero, a priestess of Aphrodite at Sestos. Because of her position and of family opposition, they could not marry but decided to meet clandestinely every night, Leander swimming to her across the Hellespont, guided by a light from Hero's tower. One night the light blew out and Leander lost his direction, was carried off by the current, and drowned. The next morning Hero found his body washed ashore and threw herself into the current. The story of Hero and Leander has been told by countless poets, none of whom thought to provide him with a rowboat.

78. *the nest of humankind:* The Earthly Paradise is the Garden of Eden.

81. *Delectasti me:* Psalm XCII, "I will triumph in the works of Thy hands." Matilda's phrase is from verse 4: "For Thou, Lord, hast made me glad through Thy work" (*Quia delectasti me, Domine, in factura tua*). The light the psalm will give, of course, is the fact that Matilda smiles for sheer joy in God's works.

87. *what I heard a while ago:* In XXI, 40–57, Statius told Dante that no rain nor snow could fall, nor any variation in the weather occur above the Gate. Dante's confusion arises from the fact that he cannot see how to take the wind he feels, nor the waters he sees flowing, except as products of earthly weathers.

91. *That Highest Good which only Itself can please:* Two ideas central to Dante's thinking are expressed in this phrasing.

The first is Dante's idea of purification. God is conceived as perfect goodness. As such, He can be pleased only by perfect goodness. In that estate He made man. And to that spiritual state man, since the

Fall, must strive to return in order to regain God, who will take to Himself only the perfection He originally created.

The second, basic to all Dante's conception of the Earthly Paradise (and later of Heaven), is that perfection is unchangeable. God, being perfect, cannot change, since any change from perfection would necessarily be toward imperfection. It is the lot of fallen man that is beset by chance and change, he being imperfect. Thus the perfection of the fruit in the garden. And thus the perfect clearness of the waters, and the fact that they do not have their source in the chance changes of evaporation and condensation, but flow at a constant (unchanging) rate from the fountain of the Will of God.

97–99. *When vapors of the earth and water meet:* This is Dante's basic conception of the origin of storms in the clash of earthy (fiery) and watery vapors (see *Inferno,* XXIV, 145–147). *toward heat:* Toward the Sun. These vapors (evaporations) are produced by heat and seek, by natural affinity, to rise to the Sun that called them forth.

103–108. *Now since the air revolves in one conjoint . . . :* The earth is conceived as standing still while the atmosphere moves from East to West at the constant rate imparted to it, as to the heavenly spheres, by the Primum Mobile. On the earth's surface the air is deflected by many obstructions (surface turbulence) that make it flow in all directions, but at the altitude of the Earthly Paradise one experiences only the air's unperturbed original motion. This is the "mild wind" Dante felt (lines 8–9), as it is the wind that makes the whole wood murmur (lines 17–18).

109–120. (See also note to line 69.) The phrasing here seems to suggest that all earthly plants have their origins in "virtues" or "powers" (somehow distinct from seeds). They impart these virtues to the wind that bears them around the world as wind-borne gifts of Heaven. On earth, if soil and climate favor, these "virtues" cause new species to spring up (which then reproduce themselves from their own seeds). But since no earthly soil and climate is perfect (unchanging), no zone on earth can raise all plants, whereas in the Earthly Paradise *all* created plants may be found, including species unknown to mankind since the Fall.

130. *Lethe:* In classical mythology, a river of Hades from which the souls of the dead drink forgetfulness of their first existence. Dante, with his usual readiness to adapt ancient mythology to his

own purposes, places it in the Earthly Paradise, and gives it the power (directly related to its original power) of washing from the souls who drink of it every last memory of sin. Note, too, that Dante's Lethe (*Inferno,* XXXIV, 133) flows down to the bottom of Hell, bearing down to Satan, to be frozen into the filthy ice around him, the last lost vestiges of the sins of the saved.

Eunoë: Having adapted Lethe to his purpose, Dante invents as its complement Eunoë (the name meaning, literally, "good memory") and gives it the power to strengthen every memory of good deeds done. The powers of the two rivers will not operate, however, unless one drinks from them in the right order. So drinking from them is surely an allegory of the way to Heaven: one must first drink of Lethe (leave all evil behind) and then of Eunoë (reawaken and strengthen every good in the soul).

146–147. *the poets:* Virgil and Statius would be two of the poets to whom Matilda refers. Dante turns around to see how they have taken her remarks about their errors. Finding them smiling at the receipt of such enlightenment, Dante turns back to Matilda. Line 146 and some of the detail of line 148 are my own invention, forced by the requirements of form and rhyme. Dante says literally: "I turned completely round to my poets, and saw they had received her last explanation with smiles; then turned my face to the gracious lady."

Canto XXIX

THE EARTHLY PARADISE   *The Banks of Lethe*
                 The Heavenly Pageant

*Chanting a blessing on those whose sins are forgiven, Matilda
moves upstream along one bank of Lethe, and Dante keeps
pace with her on the other side. A glorious light and a sweet
melody grow on the air, filling Dante with such rapture that
he cries out against Eve's daring, through which such joys
were lost to mankind.*

*Soon thereafter he sees the approach of THE HEAVENLY
PAGEANT. It is led by SEVEN GOLDEN CANDELABRA that
paint A SEVEN-STRIPED RAINBOW on the sky. Behind them
come TWENTY-FOUR ELDERS (the Books of the Old Testa-
ment), and behind them FOUR BEASTS (the Four Gospels),
who guard A TRIUMPHAL CHARIOT (the Church), drawn
by a GRIFFON (Christ). At the right wheel of the Chariot
dance THE THREE THEOLOGICAL VIRTUES; at its left
wheel, THE FOUR CARDINAL VIRTUES. This group is fol-
lowed, in order, by TWO ELDERS representing Luke as the
author of Acts and Paul as the author of the fourteen epistles;
by FOUR ELDERS representing James, Peter, John, and Jude
as authors of the four Catholic epistles; and finally by A SIN-
GLE ELDER representing John as the author of Revelation.*

*When the Chariot reaches a point directly across from
Dante, a thunderclap resounds, and the entire pageant halts
upon that signal.*

Her words done, she began her song again—
    Beati quorum tecta sunt peccata—
    as if in love when love is free of pain.

As nymphs of old went wandering alone
   through the deep-shaded woodlands, some pursuing,   5
   and others seeking to evade the Sun,

so, then, she started up the riverside
   and, on my own bank, I kept pace with her,
   matching her little steps with shortened stride.

Some fifty paces each we moved this way,   10
   when both banks curved as one; and now I found
   my face turned to the cradle of the day.

Nor had we gone as far again, all told,
   beyond the curve, when she turned to me, saying:
   "Dear brother, look and listen." And behold!—   15

through all that everlasting forest burst
   an instantaneous flood of radiance.
   I took it for a lightning-flash at first.

But lightning comes and goes. The light I saw
   not only stayed on but grew more resplendent.   20
   "What can this be?" I asked myself in awe.

And a sweet melody filled the bright air—
   so sweet that I reproached in righteous zeal
   Eve's fatal recklessness. How could she dare?—

one woman alone, made but a moment since—   25
   all heaven and earth obedient—to refuse
   the one veil willed by High Omnipotence;

beneath which, had she stayed God's acolyte,
   I should have known before then, and for longer
   those raptures of ineffable delight.   30

My soul hung tranced in joy beyond all measure
   and yearning for yet more, as I moved on
   through those first fruits of the eternal pleasure;

when, under the green boughs that spread before us
   the air became a blaze, and the sweet sound   35
   we had been hearing grew into a chorus.

O holy, holy Virgins, if for you
   I ever suffered vigils, cold, or fasts,
   occasion spurs me now to claim my due.

Empty all Helicon! Now is the time!   40
   Urania, help me here with your full choir,
   to bring things scarce conceivable to rhyme!

I saw next, far ahead, what I believed
   were seven golden trees (at such a distance
   and in such light the eye can be deceived);   45

but in a while, when I had drawn so near
   that chance resemblances confused by distance
   no longer made false images appear,

that power that reaps for reason's mill could see
   that they were candelabra; and in the chant   50
   it heard the word *Hosanna!* ringing free.

Above the gold array flamed seven times seven
   candles more lucent than the mid-month Moon
   at midnight in the calm of clearest heaven.

I turned about, amazed at what I saw,   55
   to my good Virgil, and he answered me
   in silence, with a look of equal awe.

I turned back then to those sublimities
   that were approaching at so slow a pace
   that new brides might outdistance them with ease.   60

The lady cried: "Why have you set your mind
   so fixedly upon those living lights
   that you do not observe what comes behind?"

Then I saw people walking like attendants
   behind their lords, and clothed in robes so white   65
   earth has no snow of such a pure resplendence.

Upon my left the polished river shone
   bright as a mirror, and when I looked in
   I saw my left side there, perfectly drawn.

And when I had moved close enough to be   70
   kept at a distance by no more than water,
   I halted my slow steps, better to see.

I saw the flames advance, leaving the air
   painted behind, as if by massive strokes,
   or by bright pennons they were trailing there;   75

thus, all the trailing heavens were aglow
   with seven bands of light of the same color
   as Delia's girdle or Apollo's bow.

Those bands stretched back further than I could see,
   and the distance separating side from side   80
   came to ten paces, as it seemed to me.

And there, advancing two by two beneath
   that seven-striped sky came four-and-twenty elders,
   each crowned in glory with a lily-wreath.

And all sang with one voice, triumphantly: 85
   "Blessèd art thou among the daughters of Adam!
   Blessèd thy beauty to eternity!"

And when those souls elect, as in a dream,
   had left behind the flowers and the new grass
   that shone before me, there across the stream,   90

as star follows on star in the serene
   of heaven's height, there came on at their backs
   four beasts, and these wore wreaths of living green.

Each had three pairs of wings, and every pair
    was full of eyes. Were Argus living yet,   95
    his eyes would be most like what I saw there.

I cannot spend my rhymes as liberally
    as I should like to in describing them,
    for, reader, other needs are pressing me:

but read Ezekiel where he sets forth   100
    how they appeared to him in a great storm
    of wind and cloud and fire out of the North;

and such as he recounts, such did I see;
    except that in the number of their wings
    John differs with him, and agrees with me.   105

Within the space they guarded there came on
    a burnished two-wheeled chariot in triumph,
    and harnessed to the neck of a great Griffon

whose wings, upraised into the bands of light,
    inclosed the middle one so perfectly   110
    they cut no part of those to left or right.

Higher than sight its wing-tips soared away.
    Its bird-like parts were gold; and white the rest
    with blood-red markings. Will it serve to say

Rome never saw such a caparison,   115
    no, not for Africanus, nor yet Augustus?
    The Sun's own would seem shabby by comparison;

yes, even the Sun's own chariot, which strayed
    and was destroyed in fire by Jove's dark justice
    that day the frightened Earth devoutly prayed.   120

Beside the right wheel, dancing in a gyre,
    three maidens came. The first one was so red
    she would be barely visible in fire.

The second looked as if both flesh and bone
   were made of flawless emerald. The third   125
   seemed a new snow no slightest wind has blown.

And now the white one led the dance, and now
   the red: and from the song the red one sang
   the others took their measure, fast or slow.

Beside the left wheel, dancing in a flame   130
   of purple robes, and led by one who had
   three eyes within her head, four glad nymphs came.

Behind these seven came on, side by side,
   two elders, different in dress, but both
   by the same massive bearing dignified.   135

One showed he was a follower of the art
   of great Hippocrates, whom Nature made
   to heal the creatures dearest to her heart.

The other, his counterpart, carried a blade
   so sharp and bright that at the sight of it,   140
   even across the stream, I was afraid.

Next I saw four who walked with humble mien.
   And last of all, one who moved in a trance,
   as if asleep, but his face was firm and keen.

These seven were robed like the first twenty-four   145
   in flowing robes of white, but, for their crowns,
   it was not wreaths of lilies that they wore,

but roses and whatever blooms most red.
   One would have sworn, seeing them at a distance,
   that they were wearing flames about the head.   150

And when the chariot had reached the place
   across from me, I heard a thunderclap
   that seemed a signal to those souls in grace,

for there, in unison with the exalted
first flaming standards, all that pageant halted.   155

NOTES

2. *Beati quorum tecta sunt peccata:* This is Dante's elision of
Psalm XXXII, 1: "Blessed are they [whose transgression is for-
given] whose sins are covered."

11. *both banks curved as one:* Note the regularity (constancy,
perfection) of the river's curve.

12. *the cradle of the day:* The East.

23–30. *so sweet that I reproached . . . . :* For having thrown away
the glory of the Earthly Paradise by refusing to endure the one veil
(of ignorance) under which, had Eve been dutiful, Dante would
have known his present bliss since birth (hence, "before then, and
for longer").

33. *the eternal pleasure:* The joys of Heaven. The joys of the
Earthly Paradise are the first fruits of the great harvest to come.

37–42. INVOCATION OF THE MUSES. Dante is about to de-
scribe the entrance of the Heavenly Pageant, a spectacle of such
splendor that it is difficult to conceive, let alone put into rhyme. For
his great effort, therefore, he summons all the Muses from Helicon,
calling upon Urania to preside, since she is the Muse of Astronomy,
hence of heavenly things. (Her name in Greek means, literally, "the
heavenly one.") *O holy, holy Virgins:* The Nine Muses. *with your
full choir:* With all the other Muses.

43 ff. THE HEAVENLY PAGEANT. The Pageant Dante now de-
scribes is an allegory of the Church Triumphant in the form of a reli-
gious procession or a formal masque in which devout mummers
present themselves in allegorical guises. The center of the Pageant
is the Chariot of The Church Triumphant, guarded by the Four
Gospels, and attended on the right by the Three Theological Graces
and on the left by the Four Cardinal Virtues. The Chariot itself is
drawn by the Griffon, who represents the twofold nature of Christ
as Man and God. Before this central group walk twenty-four Elders
representing the books of the Old Testament. Behind the central

group walk seven Elders representing the books of the New Testament. The entire procession is led by seven enormous Candelabra whose candles trail a rainbow canopy across the sky representing the Seven Gifts of the Spirit under which the Church moves.

Dante has not presented any allegory of such formality up to this point, and some readers have thought the allegory of the Pageant stiff and lifeless. One should bear in mind, however, that Dante is beginning to deal, now, not with reason but with revelation, and that the increased formality of his allegory here is apt to its content, and apt again in its resemblance to the rituals of the Church whose triumph he is representing. Note too, as distinct from the rest of Dante's allegory, that these figures do not enter as themselves (St. John, for example, appears in three guises) but as heavenly beings made up to represent others.

43–51. *I saw next. . . . :* Dante sees in the distance what he takes to be seven trees of gold. Drawing nearer, he sees they are, in reality, enormous candelabra. At that point, too, he is close enough to make out that the word being sung by the chorus (line 36) which was first heard as a distant melody (line 22) is "Hosanna!" *chance resemblances:* Of the bases of the candelabra to tree trunks. *that power that reaps for reason's mill:* The discernment of the senses through which reason draws the data of nature from which it derives its concepts.

50. THE SEVEN CANDELABRA. On the Mountain the Lord specified to Moses the exact form of the seven-branched candelabra of pure gold which was to be an essential part of the tabernacle (*Exodus,* xxv, 31–37). In *Revelation,* i, 12, John had a vision of seven candelabra and interpreted them as seven churches (i, 20). Later (iv, 5) he interprets them as the Seven Gifts of the Holy Spirit (wisdom, understanding, counsel, might, knowledge, piety, and fear of the Lord). As the Candelabra advance in the van of the procession, their candles paint the sky overhead with a seven-striped rainbow that represents these Gifts. Thus, the Candelabra may be taken as the light and glory of God from which issue the Seven Gifts of the Holy Spirit. The Church follows where the Candelabra lead.

51. *Hosanna!:* (Literally, "Save, we pray!") On Palm Sunday as Christ was about to enter Jerusalem, he was hailed at Bethphage on the Mount of Olives with the words "Hosannah to the son of

David!" (*Matthew*, xxi, 9.) The chant is especially apt in that Christ, as the Griffon, is about to enter in triumph.

56. *my good Virgil:* A new and much more familiar form of address signifying Dante's new state. Dante has always referred to Virgil with titles of honor and superiority.

57. *a look of equal awe:* Allegorically: Dante, out of old habit, turns to Reason for an explanation, but finds that Reason itself is overawed. Virgil has already explained (XXVII, 129) that he has passed the limit of his understanding.

60. *new brides:* Walking back from the altar. Hence, at a very slow pace. But even that pace would easily outdistance this procession.

64. *I saw people walking:* These are the figures made up as four and twenty elders who represent the books of the Old Testament as counted by St. Jerome in his *Gallican Psalter* (the twelve minor prophets are counted as one book, and so are *Ezra-Nehemiah, I* and *II Kings, I* and *II Samuel,* and *I* and *II Chronicles*). Thus the elders represent all Revelation before Christ. They wear white robes and wreaths of lilies as symbols of the purity of their faith. John has a vision of them in *Revelation,* iv, 4–5, and explains them, there, as the Twelve Patriarchs and the Twelve Apostles. In his vision they wore crowns of gold. Their song (lines 86–87) is an adaptation of the words used by Gabriel and Elisabeth in addressing Mary at the time of the Annunciation. (*Luke,* i, 28, 42.)

78. *Delia's girdle:* The rainbow-colored halo round the Moon. Delia was another name for Diana, the Moon goddess. *Apollo's bow:* The rainbow. Apollo was, of course, the Sun.

79–81. *stretched back further than I could see:* Allegorically, the Gifts of the Holy Spirit stretch further back into time than any man can reckon. *ten paces:* May certainly be taken as the Ten Commandments in which the Seven Gifts of the Holy Spirit were revealed, and through which they may be enjoyed.

93–105. THE FOUR BEASTS. They represent the Four Gospels of Matthew, Mark, Luke, and John that follow immediately upon the Old Testament. Their wreaths of living green signify Hope. The wings may be taken as signifying the speed with which the Gospels spread through the world. The fact that there are three pairs of wings obviously suggests the Trinity, and the eyes may be taken as Omniscience which is able to see past, present, and future. That much stated, Dante refers the reader to *Ezekiel,* i, 4–14, for a detailed description, except that they are there described as having only four wings, and Dante follows John (*Revelation,* iv, 8) in giving them six.

95. *Argus:* Jove made love to Io. Juno, in wifely jealousy, turned Io into a cow and set Argus of the hundred eyes to watch her. Mercury, sent by Jove, caused Argus to fall into an enchanted sleep and cut his head off. Juno set Argus' eyes in the tail of the peacock. Dante makes the point that the peacock's eyes, bright as they are, are dead, whereas the eyes in the feathers of these beasts are alive.

106 ff. THE CHARIOT OF THE CHURCH TRIUMPHANT. Within the square guarded by the Four Gospel Beasts the Church is represented by a chariot so splendid that Rome never saw its equal, not even in the triumphs of Scipio Africanus or of Augustus. The very chariot of the Sun could not compare with it.

Its two wheels may best be taken as representing the Old and the New Testament. It is drawn by the Griffon that represents Christ, and it is flanked by the Theological Virtues and the Cardinal Virtues.

108 ff. THE GRIFFON. A mythical figure with the fore parts of an eagle and the hind parts of a lion, here meant to represent the dual role of Christ as God and Man, his bird-like part divine, his lion-like part animal, hence human, and the unity of the two a symbol of his incarnation as the Word. His upraised wings, their tips soaring higher than the sight of man can follow, extend into the seven-striped heaven and inclose the central stripe representing MIGHT as the central Gift of the Holy Spirit and as a symbol of His triumph. The Griffon's coloration is probably suggested by *Song of Solomon,* v, 10–11: "My beloved is white and ruddy, the chiefest among ten thousand. His head is as the most fine gold."

118–120. *the Sun's own chariot, which strayed . . . . :* The Chariot of the Sun was driven by Apollo. One day Phaëton, Apollo's son, tried to drive it, but could not manage the horses. The chariot swerved from its path, scorching the sky and threatening to destroy the Earth. In terror Earth prayed to Jove for deliverance, and Jove destroyed the chariot with a thunderbolt. The scar left on the sky by Phaëton's course became the Milky Way.

121–129. THE THREE THEOLOGICAL VIRTUES. They are Caritas (Christian Love), Faith, and Hope. Caritas is so red she could scarcely be seen in a fire. Faith is green, and Hope pure white. They dance in a ring at the Chariot's right wheel, and Faith and Caritas take turns leading the dance, while Hope (who cannot move except as Faith and Caritas direct) follows. Note that it is Caritas ("And the greatest of these is Charity") that sings the song to which they dance.

130–132. THE FOUR CARDINAL (OR NATURAL) VIRTUES. They are Prudence, Justice, Fortitude, and Temperance. They are dressed in the Imperial Purple, for they represent the Classical Virtues. Prudence, who leads them in their dance, has three eyes symbolizing that it is her duty to look at and consider the past, the present, and the future. Note, too, that the Classical and the Theological Virtues *must* go together if the soul is to develop.

133 ff. THE SEVEN ELDERS. These represent the remaining books of the New Testament (aside from the Four Gospels). Note that it is the books, not the persons, that are represented, for John appears three times in this procession; first as the Gospel, next as the Epistles, and finally as *Revelation.* Thus the first two are *Acts* and the Fourteen Epistles. The next four are the Catholic Epistles. And the final single figure is *Revelation.* They wear wreaths of brightest red to signify the ardor of Caritas.

136–137. *One showed he was a follower of the art of great Hippocrates:* Luke, as the author of *Acts.* In *Colossians,* iv, 14, Paul describes him as "the beloved physician." He is the doctor of souls, as Hippocrates was the doctor of bodies.

139–141. *The other, his counterpart:* The figure is Paul. The sword he carries may symbolize his martyrdom by a sword, or more aptly "the sword of the Spirit, which is the word of God." (*Ephesians,* vi, 17.) Thus he is here the taker rather than the healer of lives, as presented in the Epistles.

154–155. *the exalted first flaming standards:* The candelabra that lead the procession like pennons. *in unison:* The rear and the van of the procession stopped at the same instant.

Canto XXX

The procession halts and the Prophets turn to the Chariot and sing, "Come, my bride, from Lebanon." They are summoning BEATRICE, who appears on the left side of the Chariot, half-hidden from view by showers of blossoms poured from above by A HUNDRED ANGELS. Dante, stirred by the sight, turns to Virgil to express his overflowing emotions, and discovers that VIRGIL HAS VANISHED.

Because he bursts into tears at losing Virgil DANTE IS REPRIMANDED BY BEATRICE. The Angel Choir overhead immediately breaks into a Psalm of Compassion, but Beatrice, still severe, answers by detailing Dante's offenses in not making proper use of his great gifts. It would violate the ordering of the Divine Decree, she argues, to let Dante drink the waters of Lethe, thereby washing all memory of sin from his soul, before he had shed the tears of a real repentance.

When the Septentrion of the First Heaven,
    which does not rise nor set, and which has never
    been veiled from sight by any mist but sin,

and which made every soul in that high court
    know its true course (just as the lower Seven   5
    direct the helmsman to his earthly port),

had stopped, the holy prophets, who till then
    had walked between the Griffon and those lights,
    turned to the car like souls who cry, "Amen."

And one among them who seemed sent from Heaven   10
  clarioned: *"Veni, sponsa, de Libano,"*
  three times, with all the others joining in.

As, at the last trump every saint shall rise
  out of the grave, ready with voice new-fleshed
  to carol *Alleluliah* to the skies,   15

just so, above the chariot, at the voice
  of such an elder, rose a hundred Powers
  and Principals of the Eternal Joys,

all saying together: *"Benedictus qui venis"*;
  then, scattering flowers about on every side: 20
  "Manibus o date lilia plenis."

Time and again at daybreak I have seen
  the eastern sky glow with a wash of rose
  while all the rest hung limpid and serene,

and the Sun's face rise tempered from its rest   25
  so veiled by vapors that the naked eye
  could look at it for minutes undistressed.

Exactly so, within a cloud of flowers
  that rose like fountains from the angels' hands
  and fell about the chariot in showers,   30

a lady came in view: an olive crown
  wreathed her immaculate veil, her cloak was green,
  the colors of live flame played on her gown.

My soul—such years had passed since last it saw
  that lady and stood trembling in her presence,   35
  stupefied by the power of holy awe—

now, by some power that shone from her above
  the reach and witness of my mortal eyes,
  felt the full mastery of enduring love.

The instant I was smitten by the force,   40
   which had already once transfixed my soul
   before my boyhood years had run their course,

I turned left with the same assured belief
   that makes a child run to its mother's arms
   when it is frightened or has come to grief,   45

to say to Virgil: "There is not within me
   one drop of blood unstirred. I recognize
   the tokens of the ancient flame." But he,

he had taken his light from us. He had gone.
   Virgil had gone. Virgil, the gentle Father   50
   to whom I gave my soul for its salvation!

Not all that sight of Eden lost to view
   by our First Mother could hold back the tears
   that stained my cheeks so lately washed with dew.

"Dante, do not weep yet, though Virgil goes.   55
   Do not weep yet, for soon another wound
   shall make you weep far hotter tears than those!"

As an admiral takes his place at stern or bow
   to observe the handling of his other ships
   and spur all hands to do their best—so now,   60

on the chariot's left side, I saw appear
   when I turned at the sound of my own name
   (which, necessarily, is recorded here),

that lady who had been half-veiled from view
   by the flowers of the angel-revels. Now her eyes   65
   fixed me across the stream, piercing me through.

And though the veil she still wore, held in place
   by the wreathed flowers of wise Minerva's leaves,
   let me see only glimpses of her face,

her stern and regal bearing made me dread 70
    her next words, for she spoke as one who saves
    the heaviest charge till all the rest are read.

"Look at me well. I am she. I am Beatrice.
    How dared you make your way to this high mountain?
    Did you not know that here man lives in bliss?" 75

I lowered my head and looked down at the stream.
    But when I saw myself reflected there,
    I fixed my eyes upon the grass for shame.

I shrank as a wayward child in his distress
    shrinks from his mother's sternness, for the taste 80
    of love grown wrathful is a bitterness.

She paused. At once the angel chorus sang
    the blessed psalm: *"In te, Domine, speravi."*
    As far as *"pedes meos"* their voices rang.

As on the spine of Italy the snow 85
    lies frozen hard among the living rafters
    in winter when the northeast tempests blow,

then, melting if so much as a breath stir
    from the land of shadowless noon, flows through itself
    like hot wax trickling down a lighted taper— 90

just so I froze, too cold for sighs or tears
    until I heard that choir whose notes are tuned
    to the eternal music of the spheres.

But when I heard the voice of their compassion
    plead for me more than if they had cried out: 95
    "Lady, why do you treat him in this fashion?";

the ice, which hard about my heart had pressed,
    turned into breath and water, and flowed out
    through eyes and throat in anguish from my breast.

Still standing at the chariot's left side,   100
   she turned to those compassionate essences
   whose song had sought to move her, and replied:

"You keep your vigil in the Eternal Day
   where neither night nor sleep obscures from you
   a single step the world takes on its way;   105

but I must speak with greater care that he
   who weeps on that far bank may understand
   and feel a grief to match his guilt. Not only

by the workings of the spheres that bring each seed
   to its fit end according to the stars   110
   that ride above it, but by gifts decreed

in the largesse of overflowing Grace,
   whose rain has such high vapors for its source
   our eyes cannot mount to their dwelling place;

this man, potentially, was so endowed   115
   from early youth that marvelous increase
   should have come forth from every good he sowed.

But richest soil the soonest will grow wild
   with bad seed and neglect. For a while I stayed him
   with glimpses of my face. Turning my mild   120

and youthful eyes into his very soul,
   I let him see their shining, and I led him
   by the straight way, his face to the right goal.

The instant I had come upon the sill
   of my second age, and crossed and changed my life,   125
   he left me and let others shape his will.

When I rose from the flesh into the spirit,
   to greater beauty and to greater virtue,
   he found less pleasure in me and less merit.

He turned his steps aside from the True Way, 130
    pursuing the false images of good
    that promise what they never wholly pay.

Not all the inspiration I won by prayer
    and brought to him in dreams and meditations
    could call him back, so little did he care. 135

He fell so far from every hope of bliss
    that every means of saving him had failed
    except to let him see the damned. For this

I visited the portals of the dead
    and poured my tears and prayers before that spirit 140
    by whom his steps have, up to now, been led.

The seal Almighty God's decree has placed
    on the rounds of His creation would be broken
    were he to come past Lethe and to taste

the water that wipes out the guilty years 145
without some scot of penitential tears!"

NOTES

1. *the Septentrion of the First Heaven:* The Septentrion is the seven stars of the Big Dipper. Here Dante means the seven candelabra. They are the Septentrion of the First Heaven (the Empyrean) as distinct from the seven stars of the dipper which occur lower down in the Sphere of the Fixed Stars.

2. *which does not rise nor set:* The North Star does not rise or set north of the equator, but the Septentrion, revolving around the North Star, does go below the horizon in the lower latitudes. This Septentrion of the First Heaven, however, partaking of the perfection and constancy of Heaven, neither rises nor sets but is a constant light to mankind. So these unchanging lights guide the souls of man on high, as the "lower Seven" (line 5), in their less perfect way, guide the earthly helmsmen to their earthly ports.

7. *the holy prophets:* The twenty-four elders who represent the books of the Old Testament. (See XXIX, 64, note.)

10. *one among them: The Song of Solomon.*

11. *Veni, sponsa, de Libano:* "Come [with me] from Lebanon, my spouse." *Song of Solomon,* iv, 8. This cry, re-echoed by choirs of angels, summons Beatrice, who may be taken here as revelation, faith, divine love, hence as the bride of the spirit, to Dante (man's redeemed soul).

17–18. *a hundred Powers and Principals:* Angels.

19. *Benedictus qui venis:* "Blessed is he who cometh." (*Matthew,* xxi, 9.)

21. *Manibus o date lilia plenis:* "Oh, give lilies with full hands." These are the words of Anchises in honor of Marcellus. (*Aeneid,* VI, 883.) Thus they are not only apt to the occasion but their choice is a sweetly conceived last literary compliment to Virgil before he vanishes.

31. *a lady:* Beatrice. She is dressed in the colors of Faith (white), Hope (green), and Caritas (red).

34. *since last it saw:* Beatrice died in 1290. Thus Dante has passed ten years without sight of her.

36. *stupefied:* Dante describes the stupor of his soul at the sight of the living Beatrice in *La Vita Nuova,* XIV and XXIV. Then, however, it was mortal love; here it is eternal, and the effect accordingly greater.

54. *washed with dew:* By Virgil. See I, 124.

55. *Dante:* This is the only point in the *Commedia* at which Dante mentions his own name. Its usage here suggests many allegorical possibilities. Central to all of them, however, must be the fact that Dante, in ending one life (of the mind) and beginning a new one (of faith), hears his name. The suggestion of a second baptism is inevitable. And just as a child being baptized is struck by the priest, so Beatrice is about to strike him with her tongue before he may proceed to the holy water.

64. *that lady:* There are thirty-four Cantos in the *Inferno* and this is the thirtieth of the *Purgatorio,* hence the sixty-fourth Canto of the *Commedia.* This is the sixty-fourth line of the sixty-fourth Canto. In Dante's numerology such correspondences are always meaningful. Six plus four equals ten and ten equals the sum of the square of trinity and unity. Obviously there can be no conclusive way of establishing intent in such a structure of mystic numbering, but it certainly is worth noting that the line begins with "that lady." The Italian text, in fact, begins with *vidi la donna, i.e.,* I saw the lady [who represents the sum of the square of trinity plus unity?]. The lady, of course, is Beatrice.

68. *wise Minerva's leaves:* The olive crown.

80. *his mother's sternness:* Beatrice appears in the pageant as the figure of the Church Triumphant. The Church is the mother of the devout and though she is stern, as law decrees, her sternness is that of a loving mother.

83–84. *In te, Domine, speravi . . . pedes meos:* In mercy the Angel chorus sings Psalm XXXI, 1–8, beginning "In thee, O Lord, do I put my trust" and continuing as far as "thou hast set my feet in a large room."

85–90. *the spine of Italy:* The Apennines. *the living rafters:* The trees. *the land of shadowless noon:* Africa. In equatorial regions the noonday Sun is at the zenith over each point twice a year. Its rays then fall straight down and objects cast no shadows.

101. *compassionate essences:* The Angel chorus.

106. *greater care:* For his understanding than for your intercession.

109–11. *the workings of the spheres . . . :* The influence of the stars in their courses which incline men at birth to good or evil ends according to the astrological virtue of their conjunctions.

114. *our eyes:* Beatrice is still replying to the plea of the Angel choir. Hence "our eyes" must refer not to mortal eyes, but to the eyes of the blessed. Not even such more-than-human eyes may mount to the high place of those vapors, for that place is nothing less than the Supreme Height, since Grace flows from God Himself.

124–126. *my second age:* Beatrice's womanhood. When she had reached the full bloom of youth Dante turned from her and wrote to his *donna gentile.* Allegorically, he turned from divine "sciences" to an overreliance upon philosophy (the human "sciences"). For this sin he must suffer.

144–145. *were he to come past Lethe:* In passing Lethe and drinking its waters, the soul loses all memory of guilt. This, therefore, is Dante's last opportunity to do penance.

Canto XXXI

———————♦———————

Lethe
                                            Beatrice, Matilda

*Beatrice continues her reprimand, forcing Dante to confess
his faults until he swoons with grief and pain at the thought of
his sin. He wakes to find himself in Lethe, held in the arms of
Matilda, who leads him to the other side of the stream and
there immerses him that he may drink the waters that wipe
out all memory of sin.*

*Matilda then leads him to THE FOUR CARDINAL
VIRTUES, who dance about him and lead him before THE
GRIFFON where he may look into THE EYES OF BEA-
TRICE. In them Dante sees, in a FIRST BEATIFIC VISION,
the radiant reflection of the Griffon, who appears now in his
human and now in his godly nature.*

*THE THREE THEOLOGICAL VIRTUES now approach
and beg that Dante may behold THE SMILE OF BEATRICE.
Beatrice removes her veil, and in a SECOND BEATIFIC VI-
SION, Dante beholds the splendor of the unveiled shining of
Divine Love.*

"You, there, who stand upon the other side—"
   (turning to me now, who had thought the edge
   of her discourse was sharp, the point) she cried

without pause in her flow of eloquence,
   "Speak up! Speak up! Is it true? To such a charge   5
   your own confession must give evidence."

I stood as if my spirit had turned numb:
   the organ of my speech moved, but my voice
   died in my throat before a word could come.

Briefly she paused, then cried impatiently: 10
   "What are you thinking? Speak up, for the waters
   have yet to purge sin from your memory."

Confusion joined to terror forced a broken
   "yes" from my throat, so weak that only one
   who read my lips would know that I had spoken.   15

As an arbalest will snap when string and bow
   are drawn too tight by the bowman, and the bolt
   will strike the target a diminished blow—

so did I shatter, strengthless and unstrung,
   under her charge, pouring out floods of tears,   20
   while my voice died in me on the way to my tongue.

And she: "Filled as you were with the desire
   I taught you for That Good beyond which nothing
   exists on earth to which man may aspire,

what yawning moats or what stretched chain-lengths lay   25
   across your path to force you to abandon
   all hope of pressing further on your way?

What increase or allurement seemed to show
   in the brows of others that you walked before them
   as a lover walks below his lady's window?"   30

My breath dragged from me in a bitter sigh;
   I barely found a voice to answer with;
   my lips had trouble forming a reply.

In tears I said: "The things of the world's day,
   false pleasures and enticements, turned my steps   35
   as soon as you had ceased to light my way."

And she: "Had you been silent, or denied
   what you confess, your guilt would still be known
   to Him from Whom no guilt may hope to hide.

But here, before our court, when souls upbraid   40
   themselves for their own guilt in true remorse,
   the grindstone is turned back against the blade.

In any case that you may know your crime
   truly and with true shame and so be stronger
   against the Siren's song another time,   45

control your tears and listen with your soul
   to learn how my departure from the flesh
   ought to have spurred you to the higher goal.

Nothing in Art or Nature could call forth
   such joy from you, as sight of that fair body   50
   which clothed me once and now sifts back to earth.

And if my dying turned that highest pleasure
   to very dust, what joy could still remain
   in mortal things for you to seek and treasure?

At the first blow you took from such vain things   55
   your every thought should have been raised to follow
   my flight above decay. Nor should your wings

have been weighed down by any joy below—
   love of a maid, or any other fleeting
   and useless thing—to wait a second blow.   60

The fledgling waits a second shaft, a third;
   but nets are spread and the arrow sped in vain
   in sight or hearing of the full-grown bird."

As a scolded child, tongue-tied for shame, will stand
   and recognize his fault, and weep for it,   65
   bowing his head to a just reprimand,

so did I stand. And she said: "If to hear me
   grieves you, now raise your beard and let your eyes
   show you a greater cause for misery."

The blast that blows from Libya's hot sand,   70
   or the Alpine gale, overcomes less resistance
   uprooting oaks than I, at her command,

overcame then in lifting up my face;
   for when she had referred to it as my "beard"
   I sensed too well the venom of her phrase.   75

When I had raised my eyes with so much pain,
   I saw those Primal Beings, now at rest,
   who had strewn blossoms round her thick as rain;

and with my tear-blurred and uncertain vision
   I saw her turned to face that beast which is   80
   one person in two natures without division.

Even veiled and across the river from me
   her face outshone its first-self by as much
   as she outshone all mortals formerly.

And the thorns of my repentance pricked me so   85
   that all the use and substance of the world
   I most had loved, now most appeared my foe.

Such guilty recognition gnawed my heart
   I swooned for pain; and what I then became
   she best knows who most gave me cause to smart.   90

When I returned to consciousness at last
   I found the lady who had walked alone
   bent over me. "Hold fast!" she said, "Hold fast!"

She had drawn me into the stream up to my throat,
   and pulling me behind her, she sped on   95
   over the water, light as any boat.

Nearing the sacred bank, I heard her say
  in tones so sweet I cannot call them back,
  much less describe them here: *"Asperges me."*

Then the sweet lady took my head between   100
  her open arms, and embracing me, she dipped me
  and made me drink the waters that make clean.

Then raising me in my new purity
  she led me to the dance of the Four Maidens;
  each raised an arm and so joined hands above me.   105

"Here we are nymphs; stars are we in the skies.
  Ere Beatrice went to earth we were ordained
  her handmaids. We will lead you to her eyes;

but that your own may see what joyous light
  shines in them, yonder Three, who see more deeply,   110
  will sharpen and instruct your mortal sight."

Thus they sang, then led me to the Griffon.
  Behind him, Beatrice waited. And when I stood
  at the Griffon's breast, they said in unison:

"Look deep, look well, however your eyes may smart.   115
  We have led you now before those emeralds
  from which Love shot his arrows through your heart."

A thousand burning passions, every one
  hotter than any flame, held my eyes fixed
  to the lucent eyes she held fixed on the Griffon.   120

Like sunlight in a glass the twofold creature
  shone from the deep reflection of her eyes,
  now in the one, now in the other nature.

Judge, reader, if I found it passing strange
  to see the thing unaltered in itself   125
  yet in its image working change on change.

And while my soul in wonder and delight
    was savoring that food which in itself
    both satisfies and quickens appetite,

the other Three, whose bearing made it clear   130
    they were of higher rank, came toward me dancing
    to the measure of their own angelic air.

"Turn, Beatrice, oh turn the eyes of grace,"
    was their refrain, "upon your faithful one
    who comes so far to look upon your face.   135

Grant us this favor of your grace: reveal
    your mouth to him, and let his eyes behold
    the Second Beauty, which your veils conceal."

O splendor of the eternal living light!
    who that has drunk deep of Parnassus' waters,   140
    or grown pale in the shadow of its height,

would not, still, feel his burdened genius fail
    attempting to describe in any tongue
    how you appeared when you put by your veil

in that free air open to heaven and earth   145
    whose harmony is your shining shadowed forth!

NOTES

1. *the other side:* Of Lethe. But also the other side of the immortal
life, *i.e.,* still living.

2–3. *edge . . . point:* The image of the sword (of Justice) is carried
over from lines 56–57 of the preceding Canto. It is continued in line
42, below. So far the sword has only cut; now it pierces.

11. *the waters:* Of Lethe.

16 ff. *arbalest . . . snap . . . diminished blow:* The figure is a bit
confusing. Dante seems to say that the bolt (corresponding to an ar-

row) of a crossbow strikes the target with less force when the bow snaps. He does not stop to consider that the bolt may miss the target entirely. Nevertheless, the intent of his figure is clear enough.

25. *moats . . . chain-lengths:* These were, of course, defensive military measures. The moats guarded castles. The chains were strung to block roads, bridges, and gates. Both measures imply great labor forces. Thus the point of Beatrice's question: "What enormous forces blocked your way?" The block was, of course, within Dante himself.

42. *the grindstone is turned back against the blade:* Turning the grindstone away from the blade sharpens it. Turning it back against the blade dulls it. Thus Beatrice is saying that when a soul openly confesses in true repentance what could not in any case be hidden from God, the sword of Justice is blunted, *i.e.,* no longer cuts as deeply.

49–60. DANTE'S FOLLY. If the beauty of her earthly body was Dante's supreme joy and still decayed to mere dust, says Beatrice, how could Dante have placed his trust in any other earthly thing? *love of a maid:* Dante mentions another maiden in some of his songs but in an indefinite way. No specific reference can be attached to these words.

62. *nets:* Were sometimes used for trapping birds.

68–75. *your beard:* Beatrice means "your face," but the word choice is especially cutting. She has been accusing Dante of acting like a child or a fledgling bird. To refer to his beard, therefore, is a sarcastic way of reminding him that he is, presumably, a full-grown man. *a greater cause for misery:* The sight of her accompanied by the guilty knowledge that he had turned away from so much beauty and perfection.

80–81. *that beast which is one person in two natures:* The Griffon. He is the masque of Christ and represents His two aspects as man and God.

83. *first-self:* Her mortal self.

92. *the lady who had walked alone:* Matilda.

94. *She had drawn me into the stream:* Dante wakens to find Matilda bending over him. She has already pulled Dante into Lethe

and he is in the water up to his throat, but Matilda walks *upon* the water. The fact that this particular miracle is attributed specifically to Christ cannot fail to suggest an allegorical meaning.

97. *the sacred bank:* The far bank, the other side. One bank of Lethe is nearer the world, the other nearer Heaven. The sacred bank, moreover, lies the other side of the absolution of Lethe's water. On the near side sin may still be said to exist; on the sacred side, even the memory of sin has been washed away. Contrast Beatrice's words in line 1.

99. *Asperges me: Asperges me hyssopo, et mundabor; lavabis me, et super nivem dealbabor.* ("Purge me with hyssop, and I shall be clean; wash me, and I shall be whiter than snow.") Psalm LI. These are the words the priest utters when he sprinkles holy water over the confessed sinner to absolve him. Matilda, that is to say, is performing the office of absolution. Her action, therefore, must be seen as being directly connected with Dante's confession and repentance, for nothing else could prepare him for absolution.

104. *the Four Maidens:* The Four Cardinal Virtues: Justice, Prudence, Fortitude, and Temperance. In their present manifestation they are nymphs. In another manifestation they are the four stars Dante saw above him when he arrived at the base of the mountain. (I, 23, note.) As the Cardinal Virtues (*i.e.,* the best man can achieve without the revelation of Christ's Church) they cannot themselves bring the soul to the Second Vision (of Divine Love receiving the soul) but they can lead to the First Vision (of the Two Natures of Christ), and thence to the Three Theological Virtues, through which the Second Vision may be received.

Since Beatrice, in one of her present manifestations, represents the Authority of the Church, lines 107–108 must mean that the Four Cardinal Virtues were ordained to be the handmaidens of the Church even before it was founded, working in the virtuous pagans, and in all men, to prepare the way for the triumph of the Church.

110. *yonder Three:* The Theological Virtues: Faith, Hope, and Charity (*i.e., Caritas*).

116. *those emeralds:* The eyes of Beatrice. Dante may have intended to describe them as green (hazel) but more likely his choice of words here is meant only to signify "jewel bright." Green is, of

course, the color of Hope, and an allegorical significance may be implied in that.

118–126. THE EYES OF BEATRICE. Led by the Four Cardinal Virtues, Dante takes his place before the Griffon and receives a first beatific vision of its nature, seeing now the lion (the human) and now the eagle (the divine); now one, now the other, constantly shifting, though the Griffon itself remains immovable (*i.e.,* constant, perfect). He does not, however, see the two natures as one. For that revelation he must wait till he reaches the top of Paradiso.

Note that Dante does not achieve his revelation by looking at the Griffon itself, but rather by looking at its reflection in the eyes of Beatrice (as the Church). Thus he achieves here the first fruits of Faith, seeing as much of the nature of God as is perceivable in the first life. The final revelation can happen only in Heaven, in the rapturous presence of God.

129. *both satisfies and quickens appetite:* "They that eat me shall yet be hungry, and they that drink me shall yet be thirsty." (*Ecclesiasticus,* xxiv, 21.)

138. *the Second Beauty:* The smile of Beatrice (Divine Love). Dante was led to the First Beauty by the Four Cardinal Virtues. Now the Three Theological Virtues, as higher beings, lead him to the second, and higher, beauty, which is the joy of Divine Love in receiving the purified soul.

140. *Parnassus' waters:* The fountain of Castalia. To drink from it is to receive poetic gifts. To grow pale in the shadow of Parnassus signifies to labor at mastering the art of poetry. Note that Dante makes no effort to describe the smile of Divine Love, but only his rapture at beholding it.

145–146. *that free air:* Dante has earlier made the point that the Earthly Paradise possesses an atmosphere that is entirely unconstrained by earthly influences, but moves only in perfect harmony with the primal motion. That harmony is, however, no more than the shadow of the shining of Perfect Love.

Canto XXXII

THE EARTHLY PARADISE   *Beatrice Unveiled*
Departure of the Heavenly Pageant
Transformation of the Chariot

Beatrice unveils and for the first time in ten years Dante looks upon her face. When he recovers from that blinding sight, Dante finds the Heavenly Pageant has wheeled about and is heading east. Dante and Statius follow the Chariot to THE TREE OF GOOD AND EVIL, *which rises to vast heights but bears neither leaves nor flowers. The Griffon ties the pole of the Chariot to the Tree, and the Tree immediately breaks into leaf and flower. The Heavenly Pageant greets this wonder with a hymn unknown to mortals. Overpowered by the singing,* DANTE SLEEPS.

He awakens to find himself, as he believes at first, alone with Matilda. The Heavenly Pageant has, in fact, departed, but as Dante soon learns, Beatrice has remained behind to guard the Chariot and the Seven Nymphs have remained to attend her. She is seated upon the ground, on the roots of the tree and under its shade.

Dante then witnesses an allegorical masque of THE COR-RUPTION OF THE CHURCH THROUGH WEALTH. *First* AN EAGLE *(the Roman Empire) attacks the Tree and the Chariot. Then* A FOX *(heresy). Then the Eagle returns and covers the Chariot with its feathers. Immediately* A DRAGON *(Satan) rips at the Chariot's foundation. The Chariot then covers itself with the feathers (riches) and is converted into* A MONSTROUS BEAST *on which rides* A HARLOT *(the corrupted Papacy) attended by* A GIANT *(the French Monarchy) that beats the harlot and drags the monster into the woods and out of sight.*

322

My eyes were fixed with such intensity
    on quenching, at long last, their ten years' thirst
    that every sense but sight abandoned me.

Tranced by the holy smile that drew me there
    into the old nets, I forgot all else—   5
    my eyes wore blinders, and I could not care.

When suddenly my gaze was wrenched away
    and forced to turn left to those goddesses:
    "He stares too fixedly," I heard them say.

And as a man is blinded by the light   10
    when he has looked directly at the Sun,
    just so I found that I had lost my sight.

When I could make out lesser (I mean, of course,
    "less sensible objects") as compared to the greater
    from which I had been called away by force,   15

I saw the legion of those souls in grace
    had turned right-wheel-about, and marched back now
    with the Sun and the seven torches in its face.

As forward troops when they are giving ground
    turn under their shields, and their standards face about 20
    before the rest of the column has turned round—

just so the vanguard of that heavenly force
    had all gone by before the chariot
    had swung its pole around to the new course.

Then to their wheels the ladies turned together,   25
    and the Griffon once more pulled the sacred car,
    not ruffling so much as a single feather.

Statius and I followed across that park
    with the lady who had led me through the ford,
    behind the wheel that turned the lesser arc.   30

We marched across the sacred wood which she
   who heeded a forked tongue had left deserted,
   our steps timed by angelic melody.

We had moved on, I think, about as far
   as three good bowshots, end to end, might reach,   35
   when Beatrice descended from the car.

"Adam!" I heard all murmur, censuring him.
   Then they all formed a circle round a tree
   that bore no leaf nor flower on any limb.

It soared so high that even in woods like those   40
   the Indians know it would have seemed a wonder;
   and the crown spread out the more the more it rose.

"Blessed art thou, Griffon, whose beak hath rent
   no morsel of the sweet wood of this tree,
   for it grips the belly with a raging torment!"   45

—So shouted all the others as they stood
   about the tree. And the two-natured being:
   "Thus is preserved the seed of every good!"

Then he drew up before the widowed mast
   the chariot's pole, and what came from the tree   50
   he gave it back, and tied the two stems fast.

As in the spring on earth, when the great light
   falls mingled with the rays of those sweet stars
   that follow Pisces into Heaven's height,

the trees begin to swell, then burgeon full,   55
   each one in its own hue, before the Sun
   harnesses his team beneath the Bull—

just so the boughs that had been bare before
   took color, turning something less than rose
   and more than violet as they bloomed once more.   60

The hymn I heard those blessed souls sing then
   is not sung here, nor did I understand it;
   nor did I hear it through to the Amen.

Could I portray the eyes of Argus here,
   lulled one by one by drowsy tales of Syrinx,   65
   that time their pitiless watch cost him so dear,

as a painter paints his model, I would try
   to show exactly how I fell asleep.
   But who can image drowsiness? Not I.

Therefore, I pass to my waking, and declare   70
   a radiance tore the veil of sleep; a voice
   cried out: "Arise! What are you doing there?"

When they were shown the flowering of that Tree
   that makes the angels hungry for Its fruit
   and sets a feast in Heaven eternally,   75

Peter, John, and James, awe-stricken, fell
   into a sleep from which they were recalled
   by the same word that broke a greater spell;

and saw their company reduced, as both
   Moses and Elijah vanished from them;   80
   and saw the Master's robe change back to cloth.

Just so did I awaken from my dream
   to find, bent over me, the compassionate lady
   who had conducted me along the stream.

Fearful I cried out, "Beatrice! Where is she?"   85
   And the lady: "She is seated on the roots
   of the new foliage, as you can see,

encircled by the seven shining Graces.
   The others mount to Heaven behind the Griffon,
   intoning sweeter and profounder praises."   90

If she said more, her words were lost on me,
   for now my eyes were fixed once more on Beatrice,
   my senses closed to all that was not she.

She sat on the bare earth alone, left there
   to guard the chariot that the Biformed Beast   95
   had fastened to the tree with such great care.

A living cloister ringing her about,
   the Seven Nymphs stood, holding in their hands
   those candles no wind ever shall blow out.

"Here briefly in this forest shall you dwell;   100
   and evermore, with me, be of that Rome
   in which Christ is a Roman. Hence, look well

there at the great car, and that you may be
   a light to the dark world, when you return
   set down exactly all that you shall see."   105

Thus Beatrice; and I, devoutly bent
   at the feet of her commands, turned mind and eye
   as she had willed, in all obedient.

No flash from densest clouds when the rains fall
   from the remotest reaches of the sky   110
   ever shot down as fast out of the squall

as did the bird of Jove that I saw break
   down through the tree, ripping the flowers, the leaves,
   even the bark, with its fierce claws and beak.

He struck the chariot a tremendous blow,   115
   at which it lurched like a storm-battered ship,
   now rolled to port, now starboard, to and fro.

Next came a fox, so gaunt and angular
   it seemed to know no fit food; and it pounced
   upon the cab of the triumphal car.   120

But threatening all its filthy sins with woe
   my lady sent it reeling back from there
   as fast as such a bag of bones could go.

Then, through the tree, I saw the bird descend
   once more into the car, and shed its plumes   125
   to feather it in gold from end to end.

And from the sky, as if a heart let slip
   all of its grief in one sound, a voice cried:
   "Oh what a load you bear, my little ship!"

Then, as I watched, I saw a fissure split   130
   the earth between the two wheels, and a dragon
   rise to the car and sink its tail in it.

Much as an angry wasp draws back its stinger,
   it drew its tail back, ripping the car's floor,
   and wandered off as if it meant to linger.   135

Like rich soil left to weeds, what then remained
   covered itself with feathers, which no doubt
   had been intended to burnish what they stained.

And both the wheels and the pole were overgrown,
   and all the car to the last part, and all   140
   in less time than the lips part for a moan.

So changed, the holy ark began to sprout
   heads from its various parts: three from the pole,
   one from each corner. Seven in all grew out.

The three were horned like oxen, but the four   145
   were each armed with a single evil horn.
   No one had seen the monster's like before.

Secure as a great fortress on a crag,
   an ungirt harlot rode the beast, her eyes
   darting with avarice. Beside that hag,   150

and ready to risk all to keep her his,
    a giant strode erect, and as they passed,
    from time to time the two exchanged a kiss.

But when she turned her hungry eyes on me,   155
    her savage lover in a bestial rage
    whipped her from head to foot unmercifully.

Then in a jealous fit the brute untied
    the monster from the tree, and dragged it off
    into the woods, far toward the other side,

until between me and that doxie queen   160
on her weird beast, he made the trees a screen.

NOTES

1–9. DANTE'S RAPTURE ADMONISHED. Beatrice had died in 1290. Dante has not, therefore, seen her for ten years, and the sight of her unveiled face so draws him into the old nets (of love) that he loses track of all else until he is brought to his senses by overhearing the Three Maidens charge him with overdoing. For it is immoderate (*non è bello, i.e.,* it is not an Aristotelian mean of good conduct) to stare so intensely, even at the vision of eternal beauty, if in so doing a man loses sight of the other gifts of God. Bear in mind, too, that Dante is staring with his earthly memory of the other Beatrice. The Heavenly Beatrice has not yet been truly revealed to him. That revelation will take place in the next Canto.

16–18. The Heavenly Pageant came originally from the east. It passed Dante, executed a right-wheel-about, and is now returning, face to the east. Accordingly, it now has in its face the light of the Sun as well as that of the candelabra.

20. *under their shields:* Troops turning in retreat within range of the enemy held their shields over their heads for protection.

22. *the vanguard of that heavenly force:* The twenty-four elders.

30. *the wheel that turned the lesser arc:* The right. In making a right turn, it would swing through the lesser arc. The Poets, therefore, are walking behind the Three Theological Virtues.

36. *when Beatrice descended:* In this masque, Beatrice has entered in a chariot that represents the Church Triumphant. The procession is now moving to the tree that represents the Civil Authority of the Holy Roman Empire. Her descent in order to approach on foot signifies the humility the Church should display before civil authority, as commanded by Paul (*Romans,* xiii, 1): "Let every soul be subject unto the higher powers. For there is no power but of God: the powers that be are ordained of God." To this, as Dante's image of the ideal Church, contrast his lament for the evils that befell the Church when it grew rich and arrogant (*Inferno,* XIX, 109–111, and note), and the final allegory of the present Canto.

37–60. THE TREE OF GOOD AND EVIL. This passage contains an elaborate conception, difficult in itself, and made more difficult by much of Dante's phrasing in what is certainly his least attractive style.

The tree, to begin with, is instantly recognizable, by its resemblance to its offshoot on the ledge below, as the original Tree of Good and Evil. It is for this reason that all souls murmur against Adam at sight of it.

Then, in a second symbolism, the tree is made to represent the Holy Roman Empire, towering so high (and spreading wider as it soars) that no tree in the Indian forests (the comparison is from Virgil) could equal it. (The comparison to Indian forests implies, of course, the superiority of the Christian empire.) But though enormous, the tree is, by itself, barren.

When Christ (the Griffon) approaches the tree, all praise Him for not having eaten (peculiar diet) the sweet-tasting wood (the material riches of the Empire), for by His holy poverty in this world He escaped the bellyache of corruption (with which the Church has been plagued ever since it grew rich). The Griffon replies that only so (in holy poverty) can the seed of goodness be preserved.

To understand the Griffon's next action, it is necessary to know that the true cross, according to legend, had been cut from the Tree of Good and Evil. The Griffon draws the Chariot (the Church) to the tree and binds fast to the tree "what came from it," *i.e.,* the pole of the chariot. Thus one may understand that the pole the Griffon has been pulling (and what draws the Church forward) is the true cross. This interpretation is disputed but does have the virtue of being coherent.

Now with the Church securely bound to the Empire by the true cross, the tree that had been barren breaks into bloom, turning (lines 59–60) something less than rose and more than violet (*i.e.*, the Imperial purple).

For good measure, Dante throws in a legendary reference and several astrological ones. Sense of lines 52–57: "As in the spring on earth when the great light falls mingled with the rays of those sweet stars [of Aries, the sign in which the Sun rides from March 21 to April 19] that follow Pisces [the zodiacal sign immediately preceding Aries] the trees begin to swell, then burgeon full . . . before the Sun [Apollo, the charioteer of the Sun] harnesses his team [to bear the Sun across the sky] beneath the Bull [Taurus, the sign the Sun enters on April 20]."

64–65. *Argus . . . Syrinx:* Argus (called Panoptes or "the all-seeing") had a hundred eyes all over his body. When Jupiter was smitten by Io, Juno changed the girl into a cow and sent Argus to keep watch over her. Jupiter, in his turn, sent Mercury to lull Argus to sleep either by the magic of his flute or, in the version Dante follows, by a kind of Arabian Nights series of tales about Syrinx, who was loved by Pan, and who was changed into a reed by her sisters to save her from Pan's pursuit. His watch cost him dear because Mercury, after lulling him to sleep, cut off his head. Juno set the eyes of her dead gamekeeper into the tail of the peacock, the bird sacred to her. (See XXIX, 95, note.)

70 ff. DANTE'S DREAM AND AWAKENING. The strains of the heavenly hymn lull Dante into a blissful sleep, which may be taken as symbolizing the serenity of the Kingdom. A radiance reaches through his closed eyes and he awakens to hear a voice cry, "Arise!" This is the word with which Christ called Lazarus, among others, from the "greater spell" of death. Obviously, therefore, Dante's awakening symbolizes one more release from mortal error into eternal life. Opening his eyes, Dante finds Matilda bending over him. It was she who cried to him, and at first Dante thinks that all the others have left and that he is alone with her.

Dante then compares his experience to that of Peter, John, and James at the Transfiguration. "And after six days Jesus taketh with him Peter, and James, and John his brother, and bringeth them up into a high mountain apart, and he was transfigured before them: and his face did shine as the sun, and his garments became white as the light . . . they fell on their face, and were sore afraid. And Jesus came and touched them and said, Arise, and be not afraid. And lifting up their eyes, they saw no one, save Jesus only." (*Matthew,* xvii, 1–8.) And see also *Luke,* ix, 28–36, especially, "Now Peter and they that were with him were heavy with sleep: but when they were fully awake, they saw his glory, and the two men that stood with him."

Basing his account on these two passages, Dante adds his own allegory. The vision that is shown to the disciples becomes a vision of Christ as the Mystic Tree of Heaven (which is, of course, another aspect of the Tree of Good and Evil). The vision, however, is not of the fruit of the tree but of its flowers (line 73). It is, therefore, the vision of the flowering promise of Christ, from which will follow the fruit of eternal rejoicing. The vision is especially apt since, during Dante's sleep, Christ (the Griffon) has reascended to Heaven with most of the Heavenly Procession. There Dante shall follow him in the *Paradiso,* and there the fruit of felicity awaits.

73. *that Tree:* Christ.

81. *and saw the Master's robe change back to cloth: I.e.,* back to its mortal state, as it was before the Transfiguration.

83. *the compassionate lady:* Matilda.

85. *Fearful:* Seeing only Matilda by him, Dante is afraid that Beatrice has left.

86–90. *She is seated on the roots of the new foliage:* As Christ, after his Transfiguration, resumed his earthly appearance, so Beatrice, having entered as the figure of revelation aboard the triumphal chariot, is now seated upon the ground.

Beatrice is seated *on* the ground and *under* the new foliage (that sprang from the touch of Christ—the Griffon). Let the tree in this aspect symbolize the Holy Roman Empire, and the roots Rome. The chariot, of course, represents the Church. It rests on the roots (Rome) and is tied to the tree (the Empire). Beatrice (Divine Love) is left on earth to guard the chariot under the protective shade of the tree, while the Griffon (Christ) ascends to Heaven followed by the rest of the Heavenly Train, which is singing a hymn that is sweeter and profounder than earth can understand. Beatrice is left on earth encircled and attended by the Seven Nymphs (the Three Theological Virtues and the Four Cardinal Virtues).

109–111. Dante's meteorological figure here is based on the belief that the highest reaches of the sky are the domain of fire. The highest clouds, therefore, being closest to the sphere of fire would be especially subject to fiery influences and would give forth the most powerful lightning flashes.

112. *the bird of Jove:* The eagle. See *Ezekiel,* xvii, the Parable of the Eagles and the Cedar. There, the eagle represents the Babylonian persecution of the Jews. Here, Dante clearly enough intends its attack to symbolize the Roman persecution of the early Christians.

118. *a fox:* Is most usually taken to represent the heresies that threatened the early Church and that were repelled by the divine wisdom of the Church Fathers.

124–129. THE GIFT OF THE EAGLE. The Eagle of Imperial Rome returns and covers the car (the Church) with its feathers (riches) and a voice from Heaven cries out in grief. The grief is clearly for the evils that descended upon the Church when it grew rich. Dante must certainly have had the Donation of Constantine (see *Inferno,* XIX, 109–111, and note) in mind in the first feathering of the car. The second gift of the eagle would then symbolize the whole process whereby the temporal wealth of the Empire passed so largely into the hands of the Church.

131. *a dragon:* Satan.

135. *as if it meant to linger:* Having broken the floor of the car (the foundation of the Church, once it has been weakened by wealth), Satan would certainly not run away, but rather remain to see what other mischief he could do, wandering off only very slowly.

142–147. THE CAR TRANSFORMS ITSELF INTO A SEVEN-HEADED MONSTER. "And I saw a woman sitting upon a scarlet-colored beast full of the names of blasphemy, having seven heads and ten horns." (*Revelation,* xvii, 3.)

The Seven Heads have been interpreted in endless ingenious ways. Let them be taken as representing the Seven Deadly Sins. They thus took root in the Church as soon as it covered itself with wealth. The first three of the seven are Pride, Wrath, and Avarice. Being the worst sins, they sprout from the pole (*i.e.,* they come before the others). And since they represent offenses against both God and one's neighbors, they are represented as having two horns. The four lesser sins (Acedia, Envy, Gluttony, and Lust) offend God but not necessarily one's neighbors and they are, therefore, represented as having single horns. Thus the total of ten horns.

149–150. *an ungirt harlot:* She represents the Papacy as it existed under Boniface VIII and Clement V, the two Popes Dante most charges with corruption. (See *Inferno,* XIX, and note to 77–79.) "Ungirt" (Dante uses *sciolta,* "untied, unbound") should be understood to imply both lewdness (immodesty of dress) and lack of restraint (knowing no bounds). *her eyes darting with avarice:* Looking everywhere for plunder.

152. *a giant:* The French monarchy, and especially Philip the Fair (Philip IV, 1268–1314, crowned in 1285), who made the Papacy his puppet.

154. *But when she turned her hungry eyes on me:* The question here is why the giant beats the harlot for looking at Dante. Again, many answers have been suggested, but two seem most to the point.

If Dante is taken here as representing Italy, the whipping can only refer to Philip's humiliation of Boniface VIII (see Canto XX, 85–93, note), and the harlot's covetous glance at Dante-as-Italy would represent Boniface's intrigues with various rulers. It was these intrigues that put him most at odds with Philip.

On the other hand, Dante may be taken to represent the typical Christian who looks to the Church for guidance. The allegory would then be saying that every time the corrupt Church is stirred by a wish to return to its true pastoral mission, the French kings whip her and drag her back to sin.

158. *and dragged it off:* In 1304 Philip engineered the election of Clement V and transferred the Papal Seat (dragged it off) to Avignon.

Canto XXXIII

———⟶•◦⟵———

THE EARTHLY PARADISE   *Eunoë*
        Dante's Purification Completed

*The Seven Nymphs sing a hymn of sorrow for the grief of the
Church, and Beatrice answers with Christ's words announc-
ing his resurrection. All then move onward, Beatrice sum-
moning Dante to her side as they walk on.*

  *Beatrice begins her discourse with an obscurely worded
prophecy of the Deliverance of the Church. In much simpler
language, she then utters her FINAL REPROACH TO DANTE
for having so lost sight of the truth.*

  *Just as she finishes, the train halts before THE GREAT
SPRING from which flow the waters of both Lethe and Eu-
noë. At Beatrice's command, the Seven Nymphs lead Dante
forward and he DRINKS THE WATERS OF EUNOË. By
drinking the waters of Lethe, Dante has already forgotten all
sin and error; now every good is strengthened in him. Thus is
his FINAL PURIFICATION completed, and Dante rises
"perfect, pure, and ready for the stars."*

"*Deus, venerunt gentes*"—the Holy Seven,
    in alternating chorus through their tears,
    first three, then four, raised a sweet chant to Heaven;

and Beatrice, when she heard them mourn such loss
    sighed with a grief so deep that even Mary   5
    could not have changed more at the foot of the cross.

But when the other virgins in their choir
   fell still for her reply, she rose erect
   in holy zeal, and said, as if afire:

"*Modicum et non videbitis me;*   10
   et iterum, dearly beloved sisters,
   modicum, et vos videbitis me."

Then placing the Seven before her, she moved ahead
   with a nod to me, to the Lady, and to the Sage
   that had remained, to follow where she led.   15

So she strolled on, and she had not yet laid
   her tenth step on the sward, when she turned round
   and struck my eyes with her eyes as she said

with a serene tranquillity: "Draw near,
   that you may, if I wish to speak to you   20
   as we move on, be better placed to hear."

When I was, as I should be, at her side,
   she said: "Dear brother, why are you not moved
   to question me as we move on?"—Tongue-tied,

like one who knows his station is beneath   25
   that of the presences in which he stands,
   and cannot drag his voice across his teeth,

so did I, with a voice almost choked through,
   manage to say: "My Lady, all my need
   and all that is my good is known to you."   30

And she to me: "My wish is that you break
   the grip of fear and shame, and from now on
   no longer speak like one but half awake.

The cart the dragon broke was, and is not;
   let him whose fault that is believe God's wrath   35
   will not be calmed by soup, however hot.

The eagle you saw shed its plumes back there
   to make the cart a monster and a prey
   will not remain forever without heir;

for certain as my words, my eyes foresee,   40
   already nearing, the unstayable stars
   that bring the time in which, by God's decree,

five hundred, ten, and five shall be the sign
   of one who comes to hunt down and destroy
   the giant and his thievish concubine.   45

My prophecy, being obscure as those
   of Themis and the Sphinx, may fail to move you,
   since all such words hide what they should disclose;

but soon now, like an Oedipus reborn,
   events themselves shall solve the dark enigma,   50
   and without loss of either sheep or corn.

Note my words well, and when you give them breath,
   repeat them as I said them, to the living
   whose life is no more than a race toward death.

And when you come to write them down, make clear   55
   what you have seen of the Tree, now twice-despoiled
   since all-creating God first raised it here.

All those who rob or break those boughs commit
   a blasphemy-in-deed, offending God
   who sacred to Himself created it.   60

For just one bite, the First Soul's tears were spilt
   five thousand years and more, yearning for Him
   who suffered in His own flesh for that guilt.

Your wits must be asleep not to have known
   that a particular reason must account   65
   for its great height and its inverted crown.

Had not your idle thoughts been to your brain
   an Elsan water, and your pleasure in them
   a Pyramus to the mulberry's new stain,

those two facts surely should have made you see   70
   the justice of God's interdict shine forth
   as the moral meaning of the form of the Tree.

It is my wish—because I see your mind
   turned into stone, and like a stone, so darkened
   that the light of what I tell you strikes it blind—   75

that you bear back, if not in writing, then
   in outline, what I say, as pilgrims wreathe
   their staffs with palm to show where they have been."

And I to her: "As pressed wax will retain
   a faithful imprint of the signet ring,   80
   so is your seal imprinted on my brain.

But why do your desired words fly so high
   above my power to follow their intent
   that I see less and less the more I try?"

"They fly so high," she said, "that you may know   85
   what school you followed, and how far behind
   the truth I speak its feeble doctrines go;

and see that man's ways, even at his best,
   are far from God's as earth is from the heaven
   whose swiftest wheel turns above all the rest."   90

"But," I replied, "I have no recollection
   of ever having been estranged from you.
   Conscience does not accuse me of defection."

And she then with a smile: "If, as you say
   you lack that memory, then call to mind   95
   how you drank Lethe's waters here today.

As certainly as smoke betrays the fire,
   this new forgetfulness of your wish to stray
   betrays the sinfulness of that desire.

But I assure you that I shall select   100
   the simplest words that need be from now on
   to make things clear to your dull intellect."

Now with a brighter flame and slower pace
   the sun was holding its meridian height,
   which varies round the world from place to place,   105

when suddenly—as one who leads a line
   of travelers as their escort will stop short
   at a strange sight or an unusual sign—

so stopped the Seven at an edge of shade
   pale as a shadow cast by a cold peak   110
   on a cold stream deep in an Alpine glade.

And there ahead of them, in a single flow,
   Tigris and Euphrates seemed to rise
   and part as friends who linger as they go.

"O light and glory of mankind," I cried,   115
   "what is this flood that pours forth from one source
   and then parts from itself to either side?"

In answer to that prayer I heard the name
   "Matilda" and "ask her." Who spoke up then
   as one does who absolves himself of blame: 120

"This, and much more, I have this very day
   explained to him, and Lethe certainly
   could not have washed that memory away."

And Beatrice: "Perhaps a greater care,
   as often happens, dims his memory   125
   and his mind's eye. But see Eunoë there—

lead him, as is your custom, to the brim
  of that sweet stream, and with its holy waters
  revive the powers that faint and die in him."

Then as a sweet soul gladly shapes its own   130
  good will to the will of others, without protest,
  as soon as any sign has made it known,

so the sweet maid, taking me by the hand
  and saying in a modest voice to Statius,
  "Come you with him," obeyed the good command.   135

Reader, had I the space to write at will,
  I should, if only briefly, sing a praise
  of that sweet draught. Would I were drinking still!

But I have filled all of the pages planned
  for this, my second, canticle, and Art   140
  pulls at its iron bit with iron hand.

I came back from those holiest waters new,
  remade, reborn, like a Sun-wakened tree
  that spreads new foliage to the Spring dew

in sweetest freshness, healed of Winter's scars;   145
perfect, pure, and ready for the Stars.

NOTES

1. *Deus, venerunt gentes:* Psalm LXXIX, the lamentation for the
destruction of Jerusalem. "O God, the heathen are come into thine
inheritance; thy holy temple have they defiled; they have laid
Jerusalem on heaps." So have the later unbelievers despoiled and
defiled the Church.

3. *first three, then four:* The Seven Nymphs sing the psalm
antiphonally, the Three Theological Virtues singing first (they
being higher in the scale of things), and then the Four Cardinal
Virtues.

5–6. *even Mary could not have changed more:* The comparison is not a hyperbole. Beatrice, mourning for the crucifixion of the Church, would endure the same grief Mary suffered at the crucifixion of her son, Christ and the Church being one.

10–12. *Modicum et non videbitis me . . . :* "A little while and ye shall not see me; and again a little while, and ye shall see me [because I go to the Father]." (*John*, xvi, 16.)

These are Christ's words to his disciples, announcing his resurrection. Beatrice speaks them afire with her holy zeal in reply to the mournful psalm. She is saying, in effect, that the triumph of the True Faith shall be seen again. On one level her words may be taken to mean that the pure in heart shall rise above the corruption of the Church to see Christ again in Heaven. More likely, Dante meant that the Church shall be purged until Christ is once more truly visible in its workings.

14–15. *the Lady:* Matilda. *the Sage that had remained:* Statius. The other Sage, Virgil, has departed.

17. *her tenth step:* Every number mentioned by Dante invites allegorical conjecture, and many have taken the "ten" here to refer to the Ten Commandments. The interpretation seems doubtful, however, especially since the actual steps taken were not yet ten.

18. *struck my eyes with her eyes:* Dante takes this forceful way of emphasizing the power of her eyes. (The Lamps of Heaven?)

19. *serene tranquillity:* The change in Beatrice is not a matter of feminine mood. When Dante still had upon himself a stain of neglect, Beatrice berated him for it. But he has now done fit penance and the stain has been removed, thereby removing all cause for anger.

22. *When I was, as I should be, at her side:* Dante's whole progress up to this time has been, as it should be the object of every soul, to stand beside Divine Love.

27. *and cannot drag his voice across his teeth:* It is characteristic of Dante that a certain pungency should creep into his phrasing even at such sublime moments.

31–33. *like one but half awake:* Dante has achieved purification, and all memory of sin has been washed from him by the waters of

Lethe. He must yet drink of the waters of Eunoë, which will strengthen every good memory in him. Because he has not yet been so strengthened, he still speaks, partly, with the habituated fears and confusions of his former ways. It is these fears and confusions Beatrice is telling him to put by.

34–36. Beatrice now refers to the allegory that concluded Canto XXXII, assuring Dante, as in her answer to the psalm, that a dawn of righteousness is approaching. *was, and is not:* These are the words of John, *Revelation,* xvii, 8: "The beast thou sawest was, and is not." *soup:* In some parts of ancient Greece a murderer could protect himself from all vengeance if for nine successive days he ate soup on the grave of his victim. In Florence it became a custom to stand guard for nine days over the grave of a murdered man to see that no one ate soup upon it. The reference is a strange one, but Dante's intent is, clearly, that no such simple rite will ward off the vengeance of God.

37–39. *the eagle . . . will not remain forever without heir:* The eagle is, of course, the Roman Empire. The true heir of the Caesars, who will restore order and goodness, will come at last. Dante thought of Frederick II as the last real heir of the Caesars.

41. *the unstayable stars:* Nothing can stay the stars in their courses. Beatrice foresees propitious stars already near at hand. (God's wrath will not be stayed: *cf.* lines 35–36.)

43. *five hundred, ten, and five:* As Beatrice says in the next tercet, she is speaking in the veiled tongue of prophecy, and her words hide what they should disclose. Whatever the numerological significance Dante intended by the number, it cannot be identified. Since Dante could make himself clear enough when he wanted to, and since he goes on to have Beatrice say that her meaning is hidden, it follows, as a fair guess, that Dante deliberately kept his reference vague.

46–51. The basic sense of this passage is: "Though my way of speaking is obscure, events themselves will soon make clear my meaning." It is the mythological references that may confuse the modern reader. *Themis:* Daughter of Gaea (Earth) and Uranus (Heaven). She was the second wife of Zeus, and later, no longer as his wife, became his Goddess of Law and Order. She was noted for the obscurity of her oracles. *the Sphinx:* A monster with the head of an innocent maiden and the body of a savage beast. One of the oracles of Themis. She waited for travelers on a rock near Thebes and killed them when they failed to solve her famous riddle: "What walks on four legs in the morning, on two at noon, and on three at night?" *Oedipus:* The ill-fated King of Thebes answered properly that the riddle meant a man in the three stages of his life (for he crawls on all fours as an infant, walks on two legs in the middle of his life, and totters on two legs and a cane thereafter). The Sphinx was so enraged on hearing the right answer that she killed herself. (Dante's text reads not "Oedipus" but "the Naiads." The Naiads had no connection with the riddle. Dante's error follows a corrupt text of Ovid's *Metamorphoses,* VII, 759, which reads "Naiades"—the Naiads—for "Laiades"—son of Laius, i.e., Oedipus.) *without loss of either sheep or corn:* Themis, to avenge her oracle, sent a monstrous beast to ravage the flocks and fields of Thebes.

52. *and when you give them breath:* This phrase is my own invention, forced upon the text by the, to me, clear necessity to render line 54 with "death" as the rhyme. I hope the rendering will seem at least approximately Dantean: since the words thus far have been spoken only by Beatrice, a spirit, they have not yet been given breath, as they will be when Dante repeats them with his mortal voice.

56. *twice-despoiled:* Dante probably meant the Fall as the first despoilment of the tree, and the corruption of the Church as the second.

59. *blasphemy-in-deed:* As distinct from blasphemy-in-word and blasphemy-in-thought.

61. *the First Soul's:* Adam's.

62. *five thousand years and more:* According to *Genesis,* v, 5, Adam lived 930 years on earth. According to *Paradiso,* XXVI, 118, he then waited in Limbo for 4,302 years. Dante follows, in this, the chronology of the ecclesiastical historian Eusebius, who set Christ's birth in the year 5200 since the Creation. Christ's death, therefore (and the Harrowing of Hell, for which see *Inferno,* IV, 53, note), would have occurred in the year 5232.

65. *particular reason:* The tree is enormously tall and broadens toward the crown (hence "inverted"). The "particular reason" for such a form must have been to make the fruit inaccessible to man. The story of *Genesis,* however, indicates that Eve certainly had no trouble getting her apple. It must follow that the tree has grown since *Genesis.*

According to the chronology of Eusebius, the year 1300 would be the year 6500 since Creation—time enough for the knowledge of good and evil to show some substantial growth rings.

68–69. *an Elsan water:* The Elsa, a river of Tuscany, is so rich in lime that at some points along its course objects left in its waters will either petrify or become coated. So Dante's idle thoughts (seemingly flowing *around* his brain more than *through* it) have petrified his intellect. *a Pyramus to the mulberry's new stain:* The blood of Pyramus (and Thisbe) stained the mulberry red. (See XXVII, 37 ff., note.) So Dante's delight in his idle thoughts has stained his intellect. Lines 73–75, below, further explain Dante's meaning here.

72. *the moral meaning:* The form of the tree symbolizes its essential nature. Interpreted in the moral sense (as distinct, for example, from the allegorical narrative, or anagogical senses) the two main facts of the tree's form (its great height and inverted crown) express how far above and beyond man is the final understanding of Good and Evil. Hence the justice of God's interdict in forbidding man what lies beyond his grasp.

74. *turned into stone:* As if by Elsan waters. *so darkened:* As was the mulberry.

77–78. *as pilgrims wreathe their staffs with palm:* The palm grows in the Holy Land. Returning pilgrims wreathed their staffs with palm to prove they had been there.

86. *what school you followed:* The school of philosophy, whose error lies in placing its dependence on reason as an end, and which cannot, therefore, comprehend the mysteries of faith.

89–90. *the heaven whose swiftest wheel . . . :* The Primum Mobile, uppermost of the nine spheres. Since all the spheres turn together, the outermost must move most swiftly.

91–102. BEATRICE'S LAST REPROACH. Dante protests that he has no recollection of ever having been estranged from Beatrice, despite the fact that he had relied more heavily on human philosophy than on divine love. Beatrice, smiling, points out that he has just drunk the waters of Lethe, whose powers wipe away all memory of sin. Since they have wiped out the memory of his estrangement, it follows that the estrangement was sinful.

But Beatrice cannot mean that he sinned in following Virgil, for she herself sent him to Dante. Dante's sinful estrangement must have happened before he met Virgil. And since it was from the three beasts of worldliness that Virgil rescued Dante, setting him on the road to the mysteries of faith, worldliness (or the overexaltation of philosophy as his guide) must be the sin that estranged Dante from Beatrice. (See note to XXX, 124–126.)

103. *brighter flame and slower pace:* To an observer the Sun seems brightest at its noon height and seems to move most slowly then. (Its slowness is an illusion, as is the speed with which it seems to set once it has touched the horizon, but its brightness can be accounted for by the fact that its rays travel a vertical, and hence shortest, course through the atmosphere at noon.)

105. *varies round the world from place to place:* In one sense, the Sun is always at the meridian: it is always noon somewhere on the earth.

113. *Tigris and Euphrates:* The Tigris flows through Turkey and Iraq (ancient Chaldea) to join the Euphrates, which rises in Armenia and flows into the Persian Gulf. *Genesis,* ii, 10 ff., identifies the Euphrates as one of the four rivers of Eden, all of which rise from the same source. The rivers of Dante's Earthly Paradise are Lethe and Eunoë. They "seem to rise" as if they were Tigris and Euphrates rising from a single spring.

117. *parts from itself to either side:* The two rivers flow off in opposite directions, just as their powers, rising from one source, work in opposite ways to achieve one good.

122–123. *Lethe certainly could not have washed that memory away:* There being nothing sinful in it.

142–146. Dante ends each canticle with the word "stars," a fixed architectural device, and one that any rendition must preserve at whatever cost. Unfortunately for English renditions, the cost of forcing a rhyme for "stars" is great, and I have had to take considerable liberties. More closely rendered, these lines read: "I came back from that holiest wave [flood] made new like new trees renewed with new foliage, pure and prepared to mount to the stars."

John Ciardi

John Ciardi was a tireless twentieth-century American man of letters throughout a long and varied career. As a poet, he regularly published in all the major journals and won the Hopwood Award at the University of Michigan, the Eunice Tietjens Memorial Prize at *Poetry* magazine, the Golden Rose Medal from the New England Poetry Society, and several other honors. In 1980, the International Platform Association named him People's Poet of the Year. Counting his posthumous collections, twenty-two volumes of his poetry were published in all, including the copious *Collected Poems of John Ciardi* (1997), which puts many of Ciardi's best poems together in a single volume. There were also sixteen books of children's verse, which, among other honors, won the Junior Book Award from the Boys' Clubs of America in 1962 and the Award for Excellence in Poetry for Children in 1982 from the National Council of Teachers of English. He also edited an important 1950 anthology of the emerging poets of the 1940s, *Mid-Century American Poets*, and followed that up in 1959 with one of the freshest and most widely used poetry textbooks of the past half century, *How Does a Poem Mean?* On the lighter side, he collaborated with Isaac Asimov in 1978 and 1981 on two very popular volumes of limericks. In addition to his own work as poet, poetry anthologizer, and poetry textbook writer, John Ciardi was also a national presence as a commentator on contemporary poetry through his work as poetry editor at *Saturday Review* for about twenty years, his directorship of the Bread Loaf Writers' Conference in Vermont for seventeen years, and his work on the college lecture circuit for thirty-five years as the unofficial American Ambassador of Poetry.

Ciardi also hosted a CBS network television magazine show in 1961, *Accent*, and had a regular weekly feature for nine years called "A Word in Your Ear" on National Public Radio's *Morning Edition*. He opened up the arcane mysteries of etymology in his popular three-volume series of entertaining word histories, *A Browser's Dictionary* (I and II) and *Good Words to You* (III). For all these reasons, but perhaps first and foremost for his magnificent translation of Dante's *Divine Comedy*, John Ciardi earned his place among the important literary figures of his generation.

—Edward M. Cifelli

Selected Works by John Ciardi

Translations

Inferno. Mentor Books. NAL, 1954. Signet Classics edition, 2009.

Purgatorio. Mentor Books. NAL, 1961. Signet Classics edition, 2009.

Paradiso. Mentor Books. NAL. 1970. Signet Classics edition, 2009.

Poetry

Homeward to America. Henry Holt, 1940.

As If. Rutgers University Press, 1955.

I Marry You. Rutgers University Press, 1958.

Person to Person. Rutgers University Press, 1964.

Lives of X. Rutgers University Press, 1971.

The Birds of Pompeii. University of Arkansas Press, 1985.

The Collected Poems of John Ciardi. University of Arkansas Press, 1997.

Children's Verse

The Reason for the Pelican. Lippincott, 1959.

The Monster Den. Lippincott, 1966. Illustrated by Edward Gorey.

Doodle Soup. Houghton Mifflin, 1985.

Blabberhead, Bobble-Bud, and Spade. Anthology. Middlesex County, NJ, 1988.

Word Histories
A Browser's Dictionary. Harper, 1980.
A Second Browser's Dictionary. Harper, 1983.
Good Words to You. Harper. 1987.

Textbook
How Does a Poem Mean? Houghton Mifflin, 1959 and 1975.

Anthology
Mid-Century American Poets. Twayne, 1950

About John Ciardi

Edward M. Cifelli. *John Ciardi: A Biography*. University of
    Arkansas Press, 1997.
Vince Clemente. *John Ciardi: Measure of the Man*. Univer-
    sity of Arkansas Press, 1987.
Edward Krickel. *John Ciardi*. Twayne, 1980.

THE CIARDI TRANSLATIONS: *PURGATORIO*

CIARDI ON DANTE

1. Writing by "Itch and Twitch"

When John Ciardi's rendering of the *Purgatorio* was published by Mentor Classics in November 1961, the first incarnation of the current volume, he included in it an amplified version of his original "Translator's Note," which had appeared in the *Inferno* only seven years earlier, and he added an essay called "How to Read Dante," which he had first published as a feature story in the June 3, 1961, issue of *Saturday Review*. Both essays continue to be included in this newest edition of Ciardi's highly regarded translation of the *Purgatorio* because, taken together, they express a large part of Ciardi's thinking about translation, as well as his helpful insights on how to get started on the *Divine Comedy*. The two essays, plus the notes that follow each canto (just as necessary and forthright as they had been in the *Inferno*), reveal something else as well: Ciardi's two deep and ongoing engagements—the first between himself and Dante, and the second between himself and the reader. That dual engagement would extend for nine more years while he translated the *Paradiso* (1970), thus extending his time on the actual translation to twenty-three years in all. But in fact Dante became a lifelong engagement; Ciardi continued to speak regularly about Dante, the *Divine Comedy*, and the act and art of translation on the college-lecture circuit (and as a frequent one-term visiting professor) until he died in 1986.

Mostly in the "Translator's Note" and "How to Read Dante" (and in two other essays he would write later, which are covered in the Afterword to the new Signet Classics edition of Ciardi's *Paradiso*), Ciardi worked out for himself and his readers the principles, as far as he could identify them, that had guided his methods and decisions as a translator. He also offered practical suggestions to the English-speaking reader just beginning a relationship with a work that had been completed some six hundred and fifty years earlier, in Italian—a reader who desperately needed identifications of key characters, explanations of key theological issues, and glosses for key developments in the world of thirteenth- and fourteenth-century Italian politics. Most new readers of Dante need all the help they can get bridging the gap between Dante's time and place and our own, but in the end, regardless of the centuries separating us from Dante's Florence, Ciardi helps us to see that the *Divine Comedy* teems with people whose agonies and glories are just as human and complex as ours are today.

Throughout his long engagement with Dante's time and place and poetry, Ciardi managed to produce translations that he was, on balance, pleased with—but which, at the same time, gave him pause. Grappling with a way to capture Dante's meanings and re-create Dante's vernacular Italian in idiomatic American English, without sacrificing the poetry, occupied Ciardi deeply and guided him to decisions that, despite his personal misgivings, readers and critics have widely admired. As is so often the case with the work of John Ciardi, whether in his own adult poetry or his children's verse or his word histories or his twenty-plus years as columnist and poetry editor of *Saturday Review*, it is his sincerity, intelligence, and openness that make him approachable in his Dante translations and commentaries. He creates an intimacy with readers, who, for their part, enjoy being in his company—and enjoy as well his role as the humanizing buffer between the austere and unforgiving Dante Alighieri and themselves.

Ciardi had turned his attention to translating the *Purgatorio* immediately after the *Inferno* came out in 1954, but it was slow going. The work itself was time-consuming and uncompromising in its demands, but Ciardi was also busy with several other unyielding commitments, like teaching at Rutgers University, being an executive editor at Twayne Publishers, speaking on Dante and modern poetry on the college-lecture circuit, and publishing his own poetry. And then, in 1955, he agreed to become the director of the Bread Loaf Writers' Conference in Vermont, which had been founded by Robert Frost and a few others in the 1920s and which Frost continued to attend for the last two weeks of every August. Lastly, in 1956, at the invitation of editor Norman Cousins, Ciardi became poetry editor of *Saturday Review.*

Dante, however, was very much on Ciardi's mind when he received the Prix de Rome to work on the *Purgatorio* at the American Academy in Rome from September 1956 to September 1957. Unfortunately, Ciardi's standing obligations at *Saturday Review* (and to a lesser extent at Bread Loaf) followed him to Rome, which meant that he made less headway on his translation that year than he had hoped. (He lost several weeks at the beginning of 1957, for example, when he wrote a critical review of Anne Morrow Lindbergh's book *The Unicorn and Other Poems* and then had to reply to a firestorm of international criticism for it.) He took an unpaid leave from Rutgers for the 1959 fall term to work on the *Purgatorio*, but again his other pressing obligations kept him from completing the translation. Finally, picking away at the work whenever and wherever he could, Ciardi was able to deliver all but the last two cantos to his editor Arabel Porter at New American Library in February 1960. He felt he should have been able to deliver the *Purgatorio* quicker than that, but in fact fitting such an enormous and challenging job as this into the seven incredibly busy years since the *Inferno* had been published had taken a superhuman effort.

Porter sent Ciardi's translation to Professor Giorgio de Santillana at MIT for a report, and he wrote back within two weeks that, despite some lines that did not scan well, he was "very much pleased" with the translation. "There are points— in fact a few points—where he actually improved on the original, which is a pleasant thought." Archibald MacAllister added that he thought Ciardi's *Purgatorio* was "sensitive and perceptive" and that readers would now find it "more accessible than has hitherto been possible without a good command of the original Italian."[1]

The two essays published with the *Purgatorio*, the "Translator's Note" and "How to Read Dante," were by-products of all the years Ciardi had spent on his translations. In a sense, the essays are the results of all the decisions he had made as he worked his way through Dante's cantos and canticles. When the first fruits of that labor were published as the first five cantos of the *Inferno* in the winter 1952 issue of the *University of Kansas City Review*, Ciardi sent copies to everyone he knew who might have constructive criticism about each and every technical decision he had made. He wrote to his friend Clarence Decker, president of the University of Kansas City, that he was "delighted by its appearance" and that, while he had "really labored at it" in order to make it what he hoped was "the first translation into idiomatic English," he was very interested in what others thought of it.[2]

To fellow poet Richard Wilbur, Ciardi expressed his concern about the five-stress lines he had decided on: "I've worked many lines so that they won't come out metrically unless they're read with meaningful emphasis," Ciardi explained. He was worried that it might "stumble some readers."[3] He worried also about the number of near-rhymes he had depended on when full rhymes did not work well, in his view. In the end, as he wrote to Dudley Fitts in April 1953: "I simply decided to rhyme exactly where diction permitted and to rhyme any which way where it was a choice between rhyme and diction."[4] A third issue was the diction he'd selected—that is, the level of language as well as its appropriateness. As he put it in an essay called "Speaking of

1. Edward M. Cifelli, *John Ciardi: A Biography* (Fayetteville, AR: The University of Arkansas Press, 1997), p. 304.

2. Letter dated January 8, 1953. See *The Selected Letters of John Ciardi*, ed. Edward M. Cifelli (Fayetteville, AR: The University of Arkansas Press, 1991).

3. *Letters*, January 23, 1953.

4. Cifelli, *John Ciardi*, 173.

Books" in the July 18, 1954, issue of the *New York Times Book Review*, it was critical to avoid "the falsely genteel language" translators of Dante often fell into, and which consequently caused them to misrepresent Dante's diction. The result, Ciardi wrote, in another of his memorable captures, is "neither Italian nor English but simply Translatorese, a jargon not in the voice box of either language, but simply adrift in the vacuum between two dictionaries."

Ciardi probably worried most about his decision to abandon Dante's strict, interlocking *terza rima*. As he put it in the same letter to Fitts: "It can be made to rhyme precisely. But every version that does rhyme it, rhymes at the expense of idiomatic diction. On careful reading you can see the line being beaten into place to produce a rhyme word." Or, as he put it in the "Translator's Note": After experimenting with *terza rima*, couplets, ballad stanzas, and other ways of proceeding, "I hit on what I may as well call dummy *terza rima*, which is to say, I kept the three-line unit but rhymed only the first and third lines. And with that it began to happen, at least for me. I could persuade myself that what came was reasonably English, reasonably poetry, and reasonably faithful to Dante's pace and to his special way of using language" (page xiii).[5]

In the end, having self-analyzed endlessly over fifteen years and two canticles of the *Divine Comedy*, Ciardi opened his expanded "Translator's Note" to the *Purgatorio* by remarking forlornly, and with a kind of exhausted honesty, that "any theoretical remarks offered by a translator are bound to be an apology for his failures," that "no sane translator can allow himself to dream of success," and that the best any translator of Dante can hope for is "the best possible failure" (page ix). But then, after explaining as carefully as he could the decisions he had made and the misgivings that still worried him about a single translated tercet (and by extension to the entire translation), he thought, with the barest ray of hope, that he

5. It should be noted that "dummy" here is used in its sense of "an imitation of a real or original object, intended to be used as a practical substitute." *West's Encyclopedia of American Law.* The Gale Group, Inc., 1998. Answers.com, May 7, 2009.

might just possibly have gotten enough of what he was after to claim some modest success: "All I can really argue, as lamely as need be, is that within the essential failure, this final version *feels* enough like the original, and *feels* enough like English poetry (or at least verse) to allow me to conclude that I have probably caught it as well as I shall be able to" (page xv).

And then, in phrasing that was so completely stamped with Ciardi's own inimitable and idiomatic style that it was quoted in his *New York Times* obituary on April 2, 1986, Ciardi wrote: "What has any poet to trust more than that *feel* of the thing? Theory concerns him only until he picks up his pen, and it begins to concern him again as soon as he lays it down, but when the pen is in his hand he has to write by itch and twitch, though certainly his itch and twitch are intimately conditioned by all his past itching and twitching, and by all his past theorizing about them" (page xvi).[6]

2. Dante, Virgil, and Beatrice: "How to Read Dante"

Ciardi taught special, one-term Dante courses at the University of Florida, Northern Kentucky University, the University of Minnesota, and other schools, generally as a visiting professor. He enjoyed those classes, a resumption of his teaching career, which had officially ended in 1961, when he left Rutgers. He commented to an interviewer just after his first term back in the classroom in 1973: "I remembered what the enthusiasm for teaching was about. I think I broke through and reached some students who began by resisting me." Of his Minnesota experience, he wrote to an old friend in 1981: "It was a joy to unfold a first glimpse of Dante, as a thing the good students would have for the rest of their lives."[7] But despite the many opportunities Ciardi had to teach the *Divine*

---

6. The "Translator's Note" also appeared as "Translation: The Art of Failure" in the *Saturday Review* (October 7, 1961) and was reprinted once again in Ciardi's *Dialogue with an Audience* (Philadelphia: Lippincott, 1963), pp. 281–88.

7. Cifelli, *John Ciardi*, pp. 378 and 421.

Comedy in classrooms around the country, his greater impact as a teacher of Dante comes in the timeless translations, notes, and essays he left behind.

Among these, "How to Read Dante," the essay that had appeared in *Saturday Review* three months before being added permanently to his *Purgatorio* in 1961, captures one of Ciardi's teaching styles perfectly. It was the natural by-product of his fifteen-year tenure as a professor of English at Harvard and Rutgers, but it had other sources as well, including his time spent as editor of the Twayne Library of Modern Poetry and his early years at *Saturday Review*, where he published several articles like "Dialogue with the Audience," where the Poet and the Citizen square off and get a few things off their chests. He spoke on the same subject on the college-lecture circuit too, where Ciardi was paid well to speak to audiences about the poetry they rarely bought or read. Over the course of time, then, Ciardi had become a spokesman for modern American poetry, the mediator who could guide readers of "general culture," as he put it, in the world of "difficult" modern poets. So when it came to helping readers deal with Dante, who had the reputation of being "an immensely difficult poet" (page xvii), he was on familiar ground—helping readers through the arcane mysteries of poetry, whether it be found in the modern verse of his own time or the "modern" Italian verse of Dante's.

In "How to Read Dante," Ciardi opens by saying all one needs to get started is "some first instruction in what to look for" (page xvii), which he then proceeds to give. First he shows how precise Dante is, as for example, how we know that the narrative begins "just before dawn of Good Friday" (page xviii) in the year 1300. Dawn, the Easter weekend, the fact that Dante had gone "astray" and found himself "alone in a dark wood" (page xvii)—all suggest that it is time for a change, time to head toward the light, time for a new beginning—or as Ciardi puts it, it is "a massive symbol of rebirth" (page xviii). At that point, the essay is given over to what we learn from the beginning of the *Inferno* and how we must proceed in the reading, but it also shows us what Dante learns as he goes along, how he must proceed in his journey.

So, for example, Dante learns that the way to the heavenly

light is not direct, for it is blocked by three beasts that force him to take "the long way round" (page xx) to his salvation. We learn with Dante that we will follow him as he descends into the inferno of hell before he can begin his slow ascent into purgatory and later still to heaven. It is, indeed, the long way round, but he (and we) will have a guide, Virgil, a character to help explain all that he (and we) encounter. And later in the *Purgatorio*, at the threshold of heaven, he (and we) have the beautiful Beatrice to guide us to the pure light that is God. But if Dante on his literal journey must take "the long way round," so must the poetry take the same route, as Ciardi reminds us at the end of "How to Read Dante": "The supreme art of poetry is not to *assert* meaning but to *release* it" (page xxvii). That subtle truth accounted for Ciardi's personal fascination with the poem, for Dante's search for the words and forms that will lead to his salvation matched Ciardi's own quest as a poet to find language sufficient to "release" his own meanings, not merely to "assert" them. What Ciardi saw in Dante was not simply the great pilgrim inching his way to God, but the great craftsman who made the search for rhythm, image, diction, and form seem easy. Ciardi the journeyman poet stood in awe of Dante the master poet.

Dante is guilty of the sin of Acedia, Ciardi tells us, the one of the Seven Deadly Sins that has to do with knowing what Ciardi calls "the recognized Good" (page xxii) but not pursuing it with the single-mindedness required for salvation. That is why Dante is "astray / from the straight road" and "alone in a dark wood" and why he must take "the long way round" to heaven. And that is why he takes his journey of atonement—and why we are on it with him. Taken this way, we are not facing "an immensely difficult poet," only one whose universe and theology and politics are sufficiently removed from the twenty-first century to require notes of explanation as we move along in the narrative with Dante, Virgil, Beatrice, and the other characters who are identified along the way. Broken down this way, the *Divine Comedy* becomes a more human document, an approachable, even an inviting, classic.

Two weeks after "How to Read Dante" appeared in *Saturday Review*, the magazine printed a letter to the editor by

Frances Carter from Santa Monica, California, that no doubt has spoken for many thousands of readers, maybe even hundreds of thousands, ever since. "Though repeatedly exposed to the *Divine Comedy* through higher education," Carter wrote, "I have never before been given a footing secure enough to launch me on its journey."[8] Now she had it.

Success for a translator may be a hard concept to pin down, but untold millions have encountered Dante and his great poem through John Ciardi's translations, and it is hard to resist the conclusion that, his own self-doubts aside, Ciardi has captured such a large share of the market because he managed to capture such a large share of Dante. His performances in the *Inferno* and the *Purgatorio* had been inspired—but remarkably, the best was yet to come in the *Paradiso.*

—Edward M. Cifelli

8. Cifelli, *John Ciardi*, p. 306.